CONTRARY NOTIONS
The Michael Parenti Reader

CITY LIGHTS BOOKS
SAN FRANCISCO

Cover design: Pollen
Text design: Gambrinus

Front cover photo by: Willa Madden

Library of Congress Cataloging-in-Publication Data

Parenti, Michael, 1933-
    Contrary notions: the Michael Parenti reader.
    p. cm.
    Includes bibliographical references and index.
    ISBN-13: 978-0-87286-482-5
    ISBN-10: 0-87286-482-0
    1. United States—Social conditions—1980- 2. United States—
Politics and government. 3. World politics—1989- 4. Social
history—1970- 5. Capitalism. I. Title.

    HN59.2.P382 2007
    973.92—dc22

    2006101941

City Lights Books are published at the City Lights Bookstore,
261 Columbus Avenue, San Francisco, CA 94133.
Visit our Web site: www.citylights.com

CONTENTS

ACKNOWLEDGMENTS

My heartfelt thanks to Jenny Tayloe, Peter Livingston, and Elizabeth Valente for the assistance they rendered in the preparation of this book. A special word of thanks to my editor Gregory Ruggiero who first presented me with the idea for this reader, and persisted until I agreed to do it.

INTRODUCTION

Contained herein are the *contrary notions*, the critical analysis that is so grandly ignored or viciously misrepresented by many persons from across the political spectrum—left, right, and center. To some readers my efforts might appear one-sided, but if it is true that we need to hear all sides and not just the prevailing conventional opinion, then all the more reason why the reflections and analysis presented in this book deserve reasoned attention.

It is not demanded of readers that they embrace my views but that they reflect upon their own. How seldom we bother to explore in some critical fashion the fundamental preconceptions that shape our understanding of social and political life. How frequently, as if by reflex rather than reflection, we respond to certain cues and incantations, resisting any incongruous notion. Our opinions shelter and support us; it is an excruciating effort to submit them to reappraisal. Yet if we are to maintain some pretense at being rational creatures we must risk the discomfiture that comes with questioning the unquestionable, and try to transcend our tendencies toward mental confinement.

My intent is to proffer contrary notions, that is, critical ways of thinking about socio-political reality that will remain useful to the reader long after many of the particulars herein have slipped from his or her recall. What you are about to dip into are readings from various works of mine, from across some forty years and covering a wide range of subjects, including culture, ideology, media, environment, lifestyle, gender, race, ethnicity, wealth, class power, public policy, political life, technology, empire, history, and historiography, along with a few selections drawn directly from my personal life. Almost all these entries have been revised, expanded, updated, and, I like to think, improved. A few have never before been published. A few other selections are from publications or books of mine that are out of print and not easily accessible. This volume presents a varied sampling of my work without trying to represent every chronological phase or every subject I have ever treated.

Most of the writing herein is anchored in extensive research and is concerned with ideas and analyses that go beyond the issues of the day. I am of the opinion that there does not have to be an unbridgeable gap between scholars and lay readers. One can write in an accessible and pleasant style while dealing with complex concepts and constructs. To write clearly and understandably does not mean one is being simple or superficial. The converse is also true: to write in a dense, dull, or convoluted manner (as one is trained to do in academia) does not mean that one is being profound and insightful.

I decided not to include any of the many letters and book reviews I have published in newspapers, magazines, and journals, nor the polemical exchanges, rebuttals, and rejoinders I allowed myself to be drawn into, nor the numerous interviews I gave that have found their way into print. Letters, reviews, and interviews can provide food for thought, I think, but in a form that seems too fragmented and off-the-cuff for this volume. (For further information about me and my talks and writings, see www.michaelparenti.org.)

I hope the reader's experience with this book will be not only informational but conceptual and maybe even occasionally enlightening. Everything on the pages that follow is meant to cast light on larger sets of social relations. In one way or another, everything herein is meant to engage our concerns about social justice and human well-being. The struggle against plutocracy and the striving for peace and democracy are forever reborn. Along with the many defeats and deceits produced in this age of reactionary resurgence, there have been some worthwhile victories. And although we are here only for a limited time, I like to think that this is not true of the world itself.

—Michael Parenti

I.
THROUGH THE
LOOKING GLASS

1 MEDIA MOMENTS

For some time now I have been suffering from what I call "media moments." We all have heard of "senior moments," a term used mostly by people of mature years who suddenly experience a lapse in recall. The mind goes blank and the individual complains, "I'm having a senior moment." A media moment is a little different. It happens when you are reading or hearing what passes for the news. You are appalled and frustrated by the conservative bias, the evasions, the non sequiturs, and the outright disinformation. Your mind does not go blank; you simply wish it would.

I recall one media moment I experienced while listening to the BBC news. Now the BBC supposedly provides coverage superior to what is heard on U.S. mainstream media. It occasionally runs stories on European and Third World countries that are not likely to be carried by U.S. news sources. And BBC reporters ask confrontational questions of the personages they interview, applying a critical edge rarely shown by U.S. journalists. But the truth is, when it comes to addressing the fundamental questions of economic power, corporate dominance, and Western globalization,

BBC journalists and commentators are as careful as their American counterparts not to venture beyond the parameters of permissible opinion.

The BBC newscast segment that gave me my media moment was a special report on asthma, of all things. It began by noting that the number of asthma sufferers has been increasing at the alarming rate of 50 percent each decade. "Scientists are puzzled," for there is "no easy explanation," the narrator told us. One factor is "genetic predisposition," he said. We then heard from a British scientist who said, yes, there is definitely a hereditary factor behind asthma; it tends to run in families. Sure, I said to myself, asthma is increasing by 50 percent a decade because people with a genetic tendency toward the disease are becoming more sexually active and procreative than everyone else. I felt a media moment coming on.

There are other contributing factors to the asthma epidemic, the narrator continued, for instance "lifestyle." He interviewed another scientist who confirmed this "scientific finding." People are keeping cleaner homes, using air conditioning, and in general creating a more antiseptic lifestyle for themselves, the scientist said. This means they do not get enough exposure to pollen, dust, and dirt the way people did in the good old days. Hence, they fail to build up a proper defense to such irritants.

These comments made me think back to my younger years when I lived next to a construction site that deposited daily clouds of dust over my abode for months on end. Rather than building up a hardy resistance, I developed an acute sensitivity to dust and mold that has stayed with me to this day. Does exposure to a toxic environment really make us stronger? Looking at the evidence on cancer, lung diseases, and various occupational ailments, we would have to conclude that exposure does not inoculate us;

rather it seems to suppress or overload our immune systems, leaving us more vulnerable, not less.

The BBC report on asthma then took us to India for some *actualité*. A young man suffering from the disease was speaking in a rasping voice, telling of his affliction. This was accompanied by the squishing sound of a hand-held respirator. The victim said he had no money for medication. The narrator concluded that the disease persists among the poor in such great numbers because they cannot afford medical treatment. Yes, I said to myself, but this doesn't tell us what causes so much asthma among the poor to begin with.

Another "expert" was interviewed. He said that in India, as in most of the world, asthma is found in greatest abundance in the congested cities, less so in the suburbs, and still less in the countryside. No explanation was given for this, but by then I could figure it out for myself: the inner-city slum dwellers of Calcutta enjoy too antiseptic a lifestyle; too much air-conditioning and cleanliness has deprived them of the chance to challenge and strengthen their immune systems—unlike their country cousins who have all that pollen and earthy dust to breathe and who thereby build up a natural resistance. At this point I could feel the media moment drawing ever closer.

The BBC report makes no mention of how neoliberal "free market" policies have driven people off the land, causing an explosion in slum populations throughout the world. These impoverished urban areas produce the highest asthma rates. And the report says nothing about how, as cigarette markets in the West become saturated, the tobacco companies vigorously pursue new promotional drives in Asia, Africa, and Latin America, leading to a dramatic climb in Third World smoking rates, which certainly does not help anyone's respiratory system.

Finally the BBC narrator mentioned pollution. He said it "may" be a factor, but more study is needed. May? More study? In any case, he asked, "Is pollution really a cause or is it merely a trigger?" He seemed to be leaning toward "trigger," although by then I was having trouble seeing the difference. The media moment had come upon me full force. I began talking back at my radio, posing such cogent and measured comments as "You jackass, flunky, BBC announcer!"

Media apologists like to point out that journalists face severe constraints of time and space, and must necessarily reduce complex realities into brief reports; hence, issues are conflated, and omissions and oversights are inevitable. But this BBC report went on for some ten minutes, quite a long time by newscast standards. There would have been enough time to mention how the destruction of rain forests and the dramatic increase in industrial emissions have contributed to an alarming CO_2 buildup and a commensurate decline in the atmosphere's oxygen content. The BBC could have told us how the oil cartels have kept us hooked on fossil fuel, while refusing to develop nonpolluting, inexpensive tidal, wind, thermal, and solar energy systems.

And there would have been ample opportunity to say something about how the use of automobiles has skyrocketed throughout the entire world, causing severe damage to air quality, especially in cities. One study found that children who live within 250 feet of busy roads had a 50 percent higher risk of developing asthma than those who do not.[1] The asthma risk decreased to "normal" for children living about 600 feet or more away from a busy road. The researchers noted that major sources of air pollution like highways should not be the only cause for concern. Local roads also create a serious asthma hazard.

But rather than digging into the actual and less speculative causes of asthma, including the direct link to air pollution, this BBC report chose to be "balanced" and "objective" by blaming the victims, their genetic predisposition, their antiseptic lifestyles, and their inability to buy medications.

Newscasters who want to keep their careers afloat learn the fine art of evasion. We should not accuse them of doing a poor or sloppy job of reporting. If anything, with great skill they skirt around the most important points of a story. With much finesse they say a lot about very little, serving up heaps of junk news filled with so many empty calories and so few nutrients. Thus do they avoid offending those who wield politico-economic power while giving every appearance of judicious moderation and balance. It is enough to take your breath away.

2 LIBERAL MEDIA YET TO BE FOUND

It is widely believed that the corporate-owned news media suffer from a liberal bias. TV pundits and radio talk show commentators (many of whom are ultraconservatives), as well as right-wing political leaders have tirelessly propagated that belief. Meanwhile liberal critics who think otherwise, are afforded almost no exposure in the supposedly liberal media.

Consider the case of David Horowitz. When Horowitz was an outspoken left critic of U.S. domestic and foreign policies and an editor of the popular radical magazine *Ramparts*, the mainstream press ignored his existence. But after he and former *Ramparts* colleague Peter Colliers surfaced as born-again conservatives, the *Washington Post Magazine* gave prominent play to their "Lefties for Reagan" pronunciamento. Horowitz and Colliers soon linked up with the National Forum Foundation which dipped into deep conservative pockets and came up with munificent sums to enable the two ex-radicals to do ideological battle with the left. In short order, Horowitz, now a rightist media critic, had his own radio show and appeared with notable frequency on radio and television political talk shows to whine about how the media is monopolized by liberals.

Another example might suffice. When ABC correspondent John Stossel belatedly emerged as a laissez-faire ideologue, announcing, "it's my job to explain the beauties of the free market," his career took off. An ardent supporter of chemicalized agribusiness, Stossel claimed that organic food "could kill you" and catastrophic global warming is a "myth." He called for the privatization of Social Security, the curbing of environmental education, and the celebration of greed as a good thing for the economy. Instead of being challenged for his one-sided views, Stossel was given a seven-figure contract and a starring role in numerous TV specials.[2]

Then there are the many radio talk-show hosts, of whom Rush Limbaugh is only the best known, who rail against the "pinko press" on hundreds of television stations and thousands of radio stations owned by wealthy conservatives and underwritten by big business firms. To complain about how liberals dominate the media, the ultraconservative Limbaugh has an hour every day on network television and a radio show syndicated on over 600 stations. No liberal or progressive or far-left commentator enjoys anywhere near that kind of exposure.

Most toxic of all is Rupert Murdoch's Fox News Network. Unlike the pabulum dished out by CNN and the three traditional networks, Fox News and Fox commentators are on message every hour hammering home conservative ideological points. Daily memos come down from the corporate office at Fox telling its reporters and commentators what the story of the day should be and what point of view was expected when reporting it. Fox News reportedly quizzes journalistic applicants on whether they are registered Republicans or not. Fox dismisses the idea of an ecological crisis and is scornful of environmentalists in general. It never mentioned the numbers of U.S. casualties accumulating in Iraq, believing that this would reflect unfavorably upon the war effort of George W. Bush (hereafter referred to as Bush Jr. to distinguish him from his father who was also a president). Fox News supports U.S. military interventions around the globe, the untrammeled glories of the "free market," and just about every other reactionary cause, with a lockstep precision and persistence that is unmatched by the rest of the political spectrum.[3]

Religious media manifest the same imbalance of right over left. Liberal and often radically oriented Christians and their organizations lack the financial backing needed to gain serious media access. Many liberal Christians are busy doing good: relief work, community assistance, soup kitchens, and the like. Meanwhile right-wing fundamentalist Christians are busy doing propaganda, promoting homophobic, sexist, reactionary causes. Rightist Christian media comprise a multi-billion-dollar industry, controlling about 10 percent of all radio outlets and 14 percent of the nation's television stations.

Commentators on televangelist Pat Robertson's Christian Broadcasting Network (CBN) insist that we should get government out of our lives, yet they seem determined to get government into our bedrooms. They want government to outlaw cohabitation, birth control, adultery, and gay marriage. Many support retention of sodomy laws that dictate what sexual positions consenting married couples may take in bed. CBN commentators want government to outlaw safe and legal abortions because they believe a fertilized ovum takes precedent over the woman (or adolescent girl) carrying it. I heard one panel of CBN commentators, all women, tell listeners that abortion causes cancer. CBN opinion makers want government to require prayers in our schools and subsidize religious education. They blame the country's ills on decadent morality, homosexuality, feminism, and the loss of family values. Pat Robertson himself charged that feminism "encourages women to leave their husbands, kill their children, practice witchcraft, destroy capitalism and become lesbians."[4]

Political leaders do their share to reinforce the image of a liberal press. During the Iran-Contra affair, President Reagan likened the "liberal media" to a pack of sharks. And President Clinton, a Democrat, complained that he had "not gotten one damn bit of credit from the knee-jerk liberal press." Clinton was confused. Almost all the criticism hurled his way by the so-called liberal press came from conservative sources.

There is no free and independent press in the United States. The notion of a "free market of ideas" is as mythical as the notion of a free market of goods. Both conjure up an image of a bazaar in which many small producers sell their wares on a more or less equal footing. In fact—be it commodities or commentary—to reach a mass market you need substantial sums of money to buy exposure and distribution. Those without corporate media connections end up with a decidedly smaller clientele, assuming they are able to survive at all.

The major news media or press (the terms are used interchangeably here) are an inherent component of corporate America. As of 2007, only six giant conglomerates—Time Warner, General Electric, Viacom, Bertelsmann, Walt Disney, and

News Corporation (down from twenty-three in 1989)—owned most of the newspapers, magazines, book publishing houses, movie studios, cable channels, record labels, broadcast networks and channels, and radio and television programming in the United States, with additional holdings abroad. About 85 percent of the daily newspaper circulation in this country belongs to a few giant chains, and the trend in owner concentration continues unabated. All but a handful of the 150 movies produced each year are from six major studios. Big banks and corporations are among the top stockholders of mainstream media. Their representatives sit on the boards of all major publications and broadcast networks.[5]

Corporate advertisers exercise an additional conservative influence. They cancel accounts not only when stories reflect poorly on their product but, as is more often the case, when they perceive liberal tendencies creeping into news reports and commentary.

Not surprisingly, this pattern of ownership affects how news and commentary are produced. Media owners do not hesitate to kill stories they dislike and in other ways inject their own preferences into the news. As one group of investigators concluded years ago: "The owners and managers of the press determine which person, which facts, which version of the facts, and which ideas shall reach the public."[6] In recent times, media bosses have refused to run stories or commentaries that reflected favorably on single-payer health insurance, or unfavorably on "free trade" globalization and U.S. military intervention in other countries.

Clear Channel, corporate owner of some 1,200 radio stations, canceled an antiwar advertisement, and stopped playing songs by the Dixie Chicks after that group's lead singer uttered a critical remark about President Bush Jr. In 2004, Clear Channel sponsored jingoistic "Rally for America" events around the country in support of the U.S. invasion of Iraq. That same year the Walt Disney Co. blocked its Miramax division from distributing a documentary by Academy Award winner Michael Moore because it offered an unflattering picture of Bush. Sinclair Group, the largest owner of local TV stations in the country, censored its ABC affiliates for reading the names of U.S. soldiers killed in Iraq (because publicizing the casualties might dampen public support for the war). Sinclair sends recorded right-wing editorial commentary to its affiliates to be broadcast as local news, and regularly contributes large sums to Republican candidates.[7]

A favorite conservative hallucination is that the Public Broadcasting System is a leftist stronghold. In fact, more than 70 percent of PBS's prime-time shows are funded wholly or in major part by four giant oil companies, earning it the sobriquet of "Petroleum Broadcasting System." PBS's public affairs programs are underwritten by General Electric, General Motors, Metropolitan Life, Pepsico, Mobil, Paine Webber, and the like. A study of these shows by one media-watchdog group found that corporate representatives constitute 44 percent of the sources about the economy; liberal activists account for only 3 percent, while labor representatives are virtually shut out. Guests on NPR and PBS generally are as ideologically conservative or mainstream as any found on commercial networks.

Politically progressive documentaries rarely see the light of day on PBS. In recent years, "Faces of War" (revealing the brutality of the U.S.-backed counterinsurgency in El Salvador), "Deadly Deception" (an Academy-Award-winning critique of General Electric and the nuclear arms industry), "Panama Deception" (an Academy-Award-winning exposé of the U.S. invasion of Panama) and numerous other revealing documentaries were, with a few local exceptions, denied broadcast rights on both commercial and public television.

The spectrum of opinion on political talk shows and on the pages of most newspapers ranges from far right to moderate center. In a display of false balancing, right-wing ideologues are pitted against moderate centrists. On foreign affairs the press's role as a cheerleader of the national security state and free-market capitalism is almost without restraint. Virtually no positive exposure has been given to Third World revolutionary or reformist struggles or to protests at home and abroad against U.S. overseas interventions.

Be it the Vietnam War, the invasions of Grenada and Panama, the intervention against Nicaragua, the Gulf War massacre, and the subsequent invasions of Afghanistan and Iraq, U.S. military undertakings are portrayed as arising from noble if sometimes misplaced intentions. The media's view of the world is much the same as the view from the State Department and the Pentagon. The horrendous devastation wreaked upon the presumed beneficiaries of U.S. power generally is downplayed—as are the massive human rights violations perpetrated by U.S.-supported forces in scores of free-market client states.

If all this is true, why do conservatives complain about a liberal bias in the media? For one thing, attacks from the right help create a climate of opinion favorable to the right. Railing against the press's "liberalism" is a way of putting the press on the defensive, keeping it leaning rightward for its respectability. So liberal opinion in this country is forever striving for credibility within a conservatively defined framework.

Furthermore, ideological control is not formal and overt as with a state censor, but informal and usually implicit. Hence it works with imperfect effect. Editors sometimes are unable to see the troublesome implications of particular stories. As far as right-wingers are concerned, too much gets in that should be excluded. Their goal is not partial control of the news but perfect control, not an overbearing advantage (which they already have) but total dominance of the communication universe. Anything short of unanimous support for a rightist agenda is treated as evidence of liberal bias. Expecting the press corps to be a press chorus, the conservative ideologue, like any imperious maestro, reacts sharply to the occasionally discordant note.

The discordant notes can be real. The news media never challenge the free-market ideology but they do occasionally report unsettling events and mishaps that might put business and the national security state in a bad light: toxic waste dumping by industrial firms, price gouging by defense contractors, bodies piling up in Haiti, financial thievery on Wall Street, U.S. casualties in Iraq, and the like. These exposures are more than rightists care to hear and are perceived by them as a liberal vendetta and evidence of a liberal bias.

In order to perform their class-control function, the media must maintain some degree of credibility. To do that, they must give some attention to the realities people experience. They must deal with questions like: Why are my taxes so high? Why are people losing their jobs? Why is the river so polluted? Why is there so much corruption in business and government? Why are we spending so much on the military? Why are we always at war? The media's need to deal with such things—however haphazardly and insufficiently—is what leads conservatives to the conclusion that the media are infected with "liberal" biases.

This is the conservative problem: reality itself is radical, so we must not get too close to it. The Third World really is poor and oppressed; the U.S. often does side with Third-World plutocrats; our tax system really is regressive and favors the very richest; millions of Americans do live in poverty; the corporations do plunder and pollute the environment; real wages for blue-collar workers definitely have flattened and even declined; the superrich really are increasing their share of the pie; and global warming really is happening.

Despite its best efforts, there are limits to how much the press can finesse these kinds of realities. Although it sees the world through much the same ideological lens as do corporate and government elites, the press must occasionally report some of the unpleasantness of life, if only to maintain its credibility with a public that is not always willing to buy the far-right line. On those occasions, rightists complain bitterly about a left bias.

Rightist ideologues object not only to what the press says but to what it omits. They castigate the press for failing to tell the American people that federal bureaucrats, "cultural elites," gays, lesbians, feminists, and abortionists are destroying the nation; that God has been shut out of public life; that "secular progressives" are waging war against Christmas; that the U.S. military and corporate America are our only salvation; that litigious lawyers are undermining our business system; that there are no serious health-care problems in this country; that eco-terrorists stalk the land; that the environment is doing just fine—and other such loony tunes.

One ploy persistently used by rightists to "demonstrate" a liberal bias is to point out that journalists tend to vote for the Democrats. When polled, the Washington press corps favored Kerry over Bush in 2004 by a substantial majority. Left unmentioned is that working reporters are at the bottom of the command chain. They are not the ones who decide what gets printed and what does not. Nor do they determine which events are to be covered or ignored. Conservatives who rail against the "liberal media" have not a word to say about the rightist and ultra-rightist proclivities of media owners, publishers, corporate advertisers, network bosses, senior editors, syndicated columnists, commentators, and shock-jock talk-show hosts—those who really determine what comes across as news and opinion.[8]

Reporters often operate in a state of self-censorship and anticipatory response. They frequently wonder aloud how their boss is taking things. They recall how superiors have warned them not to antagonize big advertisers and other powerful interests. They can name journalists who were banished for turning in the wrong kind of copy too often. Still, most newspeople treat these incidents as aberrant departures from a basically professional news system, and insist they owe their souls to no one. They claim they are free to say what they like, not realizing it is because their superiors like what they say. Since they seldom cross any forbidden lines, they are not reined in and they remain unaware that they are on an ideological leash.

While incarcerated in Mussolini's dungeons from 1928 to 1937, the Italian communist and journalist Antonio Gramsci wrote about politics and culture in his prison notebooks. But he carefully had to eliminate words like "capitalism" and "class," for these might attract the attention of the fascist censor who would then stop him from doing any more writing. The fascists well understood their job was to suppress class consciousness wherever it might appear. Today most of our journalists and social commentators exercise a similar caution. However, unlike Gramsci, they are not in prison. They don't need a fascist censor breathing down their necks because they have a mainstream one implanted in their heads.

These internalized forms of self-censorship are more effective in preserving the dominant ideology than any state censor could hope to be. Gramsci knew he was being censored. Many of our newspeople and pundits think they are free as birds—and they are, as long as they fly around in the right circles.

For conservative critics, however, the right circles are neither right enough nor tight enough. Anything to the left of themselves, including moderate right and establishment centrist, is defined as "liberal" or "leftist." Their unrelenting campaign against the media helps to shift the center of political gravity in their direction. Giving generous exposure to conservative and far-right preachments, the press limits public debate to a contest between right and center, while everything substantially left of center is shut out. So the press becomes an active accomplice in maintaining its rightward bent.

On the American political scene, the center is occupied by relatively conservative members of the Democratic Leadership Council who are happy to be considered the only alternative to the ultra-right. This center is then passed off as "liberal." Meanwhile real liberalism and everything progressive have been excluded from the picture—which is what the pundits, politicians, and plutocrats want.

3 METHODS OF MEDIA MANIPULATION

Those who own and those who work for the major news media like to think they provide us with balanced coverage and objective commentary. Journalists and editors claim that occasional inaccuracies do occur in news coverage because of innocent error and everyday production problems such as deadline pressures, budgetary constraints, and the difficulty of reducing a complex story into a concise report. Furthermore, no communication system can hope to report everything, hence selectivity is unavoidable.

To be sure, such pressures and problems do exist and honest mistakes can be made, but do they really explain the media's over-all performance? True, the press must be selective, but what principle of selectivity is involved? Media bias usually does not occur in random fashion; rather it moves in more or less consistent directions, favoring management over labor, corporations over corporate critics, affluent Whites over low-income minorities, officialdom over protesters, privatization and free market "reforms" over public-sector development, U.S. dominance of the Third World over revolutionary or populist social change, and conservative commentators and columnists over progressive or radical ones.

SUPPRESSION BY OMISSION

Some critics complain that the press is sensationalistic and intrusive. In fact, the media's basic modus operandi is evasive rather than invasive. More common than the sensationalistic hype is the artful avoidance. Truly sensational stories (as opposed to sensationalistic) tend to be downplayed or completely avoided, even ones of major import. We hear about political repression perpetrated by officially designated "rogue" nations, but information about the massacres and death-squad murders perpetrated by U.S.-sponsored surrogate forces in the Third World are usually denied public airing.

In 1965 the Indonesian military—advised, equipped, trained, and financed by the U.S. military and the CIA—overthrew President Achmed Sukarno and eradicated the Indonesian Communist Party and its various allies, killing half a million people (some estimates are as high as a million) in what was the greatest act of political mass murder since the Holocaust. The generals also destroyed hundreds of clinics, libraries, schools, and community centers that had been established by the communists. Here was a sensational story if ever there was one, but it took three months before it received passing mention in *Time* magazine and yet another month before it was reported in the *New York Times*, accompanied by an editorial that actually praised the Indonesian military for "rightly playing its part with utmost caution."[9]

Over the course of forty years, the CIA involved itself with drug traffickers in Italy, France, Corsica, Indochina, Afghanistan, and Central and South America. Much of this activity was the object of extended congressional investigation—by Senator Church's committee and Congressman Pike's committee in the 1970s, and Senator Kerry's committee in the late 1980s. But the corporate mainstream media seem not to have heard about this truly sensational story.

ATTACK AND DESTROY THE TARGET

When omission proves to be an insufficient mode of censorship and a story somehow begins to reach a larger public, the press moves from artful avoidance to frontal assault in order to discredit the story.

In August 1996, the *San Jose Mercury News* ran an in-depth series by Pulitzer-winning investigative reporter Gary Webb, about the Iran-Contra crack shipments from Central America that were flooding East Los Angeles. The articles were based on a year-long investigation. Holding true to form, the major media mostly ignored the exposé. But the *Mercury News* series was picked up by some local and regional newspapers, and was flashed across the world on the Internet, copiously supplemented with pertinent documents and depositions supporting the charges against the CIA. African-American communities, afflicted by the crack epidemic, were up in arms and wanted to know more. The story became difficult to ignore.

So the major media switched to all-out assault. Hit pieces in the *Washington Post* and *New York Times* and on network television and PBS assured us that there was no evidence of CIA involvement, that Gary Webb's *Mercury News* series was "bad journalism," and that Webb was irresponsibly playing on the public's gullibility and conspiracy mania. In effect, the major media exonerated the CIA from any involvement in drug trafficking. The *Mercury News* caved in to the pressure and repudiated its own series. Webb was demoted and sent away to cover suburban news. He soon resigned. Webb's real mistake was not that he wrote falsehoods but that he ventured too far into the truth.

It should be mentioned that both the CIA and the Justice Department conducted internal investigations that belatedly vindicated Webb's findings, specifically that there were links between the CIA and drug dealers and that the U.S. government dealt with the drug traffic mostly by looking the other way.[10]

LABELING

Like all propagandists, mainstream media people seek to prefigure our perception of a subject with a positive or negative label even before anything of substance is said about the topic at hand. The function of labeling is to preempt substantive information and analysis. Some *positive* labels are: "stability," "the president's firm leadership," "a strong defense," and "a healthy economy." Indeed, not many Americans would want instability, wobbly presidential leadership, a weak defense, and a sick economy. The label defines the subject without having to deal with particular actualities that might lead us to a different conclusion.

Some common *negative* labels are: "leftist guerrillas," "Islamic terrorists," "conspiracy theory," "inner-city gangs," and "anti-American" (the latter applied to groups or leaders at home or abroad who criticize White House policy). These labels are seldom treated within a larger context of social relations and issues. Some labels the major media are not likely to employ are "class power," "class struggle," and "U.S. imperialism."

A favorite label used regularly by policymakers and faithfully repeated by media journalists and commentators is "reforms," whose meaning is inverted, being applied to any policy dedicated to *undoing* popular reforms that have been achieved after decades of struggle. So the elimination of family assistance programs is labeled "welfare reform." "Reforms" in Eastern Europe—in Yugoslavia, for example—have meant the dismantling of the public economy, its privatization at bargain prices, with a dramatic increase in unemployment and human suffering. "IMF reforms" is a euphemism for the same kind of bruising cutbacks throughout the Third World. As someone once noted, "reforms" are not the solution, they are the problem.

"Free market" and "free trade" are other pet labels left largely unexamined by those who promote them. Critics argue that free-market and free-trade policies undermine local producers, rely heavily on state subsidies to multinational corporations, destroy public sector services, and create greater gaps between rich and poor nations and between the wealthy few and the underprivileged many in every nation. Such arguments are seldom if ever considered by the major media.

A favorite negative media label is "hardline." Anyone who

resists free-market "reforms," be it in Belarus, Italy, Peru, or Yugoslavia, is labeled a "hardliner." An article in the *New York Times* used "hardline" and "hardliner" eleven times to describe Bosnian Serb leaders who opposed attempts by U.S.-supported NATO forces to close down the "hardline Bosnian Serb" radio station. The station was the only outlet in all of Bosnia that offered a critical perspective of Western military intervention and NATO bombings in Yugoslavia. The muting of this one remaining dissenting voice was described by the *Times* as "a step toward bringing about responsible news coverage in Bosnia." Toward the end of the story mention was made of "the apparent irony" of using foreign soldiers for "silencing broadcasts in order to encourage free speech." The NATO troops who carried out this task were identified with the positive label of "peacekeepers."[11]

It is no accident that labels like "hardline" are seldom subjected to precise definition.[12] The efficacy of a label is that it propagates an evocative but undefined image lacking a specific content that can be held up to the test of evidence.

TAKING IT AS A GIVEN

Frequently the media accept as given the very policy position that needs to be critically examined. Whenever the White House proposes an increase in military spending, press treatment is limited to discussing whether we are doing enough to maintain U.S. global military superiority. Little if any attention is given to those who hotly contest the gargantuan arms budget. Most pundits and journalists take it as a given that U.S. forces must be deployed around the world, must maintain military supremacy at all costs, and must expend hundreds of billions of dollars each year in the doing.

Likewise with discussions about Social Security "reform." The media take as a given the highly dubious assertion that there is a serious problem with Social Security, that the program will be insolvent twenty, thirty, or forty years hence and therefore is in need of drastic overhauling now. The enemies of Social Security have been predicting its financial collapse for the last three decades or so—while the program has continued to produce massive surpluses that end up in the general budget to be spent on other things. A minor hike in the program's tax ceiling would take care of any increased demand when the baby boomers start to retire. This point gets relatively little play.

Social Security is a three-pronged human service: in addition to retirement pensions, it provides survivors' insurance (up until the age of 18) to children in families that have lost their breadwinner, and it offers disability assistance to persons of pre-retirement age who are incapacitated by serious injury or prolonged illness. But from existing press coverage you would never know this—and most Americans do not.

FACE-VALUE TRANSMISSION

Many labels are fabricated not by news media but by officialdom. U.S. governmental and corporate leaders talk approvingly of "U.S. world leadership," "American interests," "national security," "free markets," and "globalization." The media uncritically transmit these official images without any noticeable critical comment regarding their actual content. Face-value transmission has characterized the press's performance in many areas of domestic and foreign policy, earning it such scornful nicknames as "stenographer for power" and "mouthpiece for officialdom."

When challenged on this, reporters respond that they cannot

inject their own personal critical views into their reports. Actually, no one is asking them to. My criticism is that they already do, and seldom realize it. Their conventional ideological perceptions usually coincide with those of their bosses and the other powers that be. This uniformity of bias is perceived as "objectivity."

REPETITION AND NORMALIZATION

In 2005, President Bush Jr. explained his method of exposition: "See, in my line of work you got to keep repeating things over and over and over again for the truth to sink in, to kind of catapult the propaganda."[13] Indeed, an opinion that is repeated often enough has a better chance of winning acceptability than rarely heard contrary notions. Repetition helps to create legitimacy. Before the attack on Yugoslavia, various news sources ran unsubstantiated reports about mass killings. Because of the scarcity of evidence and unreliability of reports, the word "genocide" at first appeared in these stories infrequently and in quotation marks, indicating that such a sweeping and sensationalized term was being used tentatively. But once the word was in the air, and after repeated use, the quotation marks disappeared and *genocide* it was, almost always blamed on the Serbs, and through repetition established as a firm fact impervious to contrary evidence. Indeed, evidence became quite irrelevant and remains so to this day.[14]

The September 11, 2001 terrorist attacks on the World Trade Center and the Pentagon, resulting in the loss of almost 3,000 lives, was labeled "a war" several times that very day, by NBC anchor Tom Brokaw. Brokaw exclaimed what no politician had yet dared to mouth: "This is *war!*" Other commentators and pundits quickly announced that Americans were going to have to surrender a goodly amount of their freedom in order to have more security, a theme that was picked up shortly afterward by policy-makers. Thus do media spokespersons clear away safe ground upon which political leaders may venture.

Throughout the autumn of 2002, a controversy raged within the country and across the globe as to whether the United States had the right to invade Iraq. Meanwhile the U.S. media normalized the idea of war by repeatedly running reports on the military preparedness that was taking place. "If we *do* go to war," telecasters intoned, "these are the kinds of missiles that will be used with deadly accuracy" (accompanied by footage of a missile hitting its target). Day after day, the public was treated to reports about reservists being called up, fleets taking to the seas, air attack squadrons placed at the ready, troops running through desert maneuvers in Kuwait, and military supply lines being set up in the Middle East. The face-value reportage of military preparedness made war seem more likely and acceptable.

SLIGHTING OF CONTENT

Corporate news media give much emphasis to surface happenings, to style and process, and less to substantive issues. Accounts of major strikes—on those infrequent occasions the press attends to labor struggles—tell us that negotiations are stalled, how long the strike has lasted, and what scuffles took place on the picket line. Usually missing is any reference to the *content* of the conflict, the actual grievances that drive workers reluctantly to the extreme expediency of a strike, such as cutbacks in wages and benefits, loss of seniority, safety issues, or the unwillingness of management to renew a contract.

Media pundits sometimes talk about the "broader picture." In fact, their ability or willingness to link immediate events and issues to larger social relations is almost nonexistent, nor would a broader analysis be tolerated by their bosses. Instead they regularly give us the *smaller* picture, this being a way of slighting content and remaining within politically safe boundaries. Thus the many demonstrations against international free-trade agreements beginning with NAFTA and GATT are reported, if at all, as contests between protesters and police with little reference to the issues of democratic sovereignty and unaccountable corporate power that impel the protesters.

FALSE BALANCING

In accordance with the canons of good journalism, the press is supposed to tap competing sources to get both sides of an issue. In fact, both sides are seldom accorded equal prominence. One study found that from 1997 through 2005 conservative guests on network opinion shows outnumbered liberal ones usually by three to one, while leftist radicals were too scarce even to be counted.[15] In sum, "both sides of a story" are not usually *all* sides. The whole left-progressive and radical portion of the opinion spectrum is amputated from the visible body politic.

False balancing was evident in a BBC report that spoke of "a history of violence between Indonesian forces and Timorese guerrillas"—with not a hint that the guerrillas were struggling for their lives against an Indonesian invasion force that had slaughtered some 200,000 Timorese. Instead, the genocidal invasion of East Timor was made to sound like a grudge fight, with "killings on both sides."[16] The U.S.-supported wars in Guatemala and El Salvador during the 1980s were often treated with that same kind of false balancing. Both those who burned villages and those who were having their villages burned were depicted as equally involved in a contentious bloodletting. While giving the appearance of being objective and balanced, such reports falsely neutralize their subject matter and thereby distort the issue.

FOLLOW-UP AVOIDANCE

When confronted with an unexpectedly dissident response, media hosts quickly change the subject, or break for a commercial, or inject an identifying announcement: "We are talking with [whomever]." The purpose is to avoid going any further into a politically forbidden topic, no matter how much the unwelcome comment might seem to need a follow-up query. An anchorperson for the BBC enthused: "Christmas in Cuba: for the first time in almost forty years Cubans were able to celebrate Christmas and go to church!" She then linked up with the BBC correspondent in Havana, who observed, "A crowd of two thousand have gathered in the cathedral for midnight mass. The whole thing is rather low key, very much like last year." Very much like last year? Here was something that craved clarification. Instead, the anchorperson quickly switched to another loaded comment: "Can we expect a growth of freedom with the pope's visit?"

PBS talk-show host Charlie Rose once asked a guest, whose name I did not hear, whether Castro was bitter about "the historic failure of communism." No, the guest replied, Castro is proud of what he believes communism has done for Cuba: advances in health care and education, full employment, and the elimination of the worst aspects of poverty. Rose fixed him with an unfriendly glare, then turned to another guest to ask: "What impact will the pope's visit have in Cuba?" Rose ignored the errant guest for the rest of the program.[17] Follow-up avoidance is a kind of damage control.

FRAMING

The most effective propaganda relies on framing rather than on falsehood. By bending the truth rather than breaking it, using emphasis and other auxiliary embellishments, communicators can create a desired impression without resorting to explicit advocacy and without departing too far from the appearance of objectivity. Framing is achieved in the way the news is packaged, the amount of exposure, the placement (front page or buried within, lead paragraph or last), the tone of presentation (sympathetic or slighting), the headlines and photographs, and, in the case of broadcast media, the accompanying visual and auditory effects, and placement (lead story at the top of the hour).

Newscasters use their own selves as auxiliary embellishments. They cultivate a smooth delivery and try to convey an impression of detachment that places them above the rough and tumble of their subject matter. Television commentators and newspaper editorialists and columnists affect a knowing tone designed to foster credibility and an aura of certitude, or what might be called "authoritative ignorance," as expressed in remarks like "How will this situation end? Only time will tell." Or, "No one can say for sure." Trite truisms are palmed off as penetrating truths. Newscasters learn to fashion sentences like "The space launching will take place as scheduled if no unexpected problems arise." And "Unless Congress acts soon, this bill is not likely to go anywhere." And "Because of heightened voter interest, election-day turnout is expected to be heavier than usual."

STUFF JUST HAPPENS

If we are to believe the media, stuff just happens. Many things are reported but few are explained. Little is said about how the social order is organized and for what purposes. Instead we are left to see the world as do mainstream pundits, as a scatter of events and personalities propelled by happenstance, circumstance, passing expediencies, confused intentions, bungled operations, and individual ambition—rarely a world influenced by powerful class interests. Passive voice and impersonal subject are essential rhetorical constructs for this mode of evasion. So we read or hear that "fighting broke out in the region," or "many people were killed in the disturbances," or "famine is on the increase." Recessions apparently just happen like some natural phenomenon ("our economy is in a slump"), having little to do with monetary policy and the contradictions between increased productivity and decreased buying power.

"Globalization" is one of those things that the press presents as a natural (but undefined) development. In fact, globalization is a premeditated policy pursued by transnational corporate interests throughout the world to gain an unchallengeable grip on markets. "Free trade" agreements set up international trade councils that are elected by no one, operate in secrecy without conflict of interest restrictions, and enjoy the power to overrule just about all labor, consumer, and environmental laws and all public service regulations of signatory nations. Globalization establishes the supremacy of property rights over all other rights. What we are experiencing with GATT, NAFTA, FTAA, GATS, and the WTO[18] is *de*globalization, greater concentration of politico-economic power in the hands of an international investor class, a global coup d'etat that divests the peoples of the world of protective democratic input.

Social problems are rarely associated with the politico-economic forces that create them. We are taught to rein in our own critical thinking and not ask *why* things happen the way they do. Imagine if we attempted something different. Suppose we report that the harsh labor conditions existing in so many countries generally have the backing of the military in those countries. Suppose further that we cross another line and note that these military forces are fully supported and funded by the U.S. national security state. Then suppose we cross that most serious line of all and instead of just deploring this fact we also ask *why* successive U.S. administrations have involved themselves in such pursuits throughout the world. Suppose we conclude that the whole phenomenon is consistent with a dedication to making the world safe for free-market corporate capitalism, as measured by the kinds of countries that are helped and the kinds that are attacked. Such an analysis almost certainly would receive no circulation save in a few select radical publications. We crossed too many lines, going beyond the parameters of permissible discourse. Because we tried to explain the particular situation (bad labor conditions) in terms of a larger set of social relations (transnational corporate power), our presentation would be rejected out of hand as "conspiracy theory," or "Marxist," "paranoiac," "cynical," or some other negative label that puts a foreclosure on critical thinking and evidence.

In sum, the news media's daily performance under what is called "democratic capitalism" is not a failure but a skillfully evasive success. We often hear that the press "got it wrong" or "dropped the ball" on this or that story. In fact, the media do their job quite well. Media people have a trained incapacity for the whole truth.

Once we grasp this, we move from a liberal complaint about

the press's sloppy performance to a radical analysis of how journalists and editors maintain the dominant paradigm with much craft and often with the utmost sincerity—having internalized the notions and images of the prevailing orthodoxy. We might recall Upton Sinclair's remark: "It is difficult to get a man to understand something when his salary depends upon his not understanding it."

4 OBJECTIVITY AND THE DOMINANT PARADIGM

The important legitimating symbols of our culture are mediated through a social structure that is largely controlled by centralized, moneyed organizations. This is especially true of our information universe whose mass market is pretty much monopolized by corporate-owned media.

The reporters and news editors who work for these giant multi-billion-dollar media conglomerates believe they are objective in their treatment of the news. They say they are professionals who stick to the facts with no ideological ax to grind. Fox News, a network that proffers a harsh right-wing perspective and specializes in reactionary commentary, claims to be "the only network that is fair and balanced," as its announcers sometimes say when signing off. So, too, with the many other conservative pundits and columnists who overpopulate the corporate-owned media; most seem to believe that their enunciations represent the unadorned truth. And if they do voice a personal opinion, they feel it is anchored in the facts. In short, they believe in their own objectivity.

The usual criticism of objectivity is that it does not exist. The minute one sits down to write the opening line of a story, one is making judgment calls, selecting and omitting things. The very nature of perception makes it a predominantly subjective experience. We are not just passive receptors sponging up a flow of images and information. Perception involves organizing stimuli and data into comprehensible units. In a word, perception is itself an act of selective editing.

It was recently reported that some people had their eyesight restored through new surgical procedures, after a lifetime of being blind. One of the unexpected results was that, even though the physiological mechanisms of sight were reconstructed, the patients could only divine vague shapes and shades. They could not distinguish specific objects and images, for these had never registered in their minds before. Researchers concluded that we see not just with our eyes but with our brains, and the brains of these sightless persons had never had a chance to develop the capacity to organize visual perception.

Also working against the facile professions of objectivity is the understanding that we all have our own way of looking at things. We all resemble each other in some basic ways but each of us is also a unique creation. No two persons are exactly alike. So some portion of our perceptual experience is formed idiosyncratically, situated exclusively in ourselves.

But perception is not entirely or even mostly idiosyncratic. The mental selectors and filters we use to organize our informational intake are usually *not* of our own creation. Most of our seemingly personal perceptions are shaped by a variety of things outside ourselves, such as the prevailing culture, the dominant ideology, ethical beliefs, social values and biases, available information, one's position in the social structure, and one's material interests.

Back in 1921 Walter Lippmann pointed out that much of human perception is culturally prefigured: "For the most part we do not first see and then define, we define first and then see. In the great blooming, buzzing confusion of the outer world we pick out what our culture has already defined for us and we tend to perceive that which we have picked out in the form stereotyped for us by our culture."[19] The notions that fit the prevailing climate of opinion are more likely to be accepted as objective, while those that clash with it are usually seen as lacking in credibility. More often than we realize, we accept or decline an idea, depending on its acceptability within the dominant culture.

In a fashion similar to Lippmann, Alvin Gouldner wrote about the "background assumptions" of the wider culture that are the salient factors in our perceptions. Our readiness to accept something as true, or reject it as false, rests less on its argument and evidence and more on how it aligns with the preconceived notions embedded in the dominant culture, assumptions we have internalized due to repeated exposure.[20] In our culture, among mainstream opinion makers, this unanimity of implicit bias is treated as "objectivity."

Today we rarely refer to Gouldner's background assumptions, but a current equivalent term might be the "dominant paradigm." Some people even sport bumper stickers on their vehicles that urge us to "Subvert the Dominant Paradigm." A paradigm is a basic philosophical or scientific theoretical framework from which key hypotheses can be derived and tested.[21] In popular parlance, the dominant paradigm refers to the ongoing ideological orthodoxy that predetermines which concepts and labels have credibility and which do not. It is the educated person's orthodoxy.

If what passes for objectivity is little more than a culturally defined self-confirming symbolic environment, and if real objectivity—whatever that might be—is unattainable, then it would seem that we are left in the grip of a subjectivism in which one paradigm is about as reliable (or unreliable) as another. And we are faced with the unhappy conclusion that the search for social truth involves little more than choosing from a variety of illusory symbolic configurations. As David Hume argued over two centuries ago, the problem of what constitutes reality in our images can never be resolved since our images can only be compared with other images and never with reality itself.

If so, can we ever think that one imperfect, subjective opinion is better than another? Yes, as a rough rule of thumb, those dissident opinions that are less reliant on the dominant paradigm are likely to be more vigorously challenged and better tested. People generally are receptive to a standard and familiar view, made all the more familiar through a process of repetition. They unthinkingly internalize the mainstream pronouncement and then repeat it as their own opinion, as indeed it has become.

In contrast, they approach the heterodox viewpoint and disruptive information with skepticism, assuming they ever get a chance to hear it. Having been conditioned to the conventional opinion, they are less inclined to automatically internalize unfamiliar data and analysis. Contrary notions that do not fit what they think they already know are usually not welcomed. They will sometimes even self-censor by tuning out, not listening to what is being presented once they detect an alien viewpoint. If given the choice to consider a new perspective or mobilize old arguments against it, it is remarkable how quickly they start reaching for the old arguments. All this makes dissent that much more difficult but that much more urgent.

People who never complain of the orthodoxy of their mainstream political education are the first to complain about the dogmatic "political correctness" of any challenge to it. Far from seeking a diversity of views, they defend themselves from exposure to such diversity, preferring to leave their unexamined background assumptions and conventional political opinions unruffled.

I once taught a class on the mass media at Cornell University. Midway through the course some students began to complain that they were getting only one side, one perspective. I pointed out that in fact the class discussions engaged a variety of perspectives and some of the readings were of the more standard fare. But the truth was, yes, the predominant thrust of the class and assigned readings was substantially critical of the mainstream media and corporate power in general. Then I asked them, "How many of you have been exposed to this perspective in your other social science courses?" Of the forty students—mostly seniors and juniors who had taken many other courses in political science, economics, history, sociology, psychology, anthropology, and mass communications—not one hand went up (a measure of the level of ideological diversity at Cornell). Then I asked the students, "How many of you complained to your other instructors that you were getting only one side?" Again not a hand was raised, causing me to say: "So your protest is not really that you're getting only one side but that for the first time in this class, you're departing from that one side and are being exposed to another view and you don't like it." Their quest was not to investigate heterodoxy but to insulate themselves from it.

Devoid of the supportive background assumptions of the dominant belief system, the deviant view sounds just too improbable and too controversial to be treated as reliable information. Conventional opinions fit so comfortably into the dominant paradigm as to be seen not as opinions but as statements of fact, as "the nature of things." The very efficacy of opinion manipulation rests on the fact that we do not know we are being manipulated. The most insidious forms of oppression are those that so insinuate themselves into our communication universe and the recesses of our minds that we do not even realize they are acting upon us. The most powerful ideologies are not those that prevail against all challengers but those that are never challenged because in their ubiquity they appear as nothing more than the unadorned truth.

A heterodox view provides occasion to test the prevailing orthodoxy. It opens us to arguments and information that the keepers of the dominant paradigm have misrepresented or ignored outright. The dissident view is not just another opinion among many. Its task is to contest the ruling ideology and broaden the boundaries of debate. The function of established opinion is just the opposite, to keep the parameters of debate as narrow as possible.

It is not true, however, that people are totally and rigidly unyielding when challenged in their heartfelt convictions. Confronted with incontrovertible facts that do not fit with what they believe, they sometimes concede the immediate point, but in a way that blunts its impact and keeps the orthodox view intact. I was telling someone that the 2004 presidential election was stolen, a notion that he found hard to accept because such things do not happen in our great democracy, and wasn't I succumbing to conspiracy theories? When I hastily laid out some of the evidence[22] which he could not readily refute, he conceded that such things might have happened, then added that of course there are always mishaps of one sort or another, for no election is ever perfect. So by conceding ground, he retained his basic belief, albeit slightly modified, that while there may have been irregularities here and there that might be worth looking into and correcting, that doesn't mean the election was stolen.

After all is said and done, we are not doomed to an aimless relativism. Even if the problem of perception remains epistemologically unresolved, common sense and everyday life oblige us to make judgments and act as if some images and information are more reliable than others. We may not always know what is true, but we can develop some proficiency at detecting what is false. At least for some purposes, rational mechanisms have their use in the detection of error, so that even if "naked reality" constantly eludes us, we hopefully can arrive at a closer approximation of the truth.[23]

Sometimes the orthodox view is so entrenched that evidence becomes irrelevant. But there are limits to the manipulative efficacy of propaganda. Sometimes misrepresentations can be exposed by a process of feedback, as when subsequent events fail to fulfill the original image. In such instances officialdom has difficulty finessing reality. For example, (a) in 2003–05, official propaganda promised us a quick and easy "liberation" of Iraq, but reality brought undeniably different results that challenged the official line. White House propaganda told us that U.S. troops were "gratefully received by the Iraqi people," but actually a costly and protracted war of resistance ensued. (b) White House propaganda said war was necessary to destroy Saddam Hussein's weapons of mass destruction. But the subsequent invasion revealed that such weapons did not exist, which might explain why Saddam failed to use them when invaded. (c) Propaganda in late 2003 told us that "a fanatical handful of terrorists and Baathist holdouts" were causing most of the trouble, but how could a "handful" pin down two Marine divisions and the 82nd Airborne and inflict thousands of casualties?

As with Iraq, so with Vietnam. For years, the press transmitted the official view of the Vietnam War, but while it could gloss over what was happening in Indochina, it could not totally ignore the awful actuality of the war itself. Still the dominant paradigm prevailed. For the debate on the war was limited between those who said we could win and those who said we could not. Those of us who said we should not be there no matter what the results, that we had no right to intervene and that the intervention served neither the Indochinese nor the American people, never got a platform in the mainstream media because we were deemed "ideological" and "not objective."

The dominant paradigm often can suppress and ignore the entire actuality, as with the U.S. bombing of Cambodia during the Vietnam era, a mass slaughter that the White House kept from the public and from the Congress for quite some time. But total suppression is not always possible, not even in a totalitarian state, as Hitler's minister of propaganda Dr. Joseph Goebbels discovered toward the end of World War II. Goebbels unsuccessfully tried to convince the German public that Nazi armies were winning victory after victory. But after awhile the people could not help noticing that their armies were in retreat, for the "victorious" battles were taking place in regions that kept getting increasingly closer to Germany's borders, finally penetrating the country itself.

Along with the limits of reality we have our powers of critical deduction. I believe it was the philosopher Morris Raphael Cohen who once said that thought is the morality of action, and logic is the morality of thought. One component of logic is consistency. Without doing any empirical investigation of our own, we can look at the internal evidence to find that, like any liar, the press and the officialdom it serves are filled with inconsistencies and contradictions. Seldom held accountable by the news media for what they say, policymakers can blithely produce information and opinions that inadvertently reveal the falsity of previous statements, without a word of explanation. We can point to the absence of supporting evidence and the failure to amplify. We can ask why assertions that appear again and again in the news are not measured against observable actualities. And why are certain important events and information summarily ignored? We already know the answer: it has to do with how they fit into the dominant paradigm.

There remains one hopeful thought: socialization into the conventional culture does not operate with perfect effect. If this were not so, if we were all thoroughly immersed in the dominant paradigm, then I could not have been able to record these critical thoughts and you could not have been able to understand them.

Just about all societies of any size and complexity have their dissenters and critics, or at least their quiet skeptics and nonbelievers. No society, not even the "primitive," is as neatly packaged as some outside observers would have us believe. Even among the Trobrianders, the Zuni, the Kwakiutl, and other peoples, there always were hearty skeptics who thought the myths of their culture were just that—myths, fabricated and unconvincing stories. Culture works its effects upon us imperfectly, and often that is for the best.

In our own society, reality is more a problem for the ruling class than for the rest of us. It has to be constantly finessed and misrepresented to cloak a reactionary agenda. Those at the top understand that the corporate political culture is not a mystically self-sustaining system. They know they must work tirelessly to propagate the ruling orthodoxy, to use democratic appearances to cloak plutocratic policies.[24]

So there is an element of struggle and indeterminacy in all our social realm. And sometimes there is a limit to how many misrepresentations people will swallow. In the face of monopolistic ideological manipulation, many individuals develop a skepticism or outright disaffection based on the growing disparity between social actuality and official ideology. Hence, along with institutional stability we have popular ferment. Along with elite manipulation we have widespread skepticism. Along with ruling-class coercion we have mass resistance—albeit not as much as some of us might wish.

Years ago, William James observed how custom can operate as a sedative while novelty (including dissidence) is rejected as an irritant.[25] Yet I would argue that sedatives can become suffocating after a time and irritants can enliven. People sometimes hunger for the discomforting critical perspective that gives them a more meaningful explanation of things. By being aware of this, we have a better chance of moving against the tide. It is not a matter of becoming the faithful instrument of any particular persuasion but of resisting the misrepresentations of a subtle but thoroughly ideological corporate-dominated culture. In the socio-political struggles of this world, perception and belief are key ingredients. The ideological gatekeepers know this—and so should we.

5 REPRESSION IN ACADEMIA

For some time we have been asked to believe that the quality of higher education is being devalued by the "politically correct" ideological tyranny of feminists, African-American and Latino militants, homosexuals, and Marxists. The truth may be elsewhere. The average university or college is a corporation, controlled by self-selected, self-perpetuating boards of trustees, drawn mostly from the corporate business world. Though endowed with little if any academic expertise, trustees have legal control of the property and policies of the institution. They are answerable to no one but themselves, exercising final authority over all matters of capital funding, budget, tuition, and the hiring, firing, and promotion of faculty and administrators. They even wield ultimate dominion over *curriculum*, mandating course offerings they like while canceling ones that might earn their disfavor. They also have final say regarding course requirements, cross-disciplinary programs, and the existence of entire departments and schools within the university.

On the nation's campuses there also can be found faculty members who do "risk analysis" to help private corporations make safe investments abroad. Other faculty work on consumer responses, marketing techniques, and labor unrest. Still others devise methods for controlling rebellious peoples at home and abroad, be they Latin American villagers, inner-city residents, or factory workers. Funded by corporations, conservative foundations, the Pentagon, and other branches of government, the researchers develop new technologies of destruction, surveillance, control, and counterinsurgency. (Napalm was invented at Harvard.) They develop new ways of monopolizing agricultural production and natural resources. With their bright and often ruthless ideas they help make the world safe for those who own it. In sum, the average institution of higher learning owes more to Sparta than to Athens.

On these same campuses one can find ROTC programs that train future military officers, programs that are difficult to justify by any normal academic standard. The campuses are open to recruiters from various corporations, the CIA, and the armed forces. In 1993, an advertisement appeared in student newspapers across the nation promoting "student programs and career opportunities" with the CIA. Students "could be eligible for a CIA internship and tuition assistance" and would "get hands-on experience" working with CIA "professionals." The advertisement did not explain how full-time students could get "hands-on experience" as undercover agents. Would it be by reporting on professors and fellow students who voiced iconoclastic views?

Without any apparent sense of irony, many of the faculty engaged in these worldly pursuits argue that a university should be a place apart from worldly and partisan interests, a temple of knowledge. In reality, many universities have direct investments in corporate America in the form of substantial stock portfolios. By purchase and persuasion, our institutions of higher learning are wedded to institutions of higher earning. In this respect, universities differ little from other social institutions such as the media, the arts, the church, schools, and various professions.[26]

Most universities and colleges hardly qualify as hotbeds of dissident thought. The more likely product is a mild but pervasive ideological orthodoxy. College is a place where fundamental criticisms are not totally unknown but are just in scarce supply. It is also a place where students, out of necessity or choice, mortgage their future to corporate America.[27]

Ideological repression in academia is as old as the nation itself. Through the eighteenth and nineteenth centuries, most colleges were governed by prominent churchmen and wealthy merchants and landowners who believed it their duty to ensure faculty acceptance of theological preachments. In the early 1800s, trustees at northern colleges prohibited their faculties from engaging in critical discussions of slavery; abolitionism was a taboo subject. At southern colleges, faculty devoted much of their intellectual energies to justifying slavery and injecting racial supremacist notions into various parts of the curriculum.[28] By the 1870s and 1880s, Darwinism was the great bugaboo in higher education. Presidents of nine prominent eastern colleges went on record as prohibiting the teaching of evolutionary theory.

By the 1880s, prominent businessmen came to dominate the boards of trustees of most institutions of higher learning (as they still do). Seldom hesitant to impose ideological controls, they fired faculty members who expressed heretical ideas on and off campus, who attended Populist Party conventions, championed anti-monopoly views, supported free silver, opposed U.S. military interventions abroad, or defended the rights of labor leaders and socialists.[29] Among the hundreds dismissed over the years were such notable scholars as George Steele, Richard Ely, Edward Bemis, James Allen Smith, Henry Wade Rogers, Thorstein Veblen, E. A. Ross, Paul Baran, and Scott Nearing.

The first president of Cornell, Andrew White, observed that while he believed "in freedom from authoritarianism of every kind, this freedom did not, however, extend to Marxists, anarchists, and other radical disturbers of the social order." In 1908, White's contemporary, Harvard president Charles William Elliot, expressed relief that higher education rested safely in the hands of the "public-spirited, business or professional man," away from the dangerous "class influences . . . exerted by farmers as a class, or trade unionists as a class."[30]

During World War I, university officials such as Nicholas Murray Butler, president of Columbia University, explicitly forbade faculty from criticizing the war, arguing that such heresy was no longer tolerable, for in times of war wrongheadedness was sedition and folly was treason. A leading historian, Charles Beard, was grilled by the Columbia trustees, who were concerned that his views might "inculcate disrespect for American institutions." In disgust, Beard resigned from his teaching position, declaring that the trustees and Nicholas Murray Butler sought "to drive out or humiliate or terrorize every man who held progressive, liberal, or unconventional views on political matters."[31]

Academia has seldom been receptive to persons of anticapitalist persuasion. Even during the radical days of the 1930s there were relatively few socialists or communists on college teaching staffs. Repression reached a heightened intensity during the McCarthyite witchhunts of the late 1940s and early 1950s. The rooting out of communists, Marxists, and other radicals was sometimes conducted by congressional and state legislative committees or by college administrators themselves.[32] Among the victims were those who had a past or present association with the Communist Party or one of its affiliated organizations.

One study during the McCarthy period found that, though never called before any investigative body, many faculty felt a need to prove their loyalty. Almost any criticism of the existing politico-economic order invited the suspicion that one might be harboring "communist tendencies." Those who refused to sign loyalty oaths were dismissed outright.[33] The relatively few academics who denounced the anticommunist witchhunts usually did so from an anticommunist premise, arguing that "innocent" (noncommunist) people were being silenced or hounded out of their professions. The implication was that the inquisition was not wrong, just clumsy and overdone, that it was all right to deny Americans their constitutional rights if they were "guilty," that is, really communists. The idea that Reds had as much right as anyone else to teach was openly entertained by only a few brave souls.

During the Vietnam era, things heated up. Faced with student demonstrations, sit-ins, and other disruptions, university author-ities responded with a combination of liberalizing and repressive measures. They dropped course-distribution requirements in some instances and abolished parietal rules and other paternalistic restrictions on student dormitory life. Black studies and women's studies were established, as were a number of experimental social science programs that offered more "relevant" community-ori-ented courses and innovative teaching methods.

Along with the concessions, university authorities launched a repressive counteroffensive. Student activists were singled out for disciplinary actions. Campus police forces were expanded and used to attack demonstrations, as were off-campus police and, when necessary, the National Guard. Some students were arrested and expelled. At places like Kent State and Jackson State, students were shot and killed. Radicalized faculty lost their jobs, and some, including me, were assaulted by police during campus confrontations.[34]

The purging of faculty continued through the 1970s and 1980s. Angela Davis, a communist, was let go by UCLA. Marlene Dixon, a Marxist-feminist sociologist, was fired from the University of Chicago and then from McGill University for her political activism. Bruce Franklin, a noted Melville scholar and tenured associate pro-fessor at Stanford, was fired for "inciting" students to demonstrate. Franklin later received an offer from the University of Colorado that was quashed by its board of regents, who based their decision on a packet of information supplied by the FBI that included false rumors, bogus letters, and unfavorable news articles.[35]

A graduate student at the University of California, Mario Savio, who won national prominence in the 1960s as an antiwar activist and leader of the "Free Speech Movement" on the Berkeley campus, served four months in prison for one protest activity and subsequently was denied admission into various doctoral programs in physics despite having a master's degree in the subject and a sterling academic record. He spent the rest of his life unable to gain a regular appointment in higher education. After many difficult years, Savio died in 1996 at the age of 53. His last job was as a poorly paid adjunct at Sonoma State University.[36]

At the University of Washington, Seattle, Kenneth Dolbeare's attempts to build a truly pluralistic political science department with a mix of conservative, mainstream, and radical faculty, including women and people of color, came under fire from the administration. After a protracted struggle, Dolbeare departed. All the progressive untenured members of the department were let go, as were progressive-minded members of other departments, including philosophy and economics.[37]

Similar purges occurred across the nation. Within a three-year period in the early seventies at Dartmouth College, all but one of a dozen progressive faculty, who used to lunch together, were dismissed. In 1987, four professors at the New England School of Law were fired, despite solid endorsements by their colleagues. All four were involved in the Critical Legal Studies movement, a group that studied how the law acted as an instrument of the rich and powerful.

To a long list of the purged I can add my own name. In 1972, at the University of Vermont, I was denied renewal by the board of trustees despite my publications in leading scholarly journals, and despite the support of my students, my entire department, the faculty senate, the council of deans, the provost and the president.

Unable to fault my teaching or scholarship, the trustees decided in a 15-to-4 vote that my antiwar activities constituted "unprofessional conduct."

A dozen or so years later, I went to Brooklyn College as a one-year visiting professor with the understanding that a regular position would be given to the political science department for which I could later apply. My chairman's feeling was that given my qualifications, I would no doubt be the leading candidate. The administration, however, decided against it. A short time afterward, a City University chemistry professor, John Lombardi, happened to be talking to a Brooklyn College vice president at a faculty gathering. Lombardi, who was familiar with my work, asked him why I had been let go. "We found out about him," said the vice president, who went on to indicate that the administration had discovered things about my political background that they did not like.[38]

One could add many more instances from just about every discipline, including political science, economics, anthropology, literature, history, sociology, psychology and even physics, mathematics, chemistry, and musicology. Whole departments and even whole schools and colleges have been eradicated for taking the road less traveled. At University of California, Berkeley, the entire school of criminology was abolished because many of its faculty had developed a class analysis of crime and criminal enforcement. Those who taught a more orthodox criminology were given appointments in other departments. Only the radicals were let go.

Even more frequent than the firings are the nonhirings. Highly qualified social scientists, who were also known progressives, have been turned down for positions at institutions too numerous to mention. The pattern became so pronounced at the University of Texas, Austin, in the mid-1970s, that graduate students staged a protest and charged the university with politically discriminatory hiring practices.

In 1981, the political science department of Virginia Commonwealth University invited me to become chairperson, but the decision was overruled by the dean, who announced that it was unacceptable to have a "leftist" as head of a department. She did not explain why the same rule did not hold for a rightist or centrist or feminist (she claimed to be the latter). It is evident that academia speaks with two voices. One loudly proclaims professional performance as the reigning standard. The other whispers almost inaudibly that if you cross the parameters of permissible opinion, your scholarly and pedagogical performance are of no account.

Scholars of an anticapitalist, anti-imperialist bent are regularly discriminated against in the distribution of research grants and scholarships. After writing *The Power Elite*, C. Wright Mills was abruptly cut off from foundation funding. To this day, radical academics are rarely considered for positions within their professional associations and are regularly passed over for prestigious lecture invitations, grants, and appointments to editorial boards of the more influential professional journals. Faculty are still advised to think twice about voicing controversial politico-economic perspectives. One historian writes that, when a young instructor and a group of her colleagues decided to offer "Marxism" as part of a social history course, she was warned by an older faculty member, "an ordinarily calm and rational gentleman," that it would be "unwise for their department to list a course on Marxism in the catalogue."[39]

An instructor at Seton Hill College in Pennsylvania confided to a leftist student that he subscribed to a number of left publications and was well-versed in Marxist theory but the administration refused to let him teach it. The student wrote to an associate of mine, "I've had classes with this prof for two years and never suspected." On some campuses, administrative officials have monitored classes, questioned the political content of books and films, and screened the lists of guest speakers—all in the name of scholarly objectivity and balance. In some places, however, trustees and administrators readily pay out huge sums for guest lectures by committed, highly partisan, right-wing ideologues.

The guardians of academic orthodoxy never admit that some of their decisions about hiring and firing faculty might be politically motivated. Instead they will say the candidate has not published enough articles. Or if enough, the articles are not in conventionally acceptable academic journals. Or if in acceptable journals, they are still wanting in quality and originality, or show too narrow or too diffuse a development. Seemingly objective criteria can be applied in endlessly elastic ways.

John Womack, one of the very few Marxists ever to obtain tenure at an elite university, and who became chair of the history department at Harvard, ascribes his survival to the fact that he was dealing with relatively obscure topics: "Had I been a bright young student in Russian history and taken positions perpendicular to American policy . . . I think my [academic] elders would have thought that I had a second-rate mind. Which is what you say when you disagree with somebody. You can't say, 'I disagree with the person politically.' You say, 'It's clear he has a second-rate mind.'"[40]

College administrators and department heads, whatever their scholarly output, must be ready to serve as conservative enforcers. The administration at the University of Vermont brought in someone to chair the philosophy department who, by a nine to one vote, the department had turned down as insufficiently qualified. He proceeded to purge all the nontenured and politically progressive members who had voted against him. Over the objections of the political science department of the University of Maryland, Baltimore, the chancellor gave tenure to Walter Jones, not a particularly distinguished member of the profession. Jones was then made vice-chancellor, from which position he denied tenure to a radical political scientist, overruling a unanimous recommendation of the school's promotion and tenure committee.

Professional criteria proved especially elastic for those émigrés from communist countries brought to the United States under the hidden sponsorship of national security agencies and immediately accorded choice university positions without meeting minimal academic standards. Consider the case of Soviet émigré and concert pianist Vladimir Feltsman, who, after receiving a first-rate, free musical education in the Soviet Union, defected to the United States in 1986 with the help of the U.S. embassy. In short time Feltsman gave a White House concert, was hailed by President Reagan as a "moral hero," and was set up in a posh Manhattan apartment. He then was appointed to the State University of New York at New Paltz, where he taught one class a week for twice the salary of a top-ranking professor, and was awarded an endowed chair and a distinguished fellowship. SUNY, New Paltz, itself was a poorly funded school with low salaries, heavy teaching loads, and inadequate services for students.

Mainstream academics treat their politically safe brands of teaching and research as the only ones that qualify as genuine scholarship. Such was the notion used to deny Samuel Bowles tenure at Harvard. Since Marxist economics is not really scholarly, it was argued, Bowles was neither a real scholar nor an authentic economist. Thus centrist ideologues have purged scholarly dissidents under the guise of protecting rather than violating academic standards. The decision seriously split the economics department and caused Nobel Prize winner Wassily Leontif to quit Harvard in disgust.

Radical academics have been rejected because their political commitments supposedly disallow them from objective scholarship. In fact, much of the best scholarship comes from politically committed scholars. One goal of any teacher should be to introduce students to bodies of information and analysis that have been systematically ignored or suppressed—a task that usually is better performed by iconoclasts than by those who accept existing institutional and class arrangements as the finished order of things. So it has been feminists and African-American researchers who, in their partisan urgency, have revealed the previously unexamined sexist and racist presumptions and gaps of conventional scholarship.[41] Likewise, it is leftist intellectuals (including some who are female or nonwhite) who have produced the challenging scholarship about popular struggle, political economy, and class power, subjects remaining largely untouched by centrists and conservatives.[42] In sum, a dissenting ideology can awaken us to things regularly overlooked by conventional scholarship.

Orthodox ideological strictures are applied also to a teacher's outside political activity. At the University of Wisconsin, Milwaukee, an instructor of political science, Ted Hayes, an anticapitalist, was denied a contract renewal because he was judged to have "outside political commitments" that made it impossible for him to be objective. Two of the senior faculty who voted against him were state committee members of the Republican Party in Wisconsin.[43] There was no question as to whether *their* outside political commitments interfered with their objectivity as teachers or with the judgments they made about colleagues.

Evron Kirkpatrick, who served as director of the American Political Science Association for more than twenty-five years, proudly enumerated the many political scientists who occupied public office, worked in electoral campaigns or served officialdom in various capacities.[44] His comments evoked no outcry from his mainstream colleagues on behalf of scientific detachment. It seemed there was nothing wrong with political activism as long as one played a "sound role in government" (his words) rather than a dissenting role against it. Establishment academics like Kirkpatrick never explain how they supposedly avoid injecting politics into their science while so assiduously injecting their science into politics.

How neutral in their writings and teachings were such scholars as Zbigniew Brzezinski, Henry Kissinger, Daniel Patrick Moynihan, and Jeane Kirkpatrick? Despite being proponents of American industrial-military policies at home and abroad—or because of it—they enjoyed meteoric academic careers and subsequently were selected to occupy prominent policymaking positions within conservative administrations in Washington. Outspoken political advocacy, then, is not a hindrance to one's career as long as one advocates the right things.

It is a rare radical scholar who has not encountered difficulties when seeking employment or tenure, regardless of his or her qualifications. The relatively few progressive dissidents who manage to get tenure sometimes discover that their lot is one of isolation within their own departments. They endure numerous slights and are seldom consulted about policy matters. And they are not likely to be appointed to committees dealing with curriculum, hiring, and tenure, even when such assignments would be a normal part of their responsibilities.

At the University of Washington, Philip Meranto, a tenured–

anticapitalist political scientist, was frozen out of all departmental decisions and department social life. Graduate students were advised not to take his classes. He was given the most cramped faculty office despite his senior rank and was subjected to verbal harassment from university police. He eventually resigned.

After serving for many years as a tenured senior faculty member of Queens College, CUNY, noted author and political analyst John Gerassi was moved to voice his displeasure at the treatment he had been accorded, including the case of my own candidacy. In a letter to his department colleagues, he wrote:

> I have never been asked to participate in anything mean-ingful in this department. For example, I have never been asked to be an adviser to graduates or undergraduates or [anyone else] . . . . Now since my colleagues tell me they like me, and I assume that they are not saying that just to humor me, the reason must be political. Indeed, I remember years ago when I informed my colleagues that a friend of mine who was nationally known, in fact internationally respected, Michael Parenti, who would be a great draw because of his reputation, was available for a job (at a time when the department was actually trying to fill a position), I was quickly informed that he would not be considered no matter what, and I was told in effect to stay out of department business.[45]

Gerassi concluded on an ironic note: "If nothing else, may I respectfully request that while all decisions may be made by a small group of my colleagues behind closed doors, do, please, let us know what those decisions are."

The only radical to receive tenure in the department of philosophy in the 1970s at the University of Vermont was Willard Miller, a popular teacher, published author, participant in scholarly conferences, and political activist. Though he prevailed in his battle for tenure, Miller was made to pay for it. He was denied promotion and remained an assistant professor for thirty-three years with a salary frozen for a long time at below the entry level of the lowest-paid instructor. He was passed over for sabbatical for thirteen years and finally received a one-semester leave only after threatening court action. And he was perpetually passed over for reduced teaching load, a consideration granted to his departmental colleagues on a rotation basis.[46] He died in 2005, still an assistant professor.

Campus activism did not pass away with the Vietnam era. Student protests have arisen against the nuclear arms race, the university's corporate investments in an apartheid-ruled South Africa, U.S. involvement in Central America (including the U.S. invasion of Panama), and the U.S. bombing and invasion of Iraq. There have been demonstrations in support of affirmative action, women's studies, and multiculturalism, and protests against racism, sexism, and Eurocentric biases in the curriculum. But such actions are rarely inspired by anything taught in the classroom, and often despite what is taught.

Facing a campus that is not nearly as reactionary as they would wish, ultra-conservatives rail about how academia is permeated with doctrinaire, "politically correct" leftists. This is not surprising since they describe as "leftist" anyone to the left of themselves, including mainstream centrists. Their diatribes usually are little more than attacks upon socio-political views they find intolerable and want eradicated from college curricula. Through all this, one seldom actually hears from the "politically correct" people who supposedly dominate the universe of discourse.

It was the novelist Saul Bellow who denigrated preliterate societies by asking, "Who is the Tolstoy of the Zulus? The Proust of the Papuans?" When criticized for his Eurocentrism, Bellow fired back in the nation's most prominent newspaper: "We can't open our mouths without being denounced as racists, misogynists, supremacists, imperialists or fascists."[47] Writers like Bellow, who enjoy every acclaim from conventional literary quarters and plum appointments at leading universities, and who criticize anyone they wish, apparently expect to remain above criticism themselves. And when opinions arise that challenge their unexamined biases, they have the major media through which they can reach wide audiences to complain about being unjustly muted.

Networks of well-financed, right-wing campus groups coordinate conservative activities at schools around the nation, and fund over one hundred conservative campus publications, reaching more than a million students. Such undertakings are well financed by the Scaife Foundation, the Olin Foundation, and other wealthy donors. The nearly complete lack of a similar largesse for progressive groups further belies the notion that political communication in academia is dominated by left-wingers.

In addition, we witness the growing corporate arrogation of institutional functions, and increasing dependence on private funding, all of which militates against anything resembling a radical predominance. The university's conservative board of trustees dishes out extravagant salaries to top administrators along with millions of dollars in luxury cars, luxury dwellings, and other hidden perks for themselves and university officers.[48] Meanwhile student fees are being dramatically increased, services slashed, and the numbers of low-paid and heavily exploited adjunct teachers (as opposed to fulltime professors) has increased considerably. No university is under leftist rule. The majority of students are from privileged backgrounds, careerist in their concerns, and lacking in the most basic information regarding the politico-economic realities in this country and abroad. As for the faculty, the majority are of mainstream or otherwise conventionally centrist political orientation. In the social sciences there are many more Bill Clinton Democrats than George Bush Republicans. In the business and engineering schools, and maybe also law and medicine, there sometimes are more conservatives. Conservatives seize upon the relative shortage of conservative faculty as proof of deliberate discrimination. This is an odd argument coming from them, Steven Lubet points out, since conservatives usually dismiss the scarcity of women or minorities in a workforce or student body as simply the absence of qualified applicants. That is not discrimination, they insist, it is self-selection. "Conservatives abandon these arguments however when it comes to their own prospects in academe. Then the relative scarcity of Republican professors is widely asserted as proof of willful prejudice." Lubet continues:

> Beyond the ivy walls there are many professions that are dominated by Republicans. You will find very few Democrats (and still fewer outright liberals) among the ranks of high-level corporate executives, military officers or football coaches. Yet no one complains about these imbalances, and conservatives will no doubt explain that the seeming disparities are merely the result of market forces.
>
> They are probably right. It is entirely rational for conservatives to flock to jobs that reward competition, aggression and victory at the expense of others. So it should not be surprising that liberals gravitate to professions—such as academics, journalism, social work and the

arts—that emphasize inquiry, objectivity and the free exchange of ideas. After all, teachers at all levels—from nursery school to graduate school—tend to be Democrats. Surely there cannot be a conspiracy to deny conservatives employment on kindergarten playgrounds.[49]

For years mainstream academics scorned antiwar radicals and Marxists of every stripe. Now, ironically, some of these same centrists find themselves attacked by the emboldened student ultra-conservatives who complain that exposure to liberal and "leftist" ideas deprives them of their right to academic freedom and ideological diversity. What they really are protesting is their first encounter with ideological diversity, their first exposure to a critical perspective other than the one they regularly embrace. Conservative students grumble about being denied their First Amendment rights by occasionally being required to read leftist scholars. "Where are the readings by Sean Hannity, Ann Coulter, and Bill O'Reilly?" complained one.[50] They register these complaints with college administrators, trustees, and outside conservative organizations. Accusations of partisanship hurled by the student reactionaries are themselves intensely partisan, being leveled against those who question, but never against those who reinforce, conservative orthodoxy. Thus the campus headhunters act as self-appointed censors while themselves claiming to be victims of censorship.

In recent years, the underpaid adjunct teaching staff and heavily indebted student body have found still fewer opportunities for exploratory studies and iconoclastic views. The world around us faces a growing economic inequality and a potentially catastrophic environmental crisis. Yet the predominant intellectual product in academia remains largely bereft of critical engagements with society's compelling issues. Not everything written by mainstream scholars serves the powers that be, but very little of it challenges such powers. While orthodoxy no longer goes uncontested, it still rules. Scholarly inquiry may strive to be neutral but it is never confected in a neutral universe of discourse. It is always subjected to institutional and material constraints that shape the way it is produced, funded, distributed, and acknowledged. Money speaks louder than footnotes.

NOTES

1. *New York Times,* 9 May 2006.
2. Mark Dowie, "A Teflon Correspondent," *Nation,* 7 January 2002.
3. *New York Times,* 6 September 2005; and see. *Outfoxed: Rupert Murdoch's War on Journalism,* documentary by Robert Greenwald, 2004.
4. Quoted in *Nation,* 10 January 2000.
5. See Ben Bagdikian, *The New Media Monopoly* (Beacon Press, 2004).
6. Commission on Freedom of the Press, quoted in Robert Cirino, *Don't Blame the People* (Vintage, 1972). 47.
7. *San Francisco Chronicle,* 12 July and 14 October 2004; *New York Times,* 31 March 2003 and 4 May 2004.
8. As an example of this conservative media critic, see bully-boy Fred Barnes, "Is the Mainstream Media Fair and Balanced?" *Imprimis,* August 2006.
9. *New York Times,* 5 April 1966.
10. See Gary Webb, *Dark Alliance: The CIA, the Contras, and the Crack Cocaine Explosion* (Seven Stories, 1998)
11. *New York Times,* 21 October 1997.
12. For further discussion of the left, right and center labels, see herein selection 21, "Left, Right, and the 'Extreme Moderates.'"
13. Quoted in Amy Goodman and David Goodman, "The War on Truth," http://towardfreedom.com/home/content/view/889, 20 September 2006.
14. For further discussion of this herein, see selection 31, "The Rational Destruction of Yugoslavia."
15. Report by MediaMatters, http://mediamatters.org, 15 February 2006.
16. BBC World Service report, 11 December 1997.
17. Charlie Rose Show, NPR, 22 January 1998.
18. General Agreement on Tariffs and Trade (GATT), Free Trade Area of the Americas (FTAA), General Agreement on Trade in Services (GATS), World Trade Organization (WTO).

19. Walter Lippmann, *Public Opinion* (Free Press, 1960 [1921]), 81.
20. Alvin W. Gouldner, *The Coming Crisis of Western Sociology* (Basic Books, 1970).
21. The dominant scientific paradigm is established presumably on the basis of thorough testing and is accepted because it has been used many times with apparent success. "Paradigm change" refers to momentous shifts in basic models of conception and investigation, for instance, the shift from Newtonian physics to Einstein's theory of relativity. See Thomas S. Kuhn, *The Structure of Scientific Revolutions* (University of Chicago Press, 1962).
22. See selection 6, "The Stolen Presidential Elections."
23. See Kenneth Boulding, "Learning and Reality-Testing Process in the International System," *International Affairs*, v. 21 (1967).
24. For a fuller exposition of this, see my *Democracy for the Few*, 8th ed. (Wadsworth/Thomson, 2007).
25. William James, "The Sentiment of Rationality," in his *Essays in Pragmatism* (Hafner, 1948), 13.
26. For a fuller discussion of this point, see herein selection 27, "Monopoly Culture and Social Legitimacy."
27. For an early critique, see Thorstein Veblen's classic: *The Higher Learning in America: A Memorandum on the Conduct of Universities by Business Men* (B.W. Huebsch, 1918). On who dominates the university and who is served by it, see David N. Smith, *Who Rules the Universities?* (Monthly Review Press, 1974) John Trumpbour (ed.), *How Harvard Rules: Reason in the Service of Empire* (South End Press, 1989); and Geoffry D. White and Flannery Hauck, *Campus Inc.*(Prometheus, 2000). That the university is an extension of the ideological conformity found in primary and secondary schools is suggested by such works as Joel Spring, *Education and the Rise of the Corporate State* (Beacon Press, 1972).
28. Donald Tewksbury, *The Founding of American Colleges and Universities Before the Civil War* (Archon Press, 1965).
29. Richard Hofstadter and Walter Metzger, *The Development of Academic Freedom in the United States* (Columbia University Press, 1955).
30. The White and Elliot quotations are from Smith, *Who Rules the Universities?*, 85–86 and 88.
31. Richard Hofstadter and Wilson Smith, *American Higher Education*, vol. 2 (University of Chicago Press, 1961), 883–892. See also Scott Nearing, *The Making of an American Radical: A Political Autobiography* (Harper & Row, 1972).
32. See the discussion in Ellen Schrecker, *No Ivory Tower* (Oxford University Press, 1986); and in regard to a specific discipline, see David Price, *Threatening Anthropology: McCarthyism and the FBI's Surveillance of Activist Anthropologists* (Duke University Press, 2004).

33. Paul Lasersfeld and Wagner Thielens Jr., *The Academic Mind* (Free Press, 1958), 52–53 and passim; also Robert MacIver, *Academic Freedom in Our Time* (Columbia University Press, 1955).

34. For details, see my "Struggles in Academe, A Personal Account," in Michael Parenti, *Dirty Truths* (City Lights Books, 1996), 235–252.

35. Angela Davis, *If They Come in the Morning* (New American Library, 1971); Marlene Dixon, *Things Which Are Done in Secret* (Black Rose Books, 1976); Philip Meranto and Matthew Lippman, *Guarding the Ivory Tower: Repression and Rebellion in Higher Education* (Lucha Publications, 1985), chapter 5.

36. *San Francisco Chronicle*, 8 December 1996.

37. Meranto and Lippman, *Guarding the Ivory Tower*, chapter 4.

38. This exchange was reported to me by Lombardi.

39. Ellen Schrecker, "Academic Freedom," in Cariag Kaplan and Ellen Schrecker (eds.), *Regulating the Intellectuals* (Praeger, 1983).

40. Womack quoted in *Washington Post*, 1 January 1983.

41. Florence Howe and Paul Lanter, *The Impact of Women's Studies on the Campus and the Disciplines* (National Institute of Education, 1980); Alan Colon, "Critical Issues in Black Studies: A Selective Analysis," *Journal of Negro Education*, 53, (December 1984), 274–281; Carols Brossard, "Classifying Black Studies Programs," *Journal of Negro Education*, 53 (November 1984), 282–290.

42. Bertell Ollman and Edward Vernoff (eds.), *The Left Academy: Marxist Scholarship on American Campuses* (McGraw Hill, 1982); and my article "Political Science Fiction," in Parenti, *Dirty Truths*, 221–233.

43. Ted Hayes, conversation with me, July 1979.

44. Evron Kirkpatrick, comments in *PS* (publication of the American Political Science Association), Summer 1981, 597.

45. John Gerassi, correspondence to his department, 15 May 1994, made available to me by Gerassi.

46. Willard Miller interviewed by me, 11 July 1994.

47. Saul Bellow, op-ed, *New York Times*, 10 March 1994.

48. *San Francisco Chronicle*, 2 June 2006.

49. *San Francisco Chronicle*, 2 December 2004.

50. Oneida Meranto, "The Third Wave of McCarthyism: Co-opting the Language of Inclusivity." *New Political Science*, 27 June 2005, 221.

II.

STEALING OUR BIRTHRIGHT

6 THE STOLEN PRESIDENTIAL ELECTIONS

In one of the closest contests in U.S. history, the 2000 presidential election between Democratic Vice-President Al Gore and Republican governor of Texas George W. Bush (Bush Jr.), the final outcome hinged on how the vote went in Florida. Independent investigations in that state revealed serious irregularities directed mostly against ethnic minorities and low-income residents who usually voted heavily Democratic. Some 36,000 newly registered voters were turned away because their names had never been added to the voter rolls by Florida's secretary of state Kathleen Harris. By virtue of the office she held, Harris presided over the state's election process while serving as an active member of Bush Jr.'s statewide campaign committee. Other voters were turned away because they were declared—almost always incorrectly—"convicted felons." In several Democratic precincts, state officials closed the polls early, leaving lines of would-be voters stranded.

Under orders from Governor Jeb Bush (Bush Jr.'s brother), state troopers near polling sites delayed people for hours while searching their cars. Some precincts required two photo IDs which many citizens do not have. The requirement under Florida law was only one photo ID. Passed just before the election, this law itself posed a special difficulty for low-income or elderly voters who did not have driver's licenses or other photo IDs. Uncounted ballot boxes went missing or were found in unexplained places or were never collected from certain African-American precincts. During the recount, GOP agitators shipped in from Washington, D.C., by the Republican national leadership stormed the Dade County Canvassing Board, punched and kicked one of the officials, shouted and banged on their office doors, and generally created a climate of intimidation that caused the board to abandon its recount and accept the dubious pro-Bush tally.[1]

Then a 5–4 conservative majority on the U.S. Supreme Court in a logically tortuous decision ruled that a complete recount in Florida would violate the Fourteenth Amendment's equal protection clause because different counties have different ways of counting the votes. At that point Gore was behind by only a few hundred or so votes in Florida and was gaining ground with each attempt at a recount. By preventing a complete tally, the justices handed Florida's electoral votes and the presidency to Bush, a stolen election in which the conservative activists on the Supreme Court played a key role.

Even though Bush Jr. lost the nation's popular vote to Gore by over half a million, he won the electoral college and the presidency itself. Florida was not the only problem. Similar abuses and mistreatment of voters and votes occurred in other parts of the country. A study by computer scientists and social scientists estimated that four to six million votes were left uncounted in the 2000 election.[2]

The 2004 presidential contest between Democratic challenger Senator John Kerry and the incumbent president George W. Bush amounted to another stolen election. Some 105 million citizens voted in 2000, but in 2004 the turnout climbed to at least 122 million. Pre-election surveys indicated that among the record 16.8 million new voters Kerry was a heavy favorite, a fact that went largely unreported by the press. In addition, there were about two million progressives who had voted for Ralph Nader in 2000 who switched to Kerry in 2004. Yet the official 2004 tallies showed Bush Jr. with 62 million votes, about 11.6 million more than he got in 2000. Meanwhile Kerry showed only eight million more votes than Gore received in 2000. To have achieved his remarkable 2004 tally, Bush would have needed to have kept virtually all his 50.4 million from 2000, plus a huge majority of the new voters, plus a large share of the very liberal Nader defectors. Nothing in the campaign and in the opinion polls suggest such a mass crossover. The numbers simply do not add up.

In key states like Ohio, the Democrats achieved immense success at registering new voters, outdoing the Republicans by as much as five to one. Moreover the Democratic party was unusually united around its candidate—or certainly against the incumbent president. In contrast, prominent elements within the GOP displayed open disaffection, publicly voicing serious misgivings about the Bush administration's huge budget deficits, reckless foreign policy, theocratic tendencies, and threats to individual liberties. Sixty newspapers that had endorsed Bush in 2000 refused to do so in 2004; forty of them endorsed Kerry.[3]

All through election day 2004, exit polls showed Kerry ahead by 53 to 47 percent, giving him a nationwide edge of about 1.5 million votes, and a solid victory in the electoral college. Yet strangely enough, the official tally gave Bush the election by two million votes. What follows are examples of how the GOP "victory" was secured.[4]

In some places large numbers of Democratic registration forms disappeared, along with absentee ballots and provisional ballots. Sometimes absentee ballots were mailed out to voters just before election day, too late to be returned on time, or they were never mailed at all.

Overseas ballots normally distributed reliably by the State Department were for some reason distributed by the Pentagon in 2004. Nearly half of the six million American voters living abroad—a noticeable number of whom formed anti-Bush organizations—never received their ballots or got them too late to vote. Military personnel, usually more inclined toward supporting the president, encountered no such problems with their overseas ballots. A person familiar with my work, Rick Garves, sent me this account of his attempt to cast an overseas ballot:

> I filled out the forms to register to vote absentee since I live here in Sweden. They were even done at a meeting for "Democrats Abroad in Stockholm." I mailed the forms and when I got my packet back I looked at it and they had me as being in the military. Of course I am not and never have been. I also never checked any boxes on the forms even remotely close to anything insinuating that I was in the military.
>
> So there was not enough time to fix the "error" and I did not even bother to vote because I knew they would check and find that I am not in the military and my vote would be invalidated. I now wonder even more if that happened because of the Pentagon taking over the handling of the absentee voter registration and too, how many more overseas voters had the same problem?

Tens of thousands of Democratic voters were stricken from the rolls in several states because of "felonies" never committed, or committed by someone else, or for no given reason. Registration books in Democratic precincts were frequently out-of-date or incomplete.

Voter Outreach of America, a company funded by the Republican National Committee, collected thousands of voter registration forms in Nevada, promising to turn them in to public officials, but then systematically destroyed the ones belonging to Democrats.

Democratic precincts—enjoying record turnouts—were deprived of sufficient numbers of polling stations and voting machines, and many of the machines they had kept breaking down. After waiting long hours many people went home without voting. The noted political analyst and writer, Gregory Elich, sent me this account of his election day experience:

> I recall being surprised when I went to vote before work here in Ohio in 2004. Normally, at election time, I can go to the polling place before work, walk in and be in a voting booth in less than two minutes, even in a presidential election. In 2004, when I arrived I saw a long, snaking line of people. I waited twenty minutes, and the line barely moved. It was clear I would be late for work if I persisted, so I left and decided to take an hour or so of vacation time in the middle of the day to vote. I thought surely, in the middle of the work day, the line would not be bad. The line was worse, and it took me close to two hours to vote.
>
> My neighborhood is about 65 to 70 percent African-American. The next day, in conversation with an African-American co-worker, she told me that she waited

in line for four hours. And I heard stories later of people waiting as long as 7 hours. I also stopped at the post office, and voting was a topic of conversation for those of us in the post office line. The man ahead of me, who lived in a well-to-do neighborhood said he was surprised to hear the stories, because it only took him two minutes to vote. Just anecdotal stories, but there were so many more, that there certainly seemed to be a pattern in regard to wealthy vs. working class neighborhoods.

Pro-Bush precincts almost always had enough voting machines, all working well to make voting quick and convenient. A similar pattern was observed with student populations in several states: students at conservative Christian colleges had little or no wait at the polls, while students from liberal arts colleges were forced to line up for as long as ten hours, causing many to give up.

In Lucas County, Ohio, one polling place never opened; the voting machines were locked in an office and apparently no one could find the key. In Hamilton County many absentee voters could not cast a Democratic vote for president because John Kerry's name had been "accidentally" removed when Ralph Nader was taken off the ballot.

A polling station in a conservative evangelical church in Miami County, Ohio, recorded an impossibly high turnout of 98 percent, while a polling place in Democratic inner-city Cleveland recorded an impossibly low turnout of 7 percent.

Latino, Native American, and African-American voters in New Mexico who favored Kerry by two to one were five times more likely to have their ballots spoiled and discarded in districts supervised by Republican election officials. Many were readily given provisional ballots that subsequently were never counted. In these same Democratic areas Bush "won" an astonishing 68 to 31 percent upset victory. One Republican judge in New Mexico discarded hundreds of provisional ballots cast for Kerry, accepting only those that were for Bush.

Cadres of right-wing activists, many of them religious fundamentalists, were financed by the Republican Party. Deployed to key Democratic precincts, they handed out flyers warning that voters who had unpaid parking tickets, an arrest record, or owed child support would be arrested at the polls—all untrue. They went door to door offering to "deliver" absentee ballots to the proper office, and announcing that Republicans were to vote on Tuesday (election day) and Democrats on Wednesday.

Democratic poll watchers in Ohio, Arizona, and other states, who tried to monitor election night vote counting, were menaced and shut out by squads of GOP toughs. In Warren County, Ohio, immediately after the polls closed, Republican officials announced a "terrorist attack" alert, and ordered the press to leave. They then moved all ballots to a warehouse where the counting was conducted in secret, producing an amazingly high tally for Bush, some 14,000 more votes than he had received in 2000. It wasn't the terrorists who attacked Warren County.

Bush Jr. also did remarkably well with phantom populations. The number of his votes in Perry and Cuyahoga counties in Ohio exceeded the number of registered voters, creating turnout rates as high as 124 percent. In Miami County, Ohio, nearly 19,000 additional votes eerily appeared in Bush's column *after* all precincts had reported. In a small conservative suburban precinct of Columbus, where only 638 people were registered, the touch-screen machines tallied 4,258 votes for Bush.

In almost half of New Mexico's counties, more votes were reported than were recorded as being cast, and the tallies were consistently in Bush's favor. These ghostly results were dismissed by New Mexico's Republican Secretary of State as an "administrative lapse."

Exit polls showed Kerry solidly ahead of Bush Jr. in both the popular vote and the electoral college. Exit polls are an exceptionally accurate measure of elections. In the last three elections in Germany, for example, exit polls were never off by more than three-tenths of one percent. Unlike ordinary opinion polls, the exit sample is drawn from people who have actually just voted. It rules out those who say they will vote but never make it to the polls, those who cannot be sampled because they have no telephone or otherwise cannot be reached at home, those who are undecided or who change their minds about whom to support, and those who are turned away at the polls for one reason or another. Exit polls have come to be considered so reliable that international organizations use them to validate election results in countries around the world.

Republicans argued that in 2004 the exit polls were inaccurate because they were taken only in the morning when Kerry voters came out in greater numbers. (Apparently Bush voters are late sleepers.) In fact, the polling was done at random intervals all through the day, and the evening results were as favorable to Kerry as the earlier sampling. It was also argued that exit pollsters focused more on women (who favored Kerry) than men, or perhaps large numbers of taciturn Republicans were less inclined than chatty Democrats to talk to pollsters. No evidence was put forth to substantiate these fanciful speculations.

Most revealing, the discrepancies between exit polls and official tallies were never random but worked to Bush's advantage in ten of eleven swing states that were too close to call, sometimes by as much as 9.5 percent as in New Hampshire, an unheard of margin of error for an exit poll. In Nevada, Ohio, New Mexico, and Iowa exit polls registered solid victories for Kerry, yet the official tally in each case went to Bush, a mystifying outcome.

In states that were not hotly contested the exit polls proved quite accurate. Thus exit polls in Utah predicted a Bush victory of 70.8 to 26.4 percent; the actual result was 71.1 to 26.4 percent. In Missouri, where the exit polls predicted a Bush victory of 54 to 46 percent, the final result was 53 to 46 percent.

One explanation for the strange anomalies in vote tallies was found in the widespread use of touchscreen electronic voting machines. These machines produced results that consistently favored Bush over Kerry, often in chillingly consistent contradiction to exit polls.

In 2003 more than 900 computer professionals had signed a petition urging that all touchscreen systems include a verifiable audit trail. Touchscreen voting machines can be easily programmed to go dead on election day or throw votes to the wrong candidate or make votes disappear while leaving the impression that everything is working fine. A tiny number of operatives can easily access the entire computer network through one machine and thereby change votes at will. The touchscreen machines use trade-secret code, and are tested, reviewed, and certified in complete secrecy. Verified counts are impossible because the machines leave no reliable paper trail.

Since the introduction of touchscreen voting, anomalous congressional election results have been increasing. In 2000 and 2002, Senate and House contests and state legislative races in North Carolina, Nebraska, Alabama, Minnesota, Colorado, and elsewhere produced dramatic and puzzling upsets, always at the expense of Democrats who were substantially ahead in the polls. All of Georgia's voters used Diebold touchscreen machines in

2002, and Georgia's incumbent Democratic governor and incumbent Democratic senator, who were both well ahead in the polls just before the election, lost in amazing double-digit voting shifts.

In some counties in Texas, Virginia, and Ohio, voters who pressed the Democrat's name found that the GOP candidate was chosen. It never happened the other way. No one reported choosing a Republican and ending up with the Democrat. In Cormal County, Texas, three GOP candidates won the touchscreen contest by exactly 18,181 votes apiece, a near statistical impossibility.

This may be the most telling datum of all: In New Mexico in 2004, Kerry lost all precincts equipped with touchscreen machines, irrespective of income levels, ethnicity, and past voting patterns. The only thing that consistently correlated with his defeat in those precincts was the presence of the touchscreen machine itself. In Florida, Bush registered inexplicably sharp jumps in his vote (compared to 2000) in counties that used touchscreen machines, including counties that had shown record increases in Democratic voter registration.[5]

In sum, despite an arsenal of foul ploys that prevented people from voting, those who did get to vote still went decisively for Kerry—but had their votes subverted by a rigged system.

Companies like Diebold, Sequoia, and ES&S that market the touchscreen machines are owned by militant supporters of the Republican party. These companies have consistently refused to allow election officials to evaluate the secret voting machine software. Apparently corporate trade secrets are more important than voting rights. In effect, corporations have privatized the electoral system, leaving it susceptible to fixed outcomes. *Caveat emptor.*

Postscript: In the 2006 mid-term congressional elections, the Democrats won back the House with a thirty-seat majority and the Senate by one seat. This might lead us to conclude that honest elections won the day. To be sure, the U.S. electoral system is a patchwork of fifty different state systems, all with additional county-level variations. So there must have been honestly conducted electoral proceedings in many parts of the country.

Still, what has to be explained is why the Democratic victory was so relatively slim. Given the massive crossover reported in the polls, why was it not a landslide of greater magnitude? From 15 to 30 percent of erstwhile Republican voters reportedly either switched or stayed home. Most Democratic gains in 2006 were in White, suburban, middle-class districts.[6] Meanwhile traditional Democratic strongholds held fairly firm. It seems the Republicans lost because while they focused on trying to suppress and undermine the Democratic base, they lost a large chunk of their own following.

In several states, residents in Democratic areas were confronted by purged registration lists, falsely based threats of arrest, and exacting voter ID requirements. Irregularities were so outrageous in Virginia that the FBI was called in. According to the polls, Senate Republican incumbent George Allen should have lost Virginia by a substantial margin instead of a few thousand votes. Touchscreen irregularities and voter discouragement tactics helped him close the gap, but not enough. In Florida's district 13, the Democratic candidate Christine Jennings lost by a few hundred votes after 18,000 ballots were lost by touchscreen machines that left no paper trail to rectify the situation.

Touchscreen machines have been variously described as "faulty," or ridden with "glitches." This is not usually the case. If it were simply a matter of malfunction, the mistakes would occur randomly, rather than consistently favoring the GOP. What we are dealing with are not faulty machines but fixed machines.

The United States is the only country (as compared to Western Europe) that makes it difficult for people to vote. Historically the hurdles have been directed at low-income voters and ethnic minorities. In 2006, various states disqualified voters if their registration information failed to match perfectly with some other record such as a driver's license (for instance, the use of a middle initial in the driver's license but not in the registration form). Because of these minor discrepancies at least 17 percent of eligible citizens in Arizona's largest county were denied registration. In some states persons who conduct voter registration drives risk criminal prosecution for harmless mistakes, including errors in collecting forms. In Florida some 50,000 voters were purged in 2004 (in addition to the many purged in 2000), many of them African Americans who still were unable to vote by 2006. In various states and counties the subterranean war against electoral democracy continues.

7 HOW THE FREE MARKET KILLED NEW ORLEANS

The free market played a crucial role in the 2005 destruction of New Orleans and the death of thousands of its residents. Forewarned that a momentous category-5 hurricane might hit that city and surrounding areas, what did officials do? They played the free market. They announced that everyone should evacuate. All were expected to devise their own way out of the disaster area by private means, just like people do when disaster hits free-market Third World countries.

It is a beautiful thing, this free market in which every individual pursues his or her own private interests and thereby effects an optimal outcome for the entire society. Thus does Adam Smith's "invisible hand" work its wonders in mysterious ways.

In New Orleans there would be none of the regimented collectivist evacuation as occurred in Cuba. When a powerful category-5 hurricane hit that island in 2004, the Castro government, abetted by neighborhood citizen committees and local Communist Party cadres, evacuated some 1.5 million people, more than 10 percent of the country's population. The Cubans lost 20,000 homes to that hurricane—but not a single person was killed, a heartening feat that went largely unmentioned in the U.S. press.

On day one of Hurricane Katrina, 29 August 2005, it was already clear that hundreds, perhaps thousands, of Americans had perished in New Orleans. Many people had "refused" to evacuate, media reporters explained, because they were just plain "stubborn."

It was not until day three that highly paid telecasters began to realize that tens of thousands of people had failed to flee because they had nowhere to go and no means of getting there. With hardly any cash at hand, and over 100,000 people without cars of their own, many had to sit tight and hope for the best. In the end, the free market did not work so well for them.

Many of these people were low-income African Americans, along with fewer numbers of poor whites. It should be remembered that most of them had jobs before the flood hit them. That's what most poor people do in this country: they work, usually quite hard at dismally paying jobs, sometimes more than one job at a time. They are poor not because they're lazy but because they are paid poverty wages while burdened by high prices, high rents, and regressive taxes.

The free market played a role in other ways. President G.W. Bush's agenda has been to cut government services to the bone and make people rely on the private sector for the things they might need. He cut $30 million in flood control appropriations. He sliced an additional $71.2 million from the budget of the New Orleans Corps of Engineers, a 44 percent reduction. Plans to fortify New Orleans levees and upgrade the system of pumping out water had to be shelved.

Personnel with the Army Corps of Engineers had started building new levees several years before Hurricane Katrina, but many of them were taken off such projects and sent to Iraq, where they were needed to assist the empire in its wars.

It was not actually the hurricane that destroyed New Orleans. Katrina swerved and hit parts of Mississippi much harder. For New Orleans most of the destruction was caused by the flood that came when the levees broke, a flood that had long been feared by many.

On day three Bush took to the airwaves, and said in a live TV interview, "I don't think anyone anticipated that breach of the levees."[7] Just another untruth tumbling from his lips. The catastrophic flooding of New Orleans had been foreseen by storm experts, engineers, Louisiana journalists, state officials, and even some federal agencies. All sorts of people had been predicting disaster for years, pointing to the danger of rising water levels and the need to strengthen the levees and pumps, and fortify the entire coastland. Bush chose not to listen.

In their campaign to starve out the public sector, reactionaries in the Bush camp allowed developers to drain vast areas of wetlands. Again, that old invisible hand of the free market was expected to take care of things. By pursuing their own private profit, the developers would supposedly devise outcomes that would benefit us all. But the Louisiana wetlands serve as a natural absorbent and barrier between New Orleans and the storms riding in from across the sea. And, for some years now, the wetlands have been disappearing at a frightening pace on the Gulf coast. All this was of no concern to the White House.

This brings us to another way that the free market helped destroy New Orleans. By relying almost entirely on fossil fuel as an energy source—far more expensive and therefore more profitable than solar, tidal, or wind power—the free market has been a great contributor to global warming. Global warming, in turn, has been causing a drastic rise in sea levels. And rising sea levels have been destroying the protective fringe of barrier islands and coastal marshlands along the Louisiana coast. "Every year," reported the *New York Times* "another 25 square miles, an area roughly the size of Manhattan, sinks quietly beneath the waves. In some places, the [Louisiana] coastline has receded 15 miles from where it was in the 1920s."[8]

Global warming also adds to the ferocity of storms. The warmer waters and warmer air create greater evaporation and allow for greater accumulation as the hurricane passes over the waters gathering strength and momentum. So Katrina went from a category 3 to a category 5 as it came across the Caribbean and into the Gulf of Mexico. A year after Katrina the Bush administration blocked the release of a revealing report by the National Oceanic and Atmospheric Administration. The report suggests that global warming is contributing to the increasing strength and frequency of hurricanes.[9] We can guess why the White House would want to suppress that kind of information.

As for the widely criticized rescue operation, free-marketeers like to say that relief to the more unfortunate among us should be left to private effort. It was a favorite preachment of President Ronald Reagan that private charity can do the job. For many crucial days leaving things to private effort indeed seemed to be the policy in New Orleans. The federal government was nowhere in sight but the Salvation Army began to muster its troops, as did many other organizations. Pat Robertson and the Christian Broadcasting Network—taking a moment off from God's work of pushing the nomination of ultra-conservative jurist John Roberts to the Supreme Court—called for donations and announced "Operation Blessing" which consisted of a highly-publicized but totally inadequate shipment of canned goods and Holy Bibles to the hurricane victims.

The Red Cross went into action, in its own peculiar way. Its message: "Don't send food or blankets; send money." Apparently the Red Cross preferred to buy its own food and blankets. It received over $800 million in three weeks after the catastrophe but had failed to distribute most of it. A caravan of doctors and nurses from Ohio, laden with medical supplies for about seven thousand people, reached the Coliseum in New Orleans only to be told by the Red Cross that they were not needed. They were turned away, even though medical personnel within the Coliseum kept asking for help.

By day three even the usually myopic media began to realize that the rescue operation was an immense failure. People were dying because relief had not arrived. Especially victimized were the infants, the elderly, the infirm, and others needing special medical attention. The authorities seemed more concerned with the looting than with rescuing people, more concerned with "crowd control," which consisted of forcing thousands to stay pent up in barren areas devoid of minimal amenities or proper shelter. The police, state troopers, National Guard, and U.S. Army personnel spent more time patrolling and pointing their guns at people than rescuing or otherwise helping them.

Questions arose that the free market seemed incapable of answering: Who was in charge of the rescue operation? Why so few helicopters and just a small force of Coast Guard crews? Why did it take helicopters five hours to lift six people out of one hospital? When would the rescue operation gather some steam? Where were the feds? Where were the buses and trucks? The shelters and portable toilets? The medical supplies and water? How was it that newscasters could get in and out of flood areas but rescuers and supplies could not?

And where was Homeland Security? What had Homeland Security done with the $33.8 billions allocated to it for fiscal 2005? By day four, almost all the major media were reporting that the federal government's response was "a national disgrace." Meanwhile Bush Jr. finally made his photo-op shirtsleeve appearance in a few well-chosen disaster areas before romping off to play golf.

By the end of the first week, as if to demonstrate that reality is irrelevant, various free-market bloggers were already claiming ideological victory. They argued that the failure to deal with the crisis is proof that "government is inept; it doesn't work." It was private individuals, charities, and corporations that pitched in to help. It was Wal-Mart that sent in three trailer trucks loaded with water, and it was the Federal Emergency Management Agency (FEMA), part of Homeland Security, that turned them away. It was private families that took the refugees into their homes, while government herded them into the Superdome.

Overlooked here is that the great outpouring of aid from private citizens, as heartening as it was, did nothing to address the problems of flood and storm, evacuation, public safety, community security, long-term individual care, rehabilitation, and infrastructure reconstruction.

To be sure, government does not work—certainly not when it is in the hands of reactionaries who have no desire to see it work. New Orleans was victimized by those right-wing ideologues who oppose the idea that government can be a salutary force in regard to social needs and human services. The White House reactionaries would be quite content to demonstrate that government is not to be counted on when it comes to helping communities (especially low-income and ethnic-minority communities that are Democratic strongholds). Thus Washington took four days to respond to requests that National Guard units from other states be allowed into Louisiana.

For all their inertia, FEMA officials played a chillingly active role in sabotaging the delivery of aid, turning away supply convoys, and warehousing or giving the runaround to the many volunteer rescue units that poured in from other states. The community organizations, churches, and other grassroots groups that took in and fed thousands of people received not a dollar of reimbursement, neither from the Red Cross nor FEMA.

Of course, it should not go unnoticed that the White House reactionaries are *selective* free-marketeers. They want to dismantle human services, get rid of public schools, public housing, and public health facilities; and they want to abolish the government's regulatory role in the corporate economy. But they also want to extend government power into other areas. They want more federal power to carry out surveillance, classify official information, control private morals, vaporize civil liberties, and suppress public protest. They want plenty of government involvement when it comes to massive public subsidies and contracts for corporate

America, limitless expansion of armaments and military technology, and perpetual overseas intervention. It is the victory of empire over republic. Government is not there to serve the people. The people are there to serve government.

In the aftermath of Hurricane Katrina, in a moment of touching irony, foreign aid was tendered by almost fifty countries, including many poorer ones such as the Dominican Republic, Honduras, India, Pakistan, Russia, and Thailand. By day seven, Mexico had sent army convoys and a navy ship laden with food, supplies, and specialists. German cargo planes came in with ready-to-eat meals and a German officer who openly expressed his concern that the meals would eventually reach the people in need. (He must have been watching the news.)

Cuba—which has a record of sending doctors to dozens of countries, including a thankful Sri Lanka during the tsunami disaster—offered almost 1,600 doctors and loads of medical supplies. Meanwhile Venezuela offered one million barrels of gasoline, $5 million in cash, water purification plants, and 50 tons of canned foods and water.

Predictably, the offers from Cuba and Venezuela were rejected by the U.S. State Department. And as of day ten, the Bush administration had nothing to say about the vast array of supplies offered by all the other countries. People throughout the world, having seen all the television images, were beginning to think that perhaps America really was not paradise on Earth. Eventually a few grudging thanks were heard from the White House. But what a deflating and insulting role reversal it was for America to be taking aid from the likes of Mexico or anyone else. America the Beautiful and Powerful, America the Supreme Rescuer and World Leader, America the Purveyor of Global Prosperity most certainly would not accept foreign aid from a Third-World communist "failure" such as Cuba.

But eventually aid sent by capitalist Honduras, capitalist Thailand and other capitalist nations was allowed in.

Postscript: To confirm the worst that has been said above, let us note that a year after the Katrina disaster, very little assistance was reaching the displaced working poor of New Orleans, most of whom were renters. An estimated 60 to 80 percent of rental units in the city were either destroyed or heavily damaged. Most of these had been occupied by low- and middle-income families. Billions in housing aid was pouring in but the bulk of it was slated for more affluent homeowners. Rents skyrocketed an average of almost 40 percent across the city in the year after Hurricane Katrina. Many lower-income residents were priced out of the market. The longer that rental properties rotted in the Louisian heat and humidity, the more difficult they were to restore. In some areas homeowners were attempting to use the recovery process to rid their neighborhoods of long-standing apartment buildings that were damaged during the storm. "The renters of New Orleans, it seems, are on their own."[10]

A native of New Orleans, Jill Pletcher, wrote to me: "The conditions here—the city itself—is in shambles. Rats and trash in all the 'off-touristy' places, which is *most* of New Orleans. It's *not* the New Orleans I grew up in. The dirty brown lines 18 feet high on the sides of familiar buildings where water sat for two weeks is a sickening sight and reminder of a national atrocity—and one that people now smirk at while they express their 'Katrina fatigue.'"[11]

What the Katrina disaster demonstrated so clearly was that the White House reactionaries had neither the desire nor the decency to provide for ordinary citizens, not even those in dire straits. In the aftermath of the hurricane, I heard someone complain, "Bush is trying to save the world when he can't even take care of his own people here at home." Not quite true. He certainly has taken very good care of his own people, that tiny fraction of one percent, the superrich. It's just that the working people of New Orleans are not part of his crowd.

8 CONSERVATIVE JUDICIAL ACTIVISM

Appearing before the Senate Judiciary Committee in 2005 as nominee for chief justice of the Supreme Court, John Roberts assured the senators that he would not be one of those noisome activist judges who inject their personal values into court decisions. Instead he would behave like "an umpire calling balls and strikes." With a completely open mind, he would judge each case solely on its own merits, with only the Constitution to guide him, he said. None of the senators doubled over with laughter.

A fortnight later, while George Bush Jr. was introducing another Court nominee—his right-wing crony Harriet Miers—he prattled on about his "judicial philosophy" and how he wanted jurists to be "strict constructionists" who cleave close to the Constitution, as opposed to loose constructionist liberals who use the Court to advance their ideological agenda. After Miers withdrew her name, Bush nominated Samuel Alito, describing him as a judge who "interprets the laws," and does not "impose his preferences or priorities on the people."

Truth be told, the Supreme Court through most of its history has engaged in the wildest *conservative* judicial activism in defense of privileged groups. Be it for slavery or segregation, child labor or the sixteen-hour workday, state sedition laws or assaults on the First Amendment—rightist judicial activists have shown an infernal agility in stretching and bending the Constitution.

Right to the eve of the Civil War, for instance, the Supreme Court asserted the primacy of property rights in slaves, rejecting all slave petitions for freedom. In the famous *Dred Scott v. Sandford* (1857), the Court concluded that, be they slave or free, Blacks were a "subordinate and inferior class of beings" without constitutional rights. Thus did reactionary judicial activists—some of them slaveholders—spin "loose constructionist" racist precepts out of thin air to lend a constitutional gloss to their beloved slavocracy.

When the federal government wanted to establish national banks, or give away half the country to speculators, or subsidize industries, or set up commissions that fixed prices and interest rates for large manufacturers and banks, or imprison dissenters who denounced war and capitalism, or use the U.S. Army to shoot workers and break strikes, or have marines kill people in Central America—the Supreme Court's conservative activists twisted the Constitution in every conceivable way to justify these acts. So much for "strict construction."

But when the federal or state governments sought to limit workday hours, set minimum wage or occupational safety standards, ensure the safety of consumer products, or guarantee the right of collective bargaining, then the Court ruled that ours was a limited form of government that could not tamper with property rights and could not deprive owner and worker of "freedom of contract."

The Fourteenth Amendment, adopted in 1868 ostensibly to establish full citizenship for African Americans, says that no state can "deprive any person of life, liberty, or property, without due process of law," nor deny any person "equal protection of the laws." In another act of pure judicial invention, a conservative

dominated Court decided that "person" really meant "corporation"; therefore the Fourteenth Amendment protected business
conglomerates from regulation by the states. To this day, corporations have legal standing as "persons" thanks to conservative
judicial activism.

Consider the conservative judicial activism perpetrated for generations against working people. Between 1880 and 1931 the courts
issued more than 1,800 injunctions to suppress labor strikes.
Labor "combinations" (unions) were declared a violation of due
process, a way of coercively extracting wealth from decent
defenseless rich employers. Collective bargaining, it was maintained, deprived both owner and worker of "freedom of
contract." By 1920, pro-business federal courts had struck down
roughly three hundred labor laws passed by state legislatures to
ease inhumane working conditions.

When Congress outlawed child labor or passed other social
reforms, conservative jurists declared such laws to be violations
of the Tenth Amendment. The Tenth Amendment says that powers not delegated to the federal government are reserved to the
states or the people. So Congress could not act. But, when states
passed social-welfare legislation, the Court's conservative activists
said such laws violated "substantive due process" (a totally fabricated oxymoron) under the Fourteenth Amendment, which says
that state governments cannot deny due process to any person. So
the state legislatures could not act.

Thus for more than fifty years, the justices used the Tenth
Amendment to stop federal reforms initiated under the Fourteenth
Amendment, and at the same time, they used the Fourteenth
Amendment to stymie state reforms initiated under the Tenth. It's
hard to get more brazenly activist than that.

A conservative Supreme Court produced *Plessy v. Ferguson* (1896), an inventive reading of the Fourteenth Amendment's equal protection clause. *Plessy* confected the "separate but equal" doctrine, claiming that the forced separation of Blacks from Whites did not impute inferiority as long as facilities were equal (which they rarely were). For some seventy years, this judicial fabrication buttressed racial segregation.

Convinced that they too were persons, women began to argue that the "due process" clauses of the Fourteenth Amendment (applying to state governments) and the Fifth Amendment (applying to the federal government) disallowed the voting prohibitions imposed on women by state and federal authorities. But in *Minor v. Happersett* (1875), a conservative Court fashioned another devilishly contorted interpretation: true, women were citizens but citizenship did not *necessarily* confer a citizen's right to suffrage. In other words, "due process," and "equal protection" applied to such "persons" as business corporations but not to women or people of African descent.

This same pattern of conservative judicial activism has continued into recent times. Bush Jr. was not the first conservative president to denounce as "judicial activism" those court decisions he disliked. Ronald Reagan did exactly the same, directing his condemnations selectively against liberal jurists. The conservative Supreme Court of Reagan's day gave agribusiness access to federally subsidized irrigation in violation of the acreage limitations set by a Democratic Congress. That same Court struck down safety regulations that had been imposed by various states on the nuclear industry.

In these and similar cases one heard no complaints from Reagan and other conservatives about judicial usurpation of policymaking powers. Judicial decisions that advanced authoritarian and corporate interests were perfectly acceptable to them. But judicial decisions that defended democratic rights and socioeconomic equality invited attacks as activist aggrandizement.

At times, presidents place themselves and their associates above accountability by claiming that the separation of powers gives them an inherent right of "executive privilege." Executive privilege has been used by the White House to withhold information on undeclared wars, illegal campaign funds, Supreme Court nominations, burglaries (Watergate), insider trading (by Bush Jr. and Cheney), and White House collusion with corporate lobbyists.

But the concept of executive privilege (i.e. unaccountable executive secrecy) exists nowhere in the Constitution or any law. Yet the right-wing activists on the Supreme Court trumpet executive privilege, deciding out of thin air that a "presumptive privilege" for withholding information belongs to the president.

In early 2006 Bush Jr. talked about "how important it is for us to guard executive privilege in order for there to be crisp decision making in the White House." Crisp? So Bush presented himself as a "strict constructionist" while making claim to a wholly extraconstitutional juridical fiction known as "executive privilege."

With staggering audacity, the Court's rightist judicial activists have decided that states cannot prohibit corporations from spending unlimited amounts on public referenda or other elections because such campaign expenditures are a form of "speech" and the Constitution guarantees freedom of speech to such "persons" as corporations. In a dissenting opinion, the liberal Justice Stevens noted, "Money is property; it is not speech." But his conservative activist colleagues preferred the more fanciful, loose constructionist interpretation.

They further ruled that "free speech" enables rich candidates to spend as much as they want on their own campaigns, and rich individuals to expend unlimited sums in any election contest. Thus both rich and poor can freely compete, one in a roar, the other in a whisper.

Right-wing judicial activism reached a frenzy point in *George W. Bush v. Al Gore.* In a 5-to-4 decision, the conservatives over-ruled the Florida Supreme Court's order for a recount in the 2000 presidential election. The justices argued with breathtaking con-trivance that since different Florida counties might use different modes of tabulating ballots, a hand recount would violate the equal protection clause of the Fourteenth Amendment. By pre-venting a recount, the Supreme Court gave the presidency to Bush.

In recent years these same conservative justices have held that the Fourteenth Amendment's equal protection clause could not be used to stop violence against women, or provide a more equitable mode of property taxes, or a more equitable distribution of funds between rich and poor school districts. But, in *Bush v. Gore* they ruled that the equal protection clause *could* be used to stop a per-fectly legal ballot recount. Then they explicitly declared that the *Bush* case could not be considered a precedent for other equal protection issues. In other words, the Fourteenth Amendment applied only when the conservative judicial activists wanted it to, as when stealing an election.

Conservatives say that judges should not try to "legislate from the bench," the way liberal activists supposedly do. But a recent Yale study reveals that conservative justices like Thomas and Scalia have a far more active rate of invalidating or reinterpreting laws than more liberal justices like Breyer and Ginsburg.[12] A sim-ilar study by a professor at the University of Kentucky College of Law came to the exact same finding: conservative judges do not just interpret the law, they refashion it—and far more often than their liberal colleagues. They are more willing than the liberals to strike down federal laws, "clearly an activist stance, since they were substituting their own judgment for that of the people's elected representatives in Congress."[13] In addition, conservative justices were more activist when it came to overturning the Court's own precedents.

Judicial activism (the reinterpretation of existing laws and court decisions) is not necessarily an undesirable thing. The Supreme Court is supposed to strike down laws or portions of laws deemed unconstitutional or otherwise grossly detrimental to our rights and well-being. Justices across the political spectrum make such judgments at times. What is reprehensible is for one side to pretend that its justices are not activist, that they show a superior regard for the Constitution, that they do not usurp power and are more objective, that they are more respectfully self-restrained than their irresponsible opponents. Thus they turn judicial activism into a partisan attack while in fact the numbers show—as does the history of the court itself—that they are guilty of doing the very thing they charge their liberal colleagues with doing.[14]

Down through the years the Court's right-wing jurists have been not only activist but downright adventuristic, showing no hesitation to invent politically partisan concepts and constructs out of thin air, eviscerate perfectly legitimate laws, shift arguments and premises as their ideology dictates, bolster an autocratic executive power, roll back substantive political and economic gains won by the populace, and weaken civil liberties, civil rights, and the democratic process itself (such as it is). The same holds true for the jurists who preside over the lower courts, which is why conservatives on the high court are quite content to let stand without review so many lower court decisions.

Perhaps one way to trim judicial adventurism is to end life tenure for federal judges, including the justices who sit on the Supreme Court. It would take a constitutional amendment, but it might be worth it. According to one poll, 91 percent of the citizenry want the terms of all federal judges to be limited.[15] Today only three states provide life tenure for state judges; the other forty-seven set fixed terms ranging from four to twelve years (usually allowing for reelection). A fixed term would still give a jurist significant independence, but would not allow him or her to remain unaccountable for an entire lifetime.

Meanwhile we should keep in mind that the right-wing aggrandizers in black robes are neither strict constructionists nor balanced adjudicators. They are unrestrained ideologues masquerading as sober defenders of lawful procedure and constitutional intent. If this is democracy, who needs oligarchy?

9 WHY THE CORPORATE RICH OPPOSE ENVIRONMENTALISM

In 1876, Marx's collaborator, Friedrich Engels, offered a prophetic caveat: "Let us not . . . flatter ourselves overmuch on account of our human conquest over nature. For each such conquest takes its revenge on us. . . . At every step we are reminded that we by no means rule over nature like a conqueror over a foreign people, like someone standing outside of nature—but that we, with flesh, blood, and brain, belong to nature, and exist in its midst. . . ."

With its never-ending emphasis on production and profit, and its indifference to environment, transnational corporate capitalism appears determined to stand outside nature. The driving goal of the giant investment firms is to convert living nature into commodities and commodities into vast accumulations of dead capital.

This capital accumulation process treats the planet's life-sustaining resources (arable land, groundwater, wetlands, forests, fisheries, ocean beds, rivers, air quality) as dispensable ingredients of limitless supply, to be consumed or toxified at will. Consequently, the support systems of the entire ecosphere—the Earth's thin skin of fresh air, water, and topsoil—are at risk, threatened by global warming, massive erosion, and ozone depletion. An ever-expanding capitalism and a fragile finite ecology are involved in a calamitous collision.

It is not true that the ruling politico-economic interests are in a state of denial about this. Far worse than denial, they have shown utter antagonism toward those who think the planet is more important than corporate profits. So they defame environmentalists as "eco-terrorists," "EPA gestapo," "Earth Day alarmists," "tree huggers," and purveyors of "Green hysteria" and "liberal claptrap." Their position was summed up by that dangerous fool, erstwhile senator Steve Symms (R-Idaho), who said that if he had to choose between capitalism and ecology, he would choose capitalism. Symms seemed not to grasp that, absent a viable ecology, there will be no capitalism or any other ism.

In July 2005, President Bush Jr. finally muttered a grudging acknowledgment: "I recognize that the surface of the Earth is warmer and that an increase in greenhouse gases caused by humans is contributing to the problem." But this belated admission of a "problem" hardly makes up for Bush's many attacks upon the environment. In recent years, Bush's people within the White House and Congress, fueled by corporate lobbyists, have supported measures to

■ allow unregulated toxic fill into lakes and harbors,

■ eliminate most of the wetland acreage that was to be set aside as reserves,

■ deregulate the production of chlorofluorocarbons (CFCs) that deplete the ozone layer,

■ eviscerate clean water and clean air standards,

■ open the unspoiled Arctic National Wildlife Refuge in Alaska to oil and gas drilling,

■ defund efforts to keep raw sewage out of rivers and away from beaches,

■ privatize and open national parks to commercial development,

■ give the remaining ancient forests over to unrestrained logging,

■ repeal the Endangered Species Act,

■ and allow mountaintop removal in mining that has transformed thousands of miles of streams and vast amounts of natural acreage into toxic wastelands.

Why do rich and powerful interests take this seemingly suicidal anti-environmental route? We can understand why they might want to destroy public housing, public education, Social Security, Medicare, and Medicaid. They and their children will not thereby be deprived of a thing, having more than sufficient private means to procure whatever services they need for themselves. But the environment is a different story. Do not wealthy reactionaries and their corporate lobbyists inhabit the same polluted planet as everyone else, eat the same chemicalized food, and breathe the same toxified air?

In fact, they do not live exactly as everyone else. They experience a different class reality, often residing in places where the air is somewhat better than in low- and middle-income areas. They have access to food that is organically raised and specially prepared. The nation's toxic dumps and freeways usually are not situated in or near their swanky neighborhoods. In fact, the superrich do not live in neighborhoods as such. They reside on landed estates with plenty of wooded areas, streams, meadows, with only a few well-monitored access roads. The pesticide sprays are not poured over their trees and gardens. Clearcutting does not desolate their ranches, estates, family forests, and prime vacation spots.

The geographer Gray Brechin was telling me about a talk he gave a few years ago to a well-heeled group at St. Francis Yacht Club. His appearance was at the invitation of a scion of two great California-South African mining fortunes. After Brechin discussed the ecological damage done in California by developers and industrialists, one of the socialites blurted out: "If things are so bad, why haven't we noticed?"

They haven't noticed because they are so comfortably insulated from the ecological devastation caused by their very own enterprises. Brechin was taken aback. He realized that like most other people, the questioner did not have "the memory to make a comparison with what once was here. All I could do was to point out the window at the empty sky and ask where the birds went, and to say that if we could see under the water, we would note a similar absence of what was once a teeming aquatic ecosystem."

Even when the corporate rich or their children succumb to a dread disease like cancer, they do not link the tragedy to environmental factors—though scientists now believe that present-day cancer epidemics stem largely from human-made causes. The plutocrats deny there is a serious problem because they themselves have created that problem and owe so much of their wealth to it.

But how can they deny the threat of an ecological apocalypse brought on by global warming, ozone depletion, disappearing top-soil, and dying oceans? Do the corporate plutocrats want to see life on Earth—including their own lives—destroyed? In the long run they indeed will be sealing their own doom, along with everyone else's. However, like us all, they live not in the long run but in the here and now. What is at stake for them is something more proximate and more urgent than global ecology. It is global capital accumulation. The fate of the biosphere seems like a far-off abstraction compared to the fate of one's immediate (and enormous) investments.

Furthermore, pollution pays, while ecology costs. Every dollar a company spends on environmental protections is one less dollar in earnings. It is more profitable to treat the environment like a septic tank, to externalize corporate diseconomies by dumping raw industrial effluent into the atmosphere, rivers, and bays, turning waterways into open sewers. Moving away from fossil fuels and toward solar, wind, and tidal energy could help avert ecological disaster, but six of the world's ten top industrial corporations are involved primarily in the production of oil, gasoline, and motor vehicles. Fossil fuel pollution means billions in profits. Ecologically sustainable forms of production directly threaten such profits.

Immense and imminent gain for oneself is a far more compelling consideration than a diffuse loss shared by the general public. The *social cost* of turning a forest into a wasteland weighs little against the *personal profit* that comes from harvesting the timber.

Now we have the "peak oil" jeremiads, replete with images of a global collapse in fossil fuel supply in a matter of a few decades at most. Such dire warnings fall on deaf ears. There is still about a trillion barrels of oil in the ground and offshore. At $100 a barrel, which is what oil will cost as it gets scarcer, we are looking at

$100 trillion in sales. And new reserves are being discovered in Africa and elsewhere just about every year. In any case, whether there is going to be lots of oil or little oil is not the question. The oil industry is not in the business of providing homes and communities with a guaranteed lifetime supply of needed fuel; it is not in the business of keeping the world's fuel supply affordable and sufficient in decades to come. It is in the business of making the largest possible profits for itself, as much and as quickly as it can, here and now. When you get down to it, all corporations are involved in fast-buck investments.

The conflict between immediate personal gain on the one hand and seemingly remote public benefit on the other operates even at the individual consumer level. Thus, it is in one's long-term interest not to operate an automobile that contributes more to environmental devastation than any other single consumer item (even if it's a hybrid). But again, we don't live in the long run, we live in the here and now, and we have an immediate everyday need for transportation, so most of us have no choice except to own and use automobiles, especially given the past undoing and present absence of viable mass transit systems and rail systems. The oil and automotive industries put "America on wheels," and then said *to hell with the environment.*

Sober business heads have refused to get caught up in doomsayer "hysteria" about ecology. Besides, there can always be found a few stray experts who will obligingly argue that the jury is still out, that there is no conclusive proof to support the "alarmists." *Conclusive* proof in this case would come only when the eco-apocalypse is upon us.

Just as corporate capitalism undermines ecology, so too is ecology profoundly subversive of capitalism. It needs planned, environmentally sustainable production rather than the rapacious, unregulated, free-market kind. It requires economical consumption rather than an artificially stimulated, ever-expanding, wasteful consumerism. It calls for natural, relatively clean and low-cost energy systems rather than high-cost, high-profit, polluting ones.

Ecology's implications for capitalism are too momentous for the capitalist to contemplate. They are more wedded to their wealth than to the Earth upon which they live, more concerned with the fate of their fortunes than with the fate of humanity. The present ecological crisis has been created by the few at the expense of the many. In other words, the struggle over environmentalism is part of the class struggle itself, a fact that seems to have escaped many environmentalists but is well understood by the plutocrats—which is why they are unsparing in their derision and denunciations of the "eco-terrorists" and "tree huggers."

Meanwhile the mechanisms of denial are in place. Already the late-night TV comedians are making light of global warming, thereby normalizing it. "It's getting so hot that Paris Hilton said she was going to wear less clothes. How is that possible?" Ha, ha, ha, that guy sure takes my mind off things. In addition there are still those few well-publicized holdout scientists, mentioned earlier, who—if they no longer actually deny the existence of global warming—do minimize its significance, telling us that, yes, the disruptions will be a bit unsettling but it's just another of those cycles that the Earth has endured during its many epochs, and the Earth has been warming for centuries.

Almost as deplorable are the scientists who warn us of the dangers of global warming, then say things like: "If it keeps up at this rate, there will be a serious climatic crisis by the end of this century." By the end of this century? that's about ninety years away;

we and almost all our kids will be dead. That makes for a lot less urgent concern. There are other scientists who manage to be even more irritating by putting the crisis even further into the future: "We'll have to stop thinking in terms of eons and start thinking in terms of centuries," one announced in the *New York Times* in 2006. If global catastrophe is a century or several centuries away, who is going to make the terribly difficult and costly decisions that are needed now?

The trouble is that global warming is not some distant urgency waiting to develop over the next century or two. It is already acting upon us with an accelerated feedback and deadly compounded effect that may be irreversible. We do not have eons or centuries or even many decades. Most of us alive today may not have the luxury of saying *"Après moi, le déluge"* because we will be around to experience the déluge ourselves. And if you think it will be "interesting" or "exciting," ask the tsunami survivors if that's how they felt. This time the plutocratic drive to "accumulate, accumulate, accumulate" may take all of us down, once and forever.

10 AUTOS AND ATOMS

Back in the late 1950s and early 1960s, America was said to have a "car culture." But the omnipresence of the automobile was something not devised by us ordinary Americans. It was the centerpiece of a national transportation system created by large corporations. Across the country in a score of cities, ecologically efficient, nonpolluting, convenient, and less costly mass-transit electric rail and trolley systems were deliberately bought out and torn up, starting in the 1930s, by the automotive, oil, tire, and highway-construction industries, using dummy corporations as fronts. The electric mass-transit systems were replaced with gas-guzzling buses, and then with more and more cars and freeways. These companies put "America on wheels," in order to make us dependent on gas-driven private vehicles, thereby maximizing profits for themselves, with no regard for the costs in money and lives, and no regard for the damage done to the environment.

For decades Americans conducted a costly and extended "romance" with that dangerous and polluting instrument of conveyance known as the automobile. Now much of the Third World is going through the same adolescent pangs for wheels. In places like China, Pakistan, India, and certain countries in Africa, people want to own cars, and in increasing numbers they are doing so.

Meanwhile for many Americans the blush of romance has faded. Many still maintain their automotive excitement but only by upping the stimulus, that is, by owning Humvees, SUVs, stunning sports cars, and other super vehicles that give them a hefty competitive edge when barreling along on the road.

There are some basic things we should say about the automobile. Every year this great wonder of modern technology kills 40,000 to 50,000 people in the United States alone and injures and cripples hundreds of thousands more. In some countries where speed limits and other traffic rules are not taken seriously, the death toll is proportionately higher. The automobile is also an ecological disaster, consuming large amounts of oxygen with the consumption of every gallon of gas, and spewing hundreds of millions of tons of lead, sulfur, carbon monoxide, carbon dioxide and a variety of other poisons every year, enough to make it the major cause of urban pollution.

Motor vehicles also add significantly to the acid rain that is killing our lakes and forests. Worst of all, they play a central role in changing the very chemical composition of our environment, contributing to global warming and all the ensuing disasters that may follow. Our cars also turn our cities and suburbs into ugly urban sprawls. More than 60 percent of the land of most U.S. cities is taken up by the movement, storage, and servicing of motorized vehicles. Recreational areas and whole neighborhoods, particularly in working-class communities, are razed to make way for costly highways. The billions spent on the construction and maintenance of freeways are a hidden but immense subsidy to the automotive and trucking industries, compliments of the U.S. taxpayer.

But let us be fair and balanced. Let us look at the advantages. We can spend hours each day in our cars—almost always one lone driver and no passengers in a vehicle built to sit five or more—hurtling along highways, courting injury and death at breakneck speeds. Or, less exciting, we can creep along in agonizing traffic jams, dying a little each time from the fumes we inhale. Here is a mode of transportation that costs the average American almost two full working days a week in car payments, auto insurance, gasoline, tolls, parking fees, traffic tickets, servicing, repairs, and taxes for highways and roads. For the less fortunate, the millions who cannot afford cars, there is the isolation, the inability to move about because public transportation is so insufficient, having been starved out by privatized vehicles. The fewer people available to ride buses, the fewer the buses, which in turn further discourages use of public transit.

Those who cannot afford a car or cannot drive for one reason or another can still feel how necessary a car becomes in a society built around vehicular traffic. The shopping mall is way off; the church and the school are in opposite directions; the movie theaters, restaurants, parks, libraries, museums and schools—assuming such things are available—are situated in widely dispersed places. Driving to them may not be easy because parking is difficult. Those people with children who need to get here and there and back again find that being the family chauffeur feels like a full-time job.

Everything in the community is spread out in order to make room for the automobile, for its movement, parking, maintenance, and storage. Urban sprawl makes public transportation that much more uneconomical for the community to support, while making a private car that much more necessary. With sprawl there is no real center to town or city, unlike Europe with its car-free promenades and piazzas, where people walk pleasant distances surrounded by lovely shops, interesting old buildings, fountains, and inviting cafés. It is not that the Europeans are so much more resourceful than we. They have been as car crazy as any of us Yanks, but fortunately their cities were build centuries before the automobile companies imposed their dictates upon urban and suburban communities. And their cars tend to be of less gargantuan dimension.

The solution to many of our woes in regard to the "car culture" is more and better public transportation. High-speed monorails can link cities and provide service to every significant area within a region or community. Nonpolluting electric cars powered by solar-feed batteries could play a major role in cleaning up the air and saving the environment. The electric cars built to satisfy California's requirement for zero-emission vehicles were among the fastest, most efficient automobiles ever built. They ran on electricity, produced no emissions or noise, and required almost no maintenance and servicing. And they put American technology at the forefront of the automotive industry. The people who got to drive them loved them. But General Motors destroyed its entire fleet of EV1 electric vehicles—not because they did not work but because they worked too well. Mass production of electric cars would have meant horrendous losses for the oil companies and for the auto servicing and repair industry that deal with the complex and costly internal combustion engine.[16] The lucky few who drove the EV1 never wanted to give it up.

Even in countries with excellent public transportation, such as the former German Democratic Republic (Communist East Germany), it soon became the rage to have a car all one's own. If given a choice between a rational public transportation system or the thrill, status, novelty, and instant mobility of a private car, too many people will go for the car.

Something has got to be done about the internal combustion engine before it does something irreversible to us—assuming it already has not. It is not a rational and survivable form of technology. Its social, ecological, and human costs are far greater than any benefit it brings.

The same holds for nuclear power, that other great technological wonder. Nuclear plants in the United States are so hazardous that insurance companies refuse to cover them. People exposed to atmospheric nuclear tests and the contaminating clouds vented from continued underground tests have suffered a variety of serious illnesses. Nuclear mishaps have occurred at reactors in a dozen states. In 1979 the nuclear plant at Three Mile Island, Pennsylvania, experienced a temporary shutdown when the reactor core overheated and almost caused a meltdown. The near disaster was well reported. Left largely unreported was the aftermath: livestock on nearby farms aborted and died prematurely, and households experienced what amounted to an epidemic of cancer, birth defects, and premature deaths.[17] The aftereffects of Three Mile Island remain one of America's best kept secrets.

In many countries, contaminating leakage is a common occurrence. Aside from a momentous accident of the kind that occurred at the Chernobyl plant in the Ukraine in 1986, there is the everyday emission of radiation caused by the mining, milling, refinement, storage, and shipment of various nuclear materials and wastes. Any amount of emission can have a damaging effect on human health. High rates of cancer have been found among persons residing close to "safe" nuclear plants. In 2004, despite all the unresolved problems facing nuclear power, Bush Jr. proposed massive subsidies for the construction of new commercial nuclear reactors.[18]

No country in the world knows what to do about a core meltdown, the results of which could be globally catastrophic.

No country in the world has a long-term technology for safe disposal of nuclear wastes, some of which remain radioactive for hundreds of thousands of years. Sweden solved its safety problem by phasing out its nuclear power and moving decisively toward sustainable and renewable energy sources. Some countries dump their radioactive nuclear waste into the ocean. Our oceans are the major source of oxygen for the planet. If they die, so do we.

The "peak oil" theorists tell us that the world's oil supply is running out. Not really, not soon enough. There are about a trillion barrels of oil left in the ground, and new reserves are being discovered every year. At $75 a barrel, that comes to $75 *trillion* dollars. The oil cartels are in no hurry to find alternative sustainable sources of energy that would seriously cut into that most profitable of all markets.

Long before we run out of fossil fuels, we are likely to run out of fresh air, clean drinking water, and a sustainable ecology. Nuclear power, automobiles, and fossil fuels like oil and coal should all be phased out. We need to develop safer, cleaner, alternative modes of energy: thermal, solar, tidal, and wind. There already exist hundreds of thousands of homes and public buildings in the world that are serviced partly or entirely by solar energy. It is the only viable direction left open to us.

One glimmer of hope lies in the fact that many private companies are thinking green. They are finding that ecologically minded forms of production can save them substantial costs. Some corporate heads are even calling upon the federal government to impose more environmentally sound regulations. Unfortunately many of our rulers are too immersed in their free-market ideology to notice that they are driving us over a cliff.

11 WHAT IS TO BE DONE?

There are those who say that we critics carp endlessly about what is wrong with the present state of affairs but we offer no solutions. In fact we critics have plenty of sensible recommendations and solutions. It is no mystery what needs to be done to bring us to a more equitable and democratic society. Here are some specific measures to consider.

AGRICULTURE AND ECOLOGY

Distribute to almost two million needy farmers much of the billions of federal dollars now handed out to rich agribusiness firms. Encourage organic farming and phase out pesticides, herbicides, chemical fertilizers, hormone-saturated meat products, and genetically modified crops. Stop the agribusiness merger-mania that now controls almost all of the world's food supply. Agribusiness conglomerates like Cargill and Continental should be broken up or nationalized.

Engage in a concerted effort at conservation and ecological restoration, including water and waste recycling and large scale composting of garbage. Stop the development of ethanol and hydrogen-cell "alternative" energies; they themselves are environmentally damaging, consuming more energy in their production than they provide for consumption, and at huge cost. Phase out dams and nuclear plants, and initiate a crash program to develop sustainable alternative energy sources. This is not impossible to do. Sweden has eliminated the use of nuclear power and may soon be completely doing away with fossil fuels, replacing them with wind, solar, thermal, and tidal energies—programs that the United States and every other country should pursue.

We need to develop rapid-mass-transit systems within and between cities for safe, economical transportation, and produce zero-emission vehicles to minimize the disastrous ecological effects of fossil fuels. Ford had electric cars as early as the 1920s. Stanford Ovshinsky, president of Energy Conversion Devices, built a newly developed electric car that had a long driving range on a battery that lasted a lifetime, used environmentally safe materials, and was easily manufactured, with operational costs that were far less than a gas-driven car—all reasons why the oil and auto industries were not supportive of electric cars and had them recalled and destroyed in California.[19]

Meanwhile around the world hundreds of millions of automobiles with internal combustion engines continue to produce enormous quantities of toxic emissions and greenhouse gases. The dangers of global warming are so immense, so compounding and fast acting that an all-out effort is needed to reverse the ecological apocalypse of flood, drought, and famine. This is the single most urgent problem the world faces (or refuses to face). Unless we move swiftly away from fossil fuels, changing direction 180 degrees, we will face a future so catastrophic that it defies description, and it may come much sooner than we think.

TAXES AND ECONOMIC REFORM

Reintroduce a steep progressive income tax for superrich individuals and corporations—without the many loopholes that still exist. Eliminate off-shore tax shelters and foreign tax credits for transnational corporations, thereby bringing in over $100 billion in additional revenues. And put a cap on corporate tax write-offs for advertising, equipment, and CEO stock options and perks. Strengthen the estate tax instead of eliminating it. Give tax relief to working people and lower income employees.

Corporations should be reduced to smaller units with employee and community control panels to protect the public's interests. As was the case in the nineteenth century, corporations should be prohibited from owning stock in other corporations. They should be granted charters only for limited times, say twenty or thirty years, and for specific business purposes, charters that can be revoked by the government for cause. Company directors should be held criminally liable for corporate malfeasance, financial swindles, and for violations of occupational safety, consumer, and environmental laws.

ELECTORAL SYSTEM

To curb the power of the moneyed interests and lobbyists, all candidates, including minor-party ones, should be provided with public financing. In addition, a strict cap should be placed on campaign spending by all party organizations, candidates and supporters. The states should institute proportional representation so that every vote will count. A party that gets 15 percent of the vote in a region will get roughly 15 percent of the seats instead of zero representation as is the case with the winner-take-all system we have now. Major parties will no longer dominate the legislature with artificially inflated majorities.[20] Also needed is a standard federal electoral law allowing uniform and easy ballot access for third parties and independents. We should abolish the electoral college to avoid artificially inflated majorities that favor the two-party monopoly and undermine the popular vote. If the president were directly elected, every vote would count, regardless of its location.

We need protection against attempts by local authorities to suppress or intimidate voters, as was done by Republican officials in several states during the stolen presidential elections of 2000 and 2004 and repeated with additional measures in 2006. As of now, in each state, elections are presided over by the secretaries of state, who often are active party partisans, as was the case in Florida and Ohio. In the 2006 gubernatorial election in Ohio, the state's secretary of state J. Kenneth Blackwell was making decisions about who could vote, while himself running as the GOP candidate for governor. He worked hard to shut down voter registration drives and purged registration lists in areas of heavily concentrated Democratic votes, just as he had done in 2004. Worse still, he presided over the counting of the ballots. What we need is a federal nonpartisan commission of professional civil servants to preside over the electoral process to insure that people are not being falsely challenged or arbitrarily removed from voter rolls. As an additional safeguard, teams of foreign observers, perhaps from the United Nations, using exit polls, should monitor election proceedings and testify as to their fairness and honesty.

Also needed are more accessible polling and registration sites in low-income areas, and an election that is held on an entire weekend instead of a work day (usually Tuesday) so that persons who must commute far and work long hours will have sufficient opportunity to get to the polls. Most important, we need paper ballots whose results can be immediately and honestly recorded in place of the touchscreen machines that so easily lead to fraudulent counts.

The District of Columbia should be granted statehood. As of now its 607,000 citizens are denied self-rule and full representation in Congress. They elect a mayor and city council but Congress and the president retain the power to overrule all the city's laws and budgets. Washington, D.C., remains one of the nation's internal colonies.

EMPLOYMENT CONDITIONS

Americans are working harder and longer for less, often without any job security. Many important vital services are needed, yet many people have no work. Job programs, more encompassing than the ones created during the New Deal, could employ people to reclaim the environment, build affordable housing and mass transit systems, rebuild a crumbling infrastructure, and provide services for the aged and infirm and for the public in general.

People could be put to work producing goods and services in competition with the private market, creating more income, more buying power, and a broader tax base. The New Deal's WPA engaged in the production of goods, manufacturing clothes and mattresses for relief clients, surgical gowns for hospitals, and canned foods for the jobless poor. This kind of not-for-profit public production to meet human needs brings in revenues to the government, both in the sales of the goods and in taxes on the incomes of the new jobs created. Eliminated from the picture is private profit for those who live off the labor of others—which explains their fierce hostility toward government attempt at direct production.

FISCAL POLICY

The national debt is a transfer payment from taxpayers to bondholders, from labor to capital, from have-nots and have-littles to the have-it-alls. Government could end deficit spending by taxing the financial class from whom it now borrows. It must stop bribing the corporate rich with investment subsidies and other guarantees. Instead it should redirect capital investments toward not-for-profit public goals. The U.S. Treasury should create and control its own currency instead of allowing the Federal Reserve and its private bankers to pocket billions every year through its privatized money supply.

GENDER, RACIAL, AND CRIMINAL JUSTICE

End racial and gender-based discriminatory practices in all institutional settings. Vigorously enforce the law to protect abortion clinics from vigilante violence, women from male abuse, minorities and homosexuals from hate crimes, and children from incest rape and other forms of adult abuse, most of which occurs within the family. Release the hundreds of political dissenters who are serving long prison terms on trumped-up charges and whose major offense is their outspoken criticism of the existing system. And release the many thousands who are enduring draconian prison sentences for relatively minor drug offenses or for defending themselves against terrible abuse by violent spouses.[21]

HEALTH CARE AND SAFETY

Allow all Americans to receive coverage similar to the Medicare now enjoyed by seniors, but with coverage for alternative health treatments as well. People of working age would contribute a sliding-scale portion of the premium through payroll deductions or estimated tax payments for the self-employed, and employers would match those payments dollar for dollar. Funding can also come from the general budget as in the single-payer plan used in Canada and other countries, providing comprehensive service to all. Under single-payer health care, the billions of dollars that are now pocketed by HMO investors, executives, and advertisers would now be used for actual medical treatment.

Thousands of additional federal inspectors are needed by the various agencies responsible for enforcement of occupational safety and consumer protection laws. "Where are we going to get the money to pay for all this?" one hears. The question is never asked in regard to the gargantuan defense budget or enormous corporate subsidies. As already noted, we can get the additional funds from a more progressive tax system and from major cuts in big business subsidies and military spending.

LABOR LAW

Abolish anti-labor laws and provide government protections to workers who now run the risk of losing their jobs because they try to organize a union in their workplace. Prohibit management's use of permanent replacement scabs for striking workers. Penalize employers who refuse to negotiate a contract after certification has been won. Repeal the restrictive "right to work" and "open shop" laws that undermine collective bargaining. Lift the minimum wage to a livable level. In California, Minnesota, and several other states, there are "living wage movements" that seek to deny contracts and public subsidies to companies that do not pay their workers a decent income.[22]

Repeal all "free trade" agreements; they place a country's democratic sovereignty in the hands of nonelective, secretive, international tribunals that undermine local economies and the lawful regulatory powers of signatory nations, while diminishing living standards throughout the world.

MILITARY SPENDING

The military spending binge of the last two decades has created a crushing tax burden, and has transformed the United States from the world's biggest creditor nation into the world's biggest debtor nation. To save hundreds of billions of dollars each year, we should clamp down on the widespread corruption and waste in military spending. We can reduce the bloated "defense" budget by two-thirds over a period of a few years—without any risk to our national security. The Pentagon now maintains a massive nuclear arsenal and other strike forces designed to fight a total war against the Soviet Union, a superpower that no longer exists. To save additional billions each year and reduce the damage done to the environment, the United States should stop all nuclear tests, including underground ones, and wage a diplomatic offensive for the eventual elimination of all nuclear weaponry in the world, including elimination of this country's arsenal. With no loss to our "national security," Washington also could save tens of billions of dollars if it stopped pursuing armed foreign interventions and dropped its Star Wars antimissile missile program.

The loss of jobs and depressive economic effects of ridding ourselves of a war economy could be mitigated by embarking upon a massive conversion to a peacetime economy, putting the monies saved from the military budget into environmental protection, human services, and other domestic needs. The shift away from war spending would greatly improve our quality of life and lead to a healthier overall economy, while bringing serious losses to profiteering defense contractors.

NATIONAL SECURITY STATE

Prohibit covert actions by intelligence agencies against anticapitalist social movements at home and abroad. End U.S.-sponsored counterinsurgency wars against the poor of the world. Eliminate all foreign aid to regimes engaged in oppressing their own peoples. The billions of U.S. tax dollars that flow into the Swiss bank accounts of foreign autocrats, militarists, and drug cartels could be better spent on human services at home. Lift the trade sanctions imposed on Cuba and other countries that have dared to deviate from the freemarket orthodoxy.

The Freedom of Information Act should be enforced instead of undermined by those up high who say they have nothing to hide, then try to hide almost everything they do.

NEWS MEDIA

The airwaves are the property of the people of the United States. As part of their public-service licensing requirements, television and radio stations should be required to give—free of charge—

public air time to all political viewpoints, including dissident and radical ones. The media should be required to give equal time to all candidates, not just Democrats and Republicans. Free air time, say, an hour a week for each party in the month before election day, as was done in Nicaragua, helps level the playing field and greatly diminishes the need to raise large sums to *buy* air time. In campaign debates, the candidates should be questioned by representatives from labor, peace, consumer, environmental, feminist, civil rights, and gay rights groups, instead of just fatuous media pundits who are dedicated to limiting the universe of discourse so as not to give offense to their corporate employers and sponsors.

SOCIAL SECURITY

Reform Social Security in a progressive way by cutting 2 percent from the current 12.4 percent Social Security flat tax rate, and offset that lost revenue by eliminating or raising the cap on how much income can be taxed. At present, earnings of more than $97,500 are exempt from FICA withholding tax. This change would give an average working family a $700 tax relief and would reverse the trend that has been raising FICA payroll taxes for low- and middle-income people while reducing taxes for the wealthy.

It is no mystery why these sensible and urgently needed reforms are not carried out. Those who have the desire for such changes have not the power. And those who have the power most certainly have not the desire, being disinclined to commit class suicide. It is not in their interest to initiate really substantive democratic reforms in the existing politico-economic system. They can be counted on to resist our efforts at just about every turn.

NOTES

1. For these various irregularities, see *New York Times*, 30 November 2000 and 15 July 2001; *Boston Globe*, 30 November 2000 and 10 March 2001. A relevant documentary is *Unprecedented: The 2000 Presidential Election*, L.A. Independent Media Center Film, 2004.

2. *New York Times*, 15 September 2002; the investigators were from California Institute of Technology and Massachusetts Institute of Technology.

3. Mark Crispin Miller, *Fooled Again: How the Right Stole the 2004 Election and Why They'll Steal the Next One Too* (Basic Books, 2005), 7–31, 262, and passim.

4. All the various instances that follow—with the exception of the Rick Garves and Gregory Elich testimonials—are from Miller, *Fooled Again*, passim; Bob Fitrakis and Harvey Wasserman, *How the GOP Stole America's 2004 Election and Is Rigging 2008* (CICJ Books/www.Freepress.org, 2005); Anita Miller (ed.), *What Went Wrong in Ohio: The Conyers Report on the 2004 Presidential Election* (Academy Chicago Publishers, 2005); Andy Dunn, "Hook & Crook," *Z Magazine*, March 2005; Greg Palast, "Kerry Won: Here Are the Facts," *Observer*, 5 November 2004; Steven F. Freeman (with Joel Bleifus), *Was the 2004 Presidential Election Stolen?* (Seven Stories, 2006).

5. Jonathan Simon and Ron Baiman, "The 2004 Presidential Election: Who Won the Popular Vote? An Examination of the Comparative Validity of Exit Polls and Vote Count Data," Freepress.org, 2 January 2004; Freeman, *Was the 2004 Presidential Election Stolen?* 99–134 and passim; Fitrakis and Wasserman, *How the GOP Stole America's 2004 Election*, 51, 55–57.

6. *New York Times*, 9 November 2006.

7. "Good Morning America," 1 September 2005

8. *New York Times*, 5 September 2005.

9. Fran Pavley and Jason Barbose, "Roadblock to Cleaner Cars," 30 October 2006.

10. See the report by Susan Saulny and Gary Rivlin, *New York Times*, 17 September 2006.

11. Jill Pletcher, email, 17 September 2006.

12. Paul Gewirtz and Chad Golder, "So Who Are the Activists?" *New York Times* op-ed, 6 July 2005.

13. "Activism Is in the Eye of the Ideologist," *New York Times* editorial, 11 September 2006. The Kentucky study was done by Professor Lori Ringhand.

14. "Activism Is in the Eye of the Ideologist."

15. Survey by the *National Law Journal*, reported in *People's Daily World*, 12 September 1986.

16. See the documentary *Who Killed the Electric Car?* (Sony Pictures Classics, 2006).

17. Karl Grossman, "Three Mile Island," *Extra!,* July/August 1993.

18. "Nuclear Power 2010," *Public Citizen*, March 2004.

19. See the documentary film, *Who Killed the Electric Car* (2006).

20. For extended discussion of this point and other things in this selection, see Michael Parenti, *Democracy for the Few*, 8ᵗʰ ed. (Wadsworth/Thomson, 2007).

21. For data and particulars, see Parenti, *Democracy for the Few*, chapters 10 and 11.

22. James Ridgeway, "Mondo Washington," *Village Voice*, 27 June 2000.

III.
LIFESTYLES AND OTHER PEOPLE

12 RACIST RULE, THEN AND NOW

There is a horrific side to American history, seldom acknowledged and rarely taught. It has to do with the countless murderous assaults perpetrated against Native Americans, Asian Americans, Mexican Americans, African Americans, immigrants, and other ethnic minorities. The period between 1835 and 1848, for instance, saw a series of aggressive incursions and then a war waged against Mexico, resulting in the U.S. takeover of approximately half of Mexico—what is now Texas, New Mexico, Arizona, Nevada, Utah, a slice of Colorado, and all of California. In the decades after 1848, 473 out of every 100,000 Mexicans in the Southwest were victims of lynchings. As Luis Angel Toro of the University of Dayton put it, "The Anglos who poured into Texas and the rest of the Southwest brought their apparatus of racial terror, developed to hold the African American people in bondage, to the newly conquered territories. Mexicans became frequent victims of beatings and lynching."[1]

There are other examples of ethnic violence almost too grim to contemplate: the four hundred years of massacres and land grabs inflicted upon indigenous Americans ("Indians"), which included the extermination of entire tribes, and the centuries of slavery inflicted upon African Americans, followed by a century of segregation. African Americans compose the ethnic group that has been most persistently assaulted by Caucasian lynch-mob violence, extending from the earliest colonial days right into the second half of the twentieth century. Let us give that terrible issue some attention (since the history textbooks seldom do), focusing on New Orleans and a few other locales at the turn of the century.

In 1900 Ida Wells-Barnett, an African-American woman of no small courage, wrote a vivid exposé of the mob atrocities that were being perpetrated against members of her race in New Orleans. To read her reports today is to peer directly into an ugly and horrific history.[2] The scenes she describes in succinct but telling detail were replicated throughout the South and in some parts of the North. To pick one of many incidents, we read that in 1899 in Maysville, Kentucky, a Black man named William Coleman—against whom there was absolutely no evidence of any crime—was slowly roasted to death by an eager crowd, "first one foot and then the other, and dragged out of the fire so that the torture might be prolonged." Describing several other autos-da-fé, Wells-Barnett remarks with bitter irony that the "ordinary procedures of hanging and shooting have been improved upon during the past ten years." Sometimes thousands of people congregated to witness the burnings.

She also provides descriptions of the more "ordinary" lynchings, shootings, and mob beatings. In most of these incidents the police either proved unable or unwilling to maintain order; occasionally they even contributed to the disorder. The hideous descriptions of racist mob madness are enough to make one ask what manner of species are humans that they would inflict such horrors upon other living beings.

If Wells-Barnett focuses on a central character, it is Robert Charles, an African American whose only crime was to resist a police beating, flee, and then fight for his life in successive gun battles. Charles was branded a "desperado" and "archfiend," capable of "diabolical coolness" in his ability to shoot back with deadly accuracy at those who tried to hunt him down. He was repeatedly described as a hardened criminal, even though he had no criminal record and seems never to have committed a crime.

Charles made a desperate last stand, single-handedly, in a small building encircled by a furious armed mob numbering in the thousands. Even as the besiegers set fire to the building, he continued exchanging gunfire with his assailants, killing five attackers and seriously wounding nine others. Finally, Wells-Barnett reports, when fire and smoke became too much to endure, Charles "appeared in the door, rifle in hand, to charge the countless guns that were drawn upon him. With a courage which was indescribable, he raised his gun to fire again, but this time it failed, for a hundred shots riddled his body and he fell dead, face fronting the mob."

In a posthumous examination of his personal effects, the police found that Charles possessed "negro periodicals and other 'race' propaganda." He was what we would today call a Black Nationalist, active in the back-to-Africa movement. Instantly he devolved from a fiendish criminal to something even worse, an "agitator" and "fanatic," a Black militant given to "wild tirades." The literature he possessed was denounced because it "attacked the White race in unstinted language and asserted the equal rights of the Negro," one report said.

"The equal rights of the Negro"—a long vicious war was being waged against that notion. For several decades before the New Orleans riots, racist violence had rampaged throughout the South, sometimes directed rather precisely against the remnants of

Reconstruction. Instigated and led by big planters, mill owners, the railroads, and White supremacists, these racist forces were determined to shatter the coalitions of abolitionists, Republicans, and Populists whose ranks consisted mostly of African Americans and some poor White farmers and small businesspeople.[3] Racist supremacy was enlisted to "keep the South safe for the White race"—which usually meant safe for the White moneyed and landed interests, a point the more impoverished lynch mob participants never seemed able to grasp.

A complicit role in the tragic events of 1900 in New Orleans was played by the White-owned press. Some of the 1900 news reports do actually offer an occasionally critical comment about the horrors perpetrated against innocent hardworking African Americans. But for the most part, the press went about its business of blaming the victims, glorifying the police, and demonizing those who fought back.

What does this sordid racist history tell us about the present? In the 1970s during a Senate committee hearing, I heard South Carolina Senator Strom Thurmond impatiently exclaim, "No one's made more progress in this country than the Nigra people." He was not really praising African Americans for the way they had struggled upward against all odds. If anything, he was voicing his annoyance at their not being grateful for all the improvements they already enjoyed. His message was: count your blessings, you've come a long way, stop being ingrates and stop griping.

In reaction to the likes of Thurmond, there are some who would claim that nothing has changed, that things today for African Americans are just as bad as they were under slavery and just as bad as during the post-Reconstruction days described by Wells-Barnett when racist mob rule was the order of the day and any Black was fair game. Since the gains won by minorities are used by racists like Thurmond as an excuse to thwart further progress, the understandable reaction of some militants is to deny that real gains have been won, and to aver that improvements can be found more in the window dressing than in the substance of things; that for every African American appointed to a high profile post in government or wherever, there are dozens of less fortunate and less visible ones being roughed up by police on streets or in jail cells, sometimes with fatal results.

But to argue that no meaningful progress has been made is to claim that history is exclusively in the hands of oppressors who are more or less omnipotent. In fact, one has to argue both sides of the street on this, in a seemingly back-and-forth manner.

First, it is important to realize that vital democratic gains have been achieved by the champions of civil rights. With incredible courage and persistence, African Americans along with some Whites have fought back and made gains against lynch-mob terrorism, segregation, sharecropper servitude, disenfranchisement, job and housing discrimination, police brutality, and every other kind of institutionalized racism.

Second, having said that advances have been made, we need to remain alert to the terrible ethno-class inequalities and oppressions that still persist within U.S. society, and the concerted assault being perpetrated by reactionaries upon the gains won by all working and middle-class people over the past century, an assault that has cost the African-American community dearly in rollbacks and cutbacks.

So we go back and forth on this issue because sometimes the gains seem important and substantive, and sometimes they indeed seem like mere tokenism or under threat of being obliterated. Old oppressions have a way of reappearing in modern dress, even if not quite as viciously and blatantly as in bygone times. When Wells-Barnett wrote in 1900, "It is now, even as it was in the days of slavery, an unpardonable sin for a Negro to resist a White man no matter how unjust or unprovoked the White man's attack may be," we might say that this still can be the case in certain situations and locales—especially if the White man is dressed in a blue uniform and wears a badge. Nowadays, too often the police commit the racist murders and beatings that the untrammeled mob used to perpetrate.[4]

Just recently, in 2005, two New Orleans police beat an unarmed 64-year-old African-American man, a retired school teacher who had been made homeless by Hurricane Katrina, an incident that leaves one with the feeling that indeed not much has changed. But we then have to reverse field and point out that the two cops were fired and charged with criminal battery.[5] In 1900, in contrast, disciplinary and legal action against police for such a crime would have been unimaginable. In fact, the police assault would probably not have even been perceived as a crime by New Orleans authorities.

It should be added that even today these officers were disciplined not because the authorities took it upon themselves to be fair-minded and tougher toward racist White cops. The officials acted because of the spotlight that was brought to bear on the incident and the pressure put upon the New Orleans police department by organized civil rights groups. And such pressure emerged and was effective because of the century of struggle against racism and the resultantly stronger egalitarian climate of opinion that obtains today.

The ruling interests of yesteryear used racism much as they do today. Racism is a way of directing the anger of exploited Whites toward irrelevant enemies, making them feel victimized by African Americans who supposedly are expecting and getting special (equal) treatment. Racism blurs and buries economic grievances. Whites are less likely to act against their bosses, being themselves too busy trying to keep African Americans down. Thus the working populace is divided against itself, making it difficult for White and Black workers to act in unison against the moneyed class.

Racism also depresses wages for all by creating super-exploited categories of workers (Blacks, women, immigrants) who toil for less because of the very limited employment choices they are accorded.

But just as there can be such a thing as "surplus repression" (overkill that becomes counterproductive in maintaining class control), so there can be such a thing as "surplus racism" which damages the community's image and limits its economic opportunities. Wells-Barnett mentioned that once the local rich White folks of New Orleans realized that mob violence was hurting investments in the region, they began to stir themselves against the race riots, not for the sake of racial justice but for the purpose of saving the city's investment credit.

Today, racism remains a handy ruling-class card to play, even while a great show is made of appointing small numbers of (relatively conservative) African Americans and other ethnic minorities to White House cabinet posts and the federal courts. Reactionary leaders cannot get away with openly inciting Caucasians against African Americans. They dare not utter racist epithets today, at least not to public audiences. But they have other buzz words and coded terms: "welfare queens," "quotas," "special interests," "inner-city residents," "criminal elements," and the like. So the plutocrats direct the legitimate grievances of the middle Americans toward innocent foes, and in return the middle Americans vote for the plutocrats thinking they are thereby defending their own precarious socio-economic interests. Thus do reactionaries continue to play off White against Black. Divide and rule—it worked back then and still does to some extent today.

All the more reason to look for ways of uniting Caucasian Americans, African Americans, and all people of color in common struggle. The road to racial justice continues to be long and hard, and sometimes it feels as if we are losing our way. Thinking about the ugly side of New Orleans in 1900 gives us a perspective on how bad things were, how bad they can get, how many gains have been made, and how important it is to continue the fight.

13 CUSTOM AGAINST WOMEN

If we uncritically immerse ourselves in the cultural context of any society, seeing it only as it sees itself, then we are embracing the self-serving illusions and hypocrisies it has of itself. Perceiving a society "purely on its own terms" usually means seeing it through the eyes of dominant groups that exercise a preponderant influence in shaping its beliefs and practices.

Furthermore, the dominant culture frequently rests on standards that are *not* shared by everyone within the society itself. So we come upon a key question: whose culture is it anyway? Too often what passes for the established culture of a society is for the most part the preserve of the privileged, a weapon used against more vulnerable elements.

This is seen no more clearly than in the wrongdoing perpetrated against women. A United Nations report found that prejudice and violence against women "remain firmly rooted in cultures around the world."[6] In many countries, including the United States, women endure discrimination in wages, occupational training, and job promotion. According to a *New York Times* report, in most of sub-Saharan Africa women cannot inherit or own land—even though they cultivate it and grow 80 percent of the continent's food.[7]

It is no secret that women are still denied control over their own reproductive activity. Throughout the world about eighty-million pregnancies a year are thought to be unwanted or ill-timed. And some twenty million unsafe, illegal abortions are performed annually, resulting in the deaths of some 78,000 women yearly, with millions more sustaining serious injury.[8] In China and other Asian countries where daughters are seen as a liability, millions of infant females are missing, having been aborted or killed at birth or done in by neglect and underfeeding.[9]

An estimated hundred million girls in Africa and the Middle East have been genitally mutilated by clitoridectomy (excision of the clitoris) or infibulation (excision of the clitoris, labia minora, and inner walls of the labia majora, with the vulva sewed almost completely shut, allowing an opening about the circumference of a pencil). The purpose of such mutilation is to drastically diminish a woman's capacity for sexual pleasure, insuring that she remains her husband's compliant possession. Some girls perish in the excision process (usually performed with no anesthetic, no sterilization procedures, and by an older female with no medical training). Long-term consequences of infibulation include obstructed menstrual flow, chronic infection, hurtful coitus, and complicated childbirth.

In much of the Middle East, women have no right to drive cars or to appear in public unaccompanied by a male relative. They have no right to initiate divorce proceedings but can be divorced at the husband's will.

In Latin American and Islamic countries, men sometimes go unpunished for defending their "honor" by killing their allegedly unfaithful wives or girlfriends. In fundamentalist Islamic Iran, the law explicitly allows for the execution of adulterous women by stoning, burning, or being thrown off a cliff. In countries such as Bangladesh and India, women are murdered so that husbands can remarry for a better dowry. An average of five women a day are burned in dowry-related disputes in India, and many more cases go unreported.[10]

In Bihar, India, women found guilty of witchcraft are still burned to death. In modern-day Ghana, there exist prison camps for females accused of being witches. In contrast, male fetish priests in Ghana have free reign with their magic practices. These priests often procure young girls from poor families that are said to owe an ancestral debt to the priest's forebears. The girls serve as the priests' sex slaves. The ones who manage to escape are not taken back by their fearful families. To survive, they must either return to the priest's shrine or go to town and become prostitutes.[11]

Millions of young females drawn from all parts of the world are pressed into sexual slavery, in what amounts to an estimated $7 billion annual business. More than a million girls and boys, many as young as five and six, are conscripted into prostitution in Asia, and perhaps an equal number in the rest of the world. Pedophiles from the United States and other countries fuel the Asian traffic. Enjoying anonymity and impunity abroad, these "sex tourists" are inclined to treat their acts of child rape as legal and culturally acceptable.[12]

In Afghanistan under the Taliban, women were captives in their own homes, prohibited from seeking medical attention, working, or going to school. The U.S. occupation of Afghanistan was hailed by President Bush Jr. as a liberation of Afghani women. In fact, most of that country remains under the control of warlords and resurgent Taliban fighters who oppose any move toward female emancipation. And the plight of rural women has become yet more desperate. Scores of young women have attempted self-immolation to escape family abuse and unwanted marriages. "During the Taliban we were living in a graveyard, but we were secure," opined one female activist. "Now women are easy marks for rapists and armed marauders."[13]

In Iraq we find a similar pattern: the plight of women actually worsening because of a U.S. invasion. Saddam Hussein's secular Baath Party created a despotic regime (fully backed by Washington during its most murderous period). But the Baathists did grant Iraqi women rights that were unparalleled in the Gulf region. Women could attend university, travel unaccompanied, and work alongside men in various professions. They could choose whom to marry or could refrain from getting married. With the growing insurgency against the U.S. occupation, however, females are now targeted by the ascendant Islamic extremists. Clerics have imposed new restrictions on them. Women are forced to wear the traditional head covering, and girls spend most of their days indoors confined to domestic chores. Most Iraqi women are now deprived of public education. Often the only thing left to read is the Koran.

Many women fear they will never regain the freedom they enjoyed under the previous regime. As one Iraqi feminist noted, "The condition of women has been deteriorating. . . . This current situation, this fundamentalism, is not even traditional. It is desperate and reactionary."[14]

For all the dramatic advances made by women in the United States, they too endure daunting victimization. Tens of thousands of them either turn to prostitution because of economic need or are forced into it by a male exploiter, only to be kept there by acts of violence and intimidation. An estimated three out of four women in the United States are victims of a violent crime sometime during their lifetime. Every day, four women are murdered by men to whom they have been close. Murder is the second leading cause of death among young American women.

In the United States domestic violence is the leading cause of injury among females of reproductive age. An estimated three million women are battered each year by their husbands or male partners, often repeatedly.

Statistically, a woman's home is her most dangerous place—if she has a man in it. This is true not only in the United States but in a number of other countries.[15] Battered women usually lack the financial means to escape, especially if they have children. When they try, their male assailants are likely to come after them and inflict still worse retribution. Police usually are of little help. Arrest is the least frequent response to domestic violence. In most states, domestic beatings are classified as a misdemeanor.[16]

In most parts of this country, if a man physically attacks another man on the street, leaving him battered and bloody, he can be charged with "felonious assault with intent to inflict serious bodily injury" and he might face five to ten years in the slammer, depending on the circumstances. But when this same man beats up his wife or female domestic partner, a whole different procedure and vocabulary is activated. For some reason the crime is reduced to a therapeutic problem. He is charged with "domestic abuse" and held overnight, if that long. And he has to agree to attend counseling sessions in which he supposedly will see the errors of his ways. If the chronic batterer knew that he would be facing five to ten years in prison, he might be more reliably deterred, as some batterers themselves have admitted.

In contrast, the women who kill their longtime male abusers in desperate acts of self-defense usually end up serving lengthy prison sentences. In recent times, women's organizations have had some success in providing havens for battered women and pressuring public authorities to move against male violence.

To conclude, those who insist that outsiders show respect for their customs may have a legitimate claim in some historic instances, or they may really be seeking license to continue oppressing the more vulnerable elements within their own society. There is nothing sacred about the status quo, and nothing sacred about culture as such. There may be longstanding practices in any culture, including our own, that are not worthy of respect. And there are basic rights that transcend all cultures, as even governments acknowledge when they outlaw certain horrific practices and sign international accords in support of human rights.[17]

14 ARE HETEROSEXUALS WORTHY OF MARRIAGE?

During 2003–2004, as heartland America gawked in horrified fascination, thousands of homosexual men married each other, as did thousands of lesbians, in San Francisco and several other obliging locales. A furious outcry was not long in coming from those who claimed to know what side of the Kulturkampf God is on. President Bush Jr. proposed an amendment to the Constitution making same-sex wedlock a federal offense. Heterosexual marriage, he declared, is "the most fundamental institution of civilization."

According to opinion polls in 2004, a majority of Americans believed that marriage should be strictly a man-woman affair. At least fourteen states had passed laws or amendments to their state constitutions banning gay marriage. Eight of these also outlawed civil unions and domestic partnerships, including heterosexual ones. It has to be man-woman *marriage* or no bonds at all.

Opponents of same-sex wedlock do not offer a single concrete example of how it would damage society. Gay marriage is legal in Belgium, the Netherlands, Canada, Norway, Sweden, Denmark, and the state of Massachusetts, and thus far it has neither impaired traditional marriage nor subverted civil order in those societies. In fact, the mentioned countries have less crime and social pathology than does the United States.

If matrimony really is such a sacred institution, why leave it entirely in the hands of heterosexuals? History gives us countless examples of how *heterosexuals* have defiled the sanctity of this purportedly God-given institution. A leader of a Michigan group called Citizens for the Protection of Marriage proclaimed that the people in his community supported "the traditional, historical, biblical definition of marriage."[18] But for millennia the traditional historical biblical marriage consisted of a bond not between a man and a woman but between a man and any number of women. Polygamy is an accepted feature in the Holy Bible itself. King Solomon, for instance, had 700 wives, not to mention 300 concubines, yet suffered not the mildest rebuke from either God or man (at least not in the Bible). Polygamy is still practiced secretly and illegally in parts of Utah among dissident Mormon splinter groups and in places like New York where it is estimated that some thousands of male immigrants from Africa have two or more wives under circumstances that prove less than happy for the women. It is seldom prosecuted.[19]

In some parts of the world today, polygamy is commonly practiced by men who have the money to buy additional wives. *Buy?*
Exactly. Too often heterosexual marriage is not a mutual bonding
but a one-sided bondage. The entrapped women have no say in
the matter. In various countries, mullahs, warlords, tribal chief-
tains, or other prestigious or prosperous males lock away as many
wives as they can get their hands on. The women often find themselves railroaded into a lifelong loveless captivity, subjected to
periodic violence, prolonged isolation, enforced illiteracy, unat-
tended illnesses, and other degrading conditions.

The defenders of straight marriage say little about how their
sanctified institution is used in some places as an instrument of
child sexual abuse and female enslavement. Girls as young as
eleven and twelve are still bartered in various parts of the world,
with a nuptial night that brings little more than child rape, often
followed by years of mistreatment by the groom and his family.

A longstanding but horrific avenue to heterosexual matrimony
is rape. In parts of southern Europe and in fifteen Latin American
countries, custom—and sometimes the penal code itself—exoner-
ates a rapist if he offers to make amends by marrying the victim,
and she accepts.[20] In Costa Rica he is released even if she refuses
the offer. Relatives often pressure the victim to accept in order to
restore honor to the family and herself. When a woman is gang
raped, *all* the rapists are likely to propose marriage in order to
evade imprisonment. "Can you imagine that a woman who has
been gang raped will then be pressured to chose which of her
attackers she wants to spend the rest of her life with?" comments
one disgusted male lawyer in Peru.[21] Such laws implicitly condone
the crime of rape by making it easily absolved with an opportunistic marriage offer.

Another practice long associated with heterosexual wedlock is its use to cement political alliances, shore up family fortunes, or advance careers. From ancient Rome to the latter-day European aristocracy, females of the best families of one nation or political faction were treated like so many gaming pieces, married off to well-placed males of another nation or faction. And not only among aristocrats. Throughout the nineteenth and early twentieth centuries, in respectable bourgeois society the suitability of a prospective spouse was just as often determined by purse and pedigree as by any genuine emotional attachment.

Throughout history marriage has been more closely linked to property than to love, usually to the benefit of the male spouse. For generations, in parts of the United States and other western countries, a married woman could not own property. She had to forfeit her family inheritance to her husband. Arranged marriages continue today in many parts of the world, with little regard for the feelings of the young women and men involved but with much concern for the dowry, social status, and financial condition of the respective families. Even in our own country there are heterosexuals who marry for money, social standing, or some other reason having little to do with personal regard and affection. Do not such opportunistic calculations devalue the institution?

Another dismal chapter in the history of heterosexual wedlock is the way it has been used to bolster racism. In some seventeen states in the United States, holy matrimony was an unholy racist institution, with laws forbidding wedlock between persons of different races. Hence for generations we lived with legally mandated same-*race* marriage. The last of these miscegenation laws was not removed from the books until 1967.

For millions of women heterosexual marriage is not a particularly uplifting or even safe institution. An estimated two million females in the United States are repeatedly battered; most are married to their attackers. Domestic violence is the single greatest cause of injury and one of the leading causes of death for U.S. women. An uncounted number of wives are raped by abusive husbands. Almost three million U.S. children reportedly are subjected to serious neglect, physical mistreatment, or incest rape by a close family member, usually a father, uncle, stepfather, grandfather, older brother, or mother. Each year tens of thousands of minors run away to escape abusive homes. Taking the sacred vows of holy matrimony is no guarantee against the foulest domestic misdeeds.

Children are as badly mistreated in traditional Christian families as in any other. Conservative religious affiliation is "one of the greatest predictors of child abuse, more so than age, gender, social class, or size of residence."[22] Nor do women fare all that well in fundamentalist households. Frequently confined to the traditional roles of wife, mother, and homemaker, they are dependent on their husbands for support and therefore more vulnerable to mistreatment. The fundamentalist clergymen they consult are often inclined to dismiss their complaints and advise them to suffer quietly like good wives as God ordained. Restrictive divorce laws and heartless cutbacks in welfare support make it still more difficult for women with children to leave oppressive and potentially lethal relationships.[23]

As women gain in education and earning power and become less economically dependent on men, they are less likely to stay in abusive marriages. In fact, they are less inclined to marry. In countries like Japan, about half of the single women from 35 to 54 have no intention of ever marrying, and over 71 percent say they never want children. Women prefer to remain single so they can "continue to maintain a wide spectrum of friends and pursue their careers," according to one report. The same trend can be observed in Singapore, South Korea, and some other countries. Despite high jobless rates, women are putting their education and careers first, showing no eagerness to submerge themselves in a traditional marriage.[24]

In the United States marriage is becoming less popular among both men and women. Census Bureau figures show that the number of unmarried men between ages 30 and 34 climbed from 9 to 33 percent over the last several decades. During that time the percentage of out-of-wedlock births more than tripled.[25] Again, if marriage is in decline, it is not because gays have been undermining it.

Millions of heterosexual couples in the United States and elsewhere find marriage to be a gratifying experience, if not for a lifetime certainly for some substantial duration. One survey reports that 38 percent of wedded Americans say they are happily married.[26] But for most U.S. marriages the predictable outcome is divorce, 51 percent to be exact. Yet society has not unraveled. Perhaps, then, marriage is *not* the most fundamental institution of civilization, the foundation of society, as Bush Jr. claims. If anything, in the more abusive households divorce is actually a blessing.

Americans are more religious than Europeans, yet they lead the world in single parenthood and divorce. According to a 2001 study by Barna Research Group Ltd., born-again Christians are just as likely to get divorced as less confirmed believers, with almost all their divorces happening "after they accepted Christ, not before." Jesus worshippers may pray together but they do not necessarily stay together. Census Bureau figures from 2003 show divorce rates are actually *higher* in areas where conservative Christians live. Bible Belt states like Kentucky, Mississippi, and Arkansas voted overwhelmingly for constitutional amendments to ban gay marriage, while having the highest divorce rates in the country, roughly twice that of more liberal states like Massachusetts.[27]

Fundamentalist keepers of public morals do bemoan the high divorce rate, but they don't rant about it the way they do about gay wedlock. The point is, if straight individuals, such as reactionary radio commentator and admitted substance abuser Rush Limbaugh, can get married and divorced repeatedly without denigrating the institution, what is so threatening about a gay union? Does Limbaugh feel that gay marriage makes a mockery of all three of his past forays into holy matrimony (and subsequent three divorces) and any future marriages he may venture upon? If anything, happy gays wanting to get into the institution might help make up for all those unhappy straights wanting to get out.

Proponents of the sanctity of heterosexual matrimony frequently prove themselves to be among the biggest moral hypocrites afoot. A prime example is Republican congressman Dan Burton of Indiana, a married father of three, and a champion of the right-wing Christian Coalition. Burton had to admit to fathering a child in an extramarital affair. He also used campaign money and federal funds to hire women of dubious credentials. He set one of them up in a house and gave her about $500,000 in payments without making clear what she did to earn so much so quickly.

Another Republican congressman, Henry Hyde of Illinois, a great proponent of "family values," was found to have carried on an adulterous affair over some years; so too Pennsylvania Republican Don Sherwood, whose extramarital girlfriend accused him in 2006 of physically abusing her. One congressman, Florida Republican Mark Foley, professed a special concern for the well-being of America's youth but himself was forced to resign from Congress when it was discovered that he had been trolling for young male pages on Capitol Hill, an addiction that Republican House leaders knew about and had covered up for many months.[28]

While preaching the sanctity of marriage, televangelist Jimmy Swaggert, married with children, was forced to admit that he was regularly patronizing a prostitute. A leading fundamentalist televangelist preacher, Rev. Ted Haggard, close ally to the Bush Jr. White House and head of a 14,000-member megachurch, vehemently denounced gay marriage and homosexuality until it was revealed that for three years he had been paying a male prostitute for monthly sexual encounters.[29] I, for one, was shocked and disgusted upon reading this particular news item. It certainly lowered my opinion of male prostitutes.

One could go on. *Freethought Today*, publication of the Freedom from Religion Foundation, every month presents two full pages of criminal cases involving scores of clergy and other religious leaders, hypocritical keepers of heterosexual family values, who are charged with sexual assault, rape, statutory rape, sodomy, coerced sex with parishioners and minors, indecent liberties with minors, molestation and sexual abuse of children (of both sexes), marriage or cohabitation with underage girls, financial embezzlement, fraud, theft, and other crimes.

As to whether children can hope to have a proper upbringing with gay parents, a judge in Arkansas ruled affirmatively in 2005. He issued a set of findings showing that children of gay and lesbian households are as well adjusted as other children, having no more academic problems or confusion about gender identity, or difficulties relating to peers, or instances of child abuse. There is no evidence, he concluded, that heterosexual parents are better at dealing with minors than gay parents.[30]

Untroubled by the absence of evidence, the New York Court of Appeals ruled in 2006 that same-sex couples have no right to marry under New York's constitution. The court ignored the Arkansas decision and the evidence upon which it was based, and fell back on folklore: "For the welfare of children, it is more important to promote stability, and to avoid instability," and "it is better, other things being equal, for children to grow up with both a mother and a father."[31]

The major purpose of marriage, argue the religiously orthodox and other homophobes, is the bearing and rearing of children. Male gay couples cannot bear children, and the New York court seemed to think that they are not sufficiently equipped to raise them. But the evidence referenced in the Arkansas case indicates that gay couples are at least as capable of proper parenting as straight couples. Futhermore, are children really the major purpose of marriage? Certainly not for the millions in childless marriages who cannot have children or do not desire children either because they are too old or too poor or just not interested or already have children from previous marriages. Should they too be denied the right to wed?

If same-sex unions do violate church teachings, then the church (or synagogue or mosque) can refuse to perform gay marriages, and many have refused. The gays I saw getting married in San Francisco's City Hall in 2004 were engaged in civil marriages, with no cleric presiding. And what I saw opened my heart. Here were people, many in longstanding relationships, who were experiencing their humanity, happy at last to have a right to marry the one they loved, happy to exercise their full citizenship and be treated as persons equal under the law. As commented one gay groom, who had been with his mate for seventeen years, "We didn't know the shame and inequality we'd been living with until we were welcomed into City Hall as equal human beings."[32]

But it is not all love and roses with gay wedlock. Less than a year after getting married, a number of same-sex couples filed for divorce, citing "irreconcilable differences," demonstrating again that gays are not that different from the rest of us.

To sum up, here are some of the things that straight-sex marriage has wrought through the ages: polygamy, child-brides, loveless arrangements, trafficked women, battered wives, bartered wives, raped wives, murdered wives, sexual slavery, incest rape, child neglect and abandonment, racist miscegenation laws, rampant hypocrisy, and astronomical divorce rates. If gays and lesbians are unqualified for marriage, what can we say about straights? The Jesus worshippers who want to prevent holy wedlock from being sullied might begin by taking an honest look at the ugly condition of so many heterosexual unions in this country and throughout the world.

15 THAT'S ITALIAN? ANOTHER ETHNIC STEREOTYPE

The several hundred or so hoodlums in the organized rackets who are of Italian descent compose but a tiny fraction of an Italian-American population estimated at over fifteen million people. Yet with the help of the news and entertainment media and persons in public life, these racketeers have become representative of an entire ethnic group. Linking Italians as an entire group with organized crime has long been one of those respectable forms of bigotry.

Back in 1961, syndicated news columnist John Crosby wrote, "I must point out that the Italians, and particularly the Sicilians, have a knack for hoodlumism and for organized crime out of proportion to most other national groups."[33] A decade later, the Oval Office tapes released during the Watergate investigation revealed President Richard Nixon saying to his assistant John Ehrlichman, "The Italians. We must not forget the Italians. . . . They're not like us. Difference is . . . they smell different. After all, you can't blame them. Oh no. Can't do that. They've never had the things we've had. . . . Of course, the trouble is . . . you can't find one that's honest."[34] Such words from a man who was driven from high office for lying, cheating, and lawbreaking.

Fast forward another dozen years or so to 1983. I am in my hotel room watching the brilliant comedian Richard Pryor doing one of his stand-ups, and suddenly I hear him say: "Not all Italians are in the mafia. They just all *work* for the mafia." The audience laughs. More recently in July 2005, on his *Prairie Home Companion* radio show, Garrison Keillor described the North End of Boston, a predominantly Italian family neighborhood with a relatively low crime rate, as "the place where, if there were such a thing as a mafia, that's where it would be." His audience thought this was uproariously funny.

There have been Irish, Jewish, Black, Latino, and even Anglo-Protestant mobsters in our history. Today we see the emergence of Russian and Asian gangsters. None of these cutthroats are representative of the larger ethnic formations from which they happened to emerge. But it is the Italian crime syndicate that has enjoyed a predominance for the last half-century, and upon whom the media have fixed. In the 1950s there was the TV series *The Untouchables*; today there is *The Sopranos*, while in the film world it is *The Godfather* and other movies too numerous to list.

Worse still, the mobsters in these flicks are sometimes depicted in a romanticized way, powerful but admirable family patriarchs who mete out a rough justice, occasionally helping the little guy. Scarce attention is given to how these gangsters actually make their living. One would never guess that they are extortionists, swindlers, drug dealers, numbers racketeers, pimps, and small-time thieves. They exploit the weak and vulnerable, maybe not as effectively as Enron, Harkin, Halliburton, and WorldCom, but viciously enough.

Just about the only positive feature of *The Sopranos* is the way it realistically depicts mobsters as ruthless "protection" racketeers who regularly victimize small business people and other hard-working folks. Distinct among mafia films is Martin Scorsese's *Goodfellas*. An exceptionally well-made movie based on a true story, *Goodfellas* divests the mafiosi of any romantic or glorified aura, revealing them to be the vicious bloodsuckers and cut-throats they really are.

Italian Americans themselves avidly watch these mafia shows for the same reason that years ago African Americans watched *Amos and Andy*, and Jewish Americans watched *The Goldbergs*. Long starved for acknowledgment from the dominant Anglo-Protestant culture, the ethnics have always looked for signs that they count for something, that they actually exist in the eyes of the wider society. The feeling of being marginalized, a stranger in one's own land, is part of what makes many ethnics so responsive to any kind of media representation, sometimes even a derogatory one. A starving person will eat foul food.

Before I finally gave up on *The Sopranos*, I found myself enjoying the arcane Southern Italian slang words and expressions that were slipped into the show's scripts. Italian dialect terms (some of them not very nice) that I had not heard since my youth in the old neighborhood I now heard on a major media show. It was a source of some satisfaction, an inside joke over America's air-waves.

Having been fed all these mafia shows, we need to remind our-selves that not all gangsters are Italian and not all Italians are gangsters. As with other ethnic groups in the last half century, Ital-ian Americans have moved in noticeable numbers into government service, political life, sports, law enforcement, educa-tion, organized labor, the professions, entertainment, and the arts. But very little of what constitutes *non-criminal* Italian-American life has been deemed worthy of cinematic treatment. (There have been some worthy exceptions such as the films *Marty, Moon-struck*, and *Dominic and Eugene.*)

When Italians actually are portrayed as law-abiding people, it is usually within the framework of working-class stereotypes: action-prone, loud-mouthed, simple-minded, visceral, living a proletarian existence worth escaping (for instance, *Saturday Night Fever, Staying Alive,* and *Hard Hat and Legs*). The media's Italian ethnic bigotry is also a class bigotry.

Additional Italian-American stereotypes can be found in the world of television advertisements, as Marco Ciolli describes it: there is the Latin lover who wins his lady with his right choice of beverage; the Mafia don ready to start a gangland massacre if the lasagna isn't *magnifico*; the nearly inarticulate disco dimwit who can barely say "Trident" as he twirls his partners around the dance floor.[35]

Above all, there are the uproarious family meal scenes of bliss-fully chattering Italians shoveling food around the table and into their mouths. In the world of commercials, Italians are repre-sented as noisy gluttons feasting with lip-smacking exuberance on endless platters of pasta, volunteering such connoisseur culinary judgments as "Mama mia! datza spicy meatball!," an expression that served as a running joke for years during the 1970s. The food stereotype has continued to this day. In 2006, a Pizza Hut television commercial featured an elderly Italian couple, dressed in the style of oldtime immigrants just getting off the boat. She exclaims "Oooh, mama mia!" when the pizza appears, and he asks her in a scolding tone, "Why you no make-uh pizza like-uh dat?"[36]

The stereotypical linking of Italians with food is so predominant as to preclude this ethnic group's association with other realms of activity (except, of course, crime). Thus a PBS documentary mini-series on the English language, written and narrated by Robert MacNeil (of *MacNeil-Lehrer News Hour* fame) dwelled at length on how various foreign languages have enriched the English language. However, Italian was something of an exception, MacNeil asserted, since the only Italian words he could find that have passed into English "all relate to food."

MacNeil should have searched a little more carefully. The food stereotype so preempted his myopic vision as to cause him to overlook such inedibles as: aggiornamento, bravo, bravado, brio, buffo, ghetto, dilettante, cognoscenti, illuminati, literati, virtuoso, crescendo, diminuendo, fresco, divertimento, falsetto, forte, fortissimo, politico, graffiti, piazza, imbroglio, inamorata, incognito, malaria, paparazzi, pietà, prima donna, diva, regatta, rotunda, impresario, piano, soprano, contralto, sotto voce, libretto, maestro, staccato, stiletto, studio, umbrella, viola, vibrato, vendetta, vista—one could go on.

Their days taken up with runs to and from the kitchen, or with shooting people in the face, Italians doubtless are a poor choice when it comes to chairing a board meeting, offering medical advice, writing a cogent social analysis, debating a public policy, arguing a court case, or conducting a scientific experiment. As Ciolli observes, "Certainly no commercial has ever shown an Italian American involved in any professional activity."[37]

It has been argued that the media merely reflect reality: after all there actually are Italian gangsters, and Italians really do like to drink wine and eat pasta (as do many other people). But such assertions overlook the distorted dimension of the "reality" presented. More often than not, the media's approach is to propagate and reinforce the cheap, facile notions about one group or another rather than challenge such views in any measured way.

If the representations can easily be made plausible, amusing, or sensational, then the corporate media will use them. The goal is to manipulate rather than educate, to reach as many people as quickly as possible with prefabricated but readily evocative images. For those on the receiving end, it's not fun.

NOTES

1. Quoted in Cristobal Cavazos, "Violence against Mexicans: A Neglected Part of Our History," *People's Weekly World,* 17 June 2006; see also Rodolfo Acuna, *Occupied America, a History of the Chicanos* (Longman, 2006).
2. Recently edited and reissued by Marcus Jacobs as: Ida B. Wells-Barnett, *Mob Rule in New Orleans* (Propaganda Press, 2006).
3. Scott Marshall, "North Carolina Confronts Shameful History," *People's Weekly World,* 18 March 2006.
4. For some of the many cases of police brutality and murder perpetrated against African Americans in recent times, see Michael Parenti, *Democracy for the Few,* 8th ed. (Wadsworth/Thomson, 2007), chapter ten, "Unequal Before the Law."
5. *Los Angeles Times,* 22 December 2005.
6. United Nations Population Fund, *State of World Population Report 2000.*
7. *New York Times,* 18 June 2004.
8. U.N. Population Fund, *State of World Population Report 2000.*
9. The disappearance of females is discernible when census data is markedly out of line with normal gender birth rates.
10. Report by the United Nations Department of Public Information DPI/1772/HR—February 1996.

11. This account given to me, 19 October 2004, by Emilie Parry, former researcher in Ghana; also see the documentary film, *Witches in Exile* (2004).

12. Andrew Cockburn, "21st Century Slavery," *National Geographic*, September 2003.

13. Quoted in John Pilger, "Afghanistan—What Good Friends Left Behind," *Guardian* (UK), 20 September 2003.

14. Yanar Mohammed quoted in Christian Parenti, *The Freedom: Shadows and Hallucinations in Occupied Iraq* (New Press, 2004), 24.

15. Elizabeth Rosenthal, "Women Face Greatest Threat of Violence at Home," *New York Times*, 6 October 2006; this article summarizes a ten-nation report by the World Health Organization.

16. Maria Roy, *The Abusive Partner* (Van Nostrand Reinhold, 1982); Richard Gelles and Murray Straus, *Intimate Violence* (Simon & Schuster, 1988).

17. For further exploration of cultural themes touched upon in this selection, see Michael Parenti, *The Culture Struggle* (Seven Stories, 2006).

18. Quoted in *San Francisco Chronicle*, 25 October 2004.

19. Nina Bernstein, "Polygamy, Praticed in Secrecy, Follows Africans to New York," *New York Times*, 23 March 2007.

20. Argentina, Brazil, Chile, Colombia, Costa Rica, the Dominican Republic, Ecuador, Guatemala, Honduras, Nicaragua, Panama, Paraguay, Peru, and Venezuela.

21. Quoted in Calvin Sims, "Justice in Peru," *New York Times* (international edition), 12 March 1997.

22. See the studies by sociologists and social psychologists cited in Kimberly Blaker, "God's Warrior Twins," *Toward Freedom*, Fall 2003.

23. Blaker, "God's Warrior Twins"; see also Kimberly Blaker (ed.) *The Fundamentals of Extremism: The Christian Right in America* (New Boston Books, 2003).

24. Jane Ganahl, "Women in Asia Are Starting to Say 'I Don't,'" *San Francisco Chronicle*, 14 November 2004.

25. U.S. Census Bureau report, Associated Press, 2 December 2004.

26. As reported in *Mother Jones*, January/February 2005.

27. *New York Times*, 20 November 2004.

28. Russ Baker, "The House Flunks Ethics," *Nation*, 15 February 1999; Dennis Bernstein and Leslie Kean, *Henry Hyde's Moral Universe* (Common Courage, 1999); *Washington Post*, 29 September to 5 October 2006.

29. *New York Times*, 3 to 5 November 2006.

30. *San Francisco Chronicle*, 1 January 2005.

31. *New York Law Journal*, 7 July 2006.

32. Quoted in Chris Thompson, "Gay Couples Aren't Inclined to Apologize," *East Bay Express*, 10-16 November 2004.

33. Crosby's column appeared in various newspapers on 22 March 1961; quoted in Richard Gambino, "Living with the Mark of Cain," *I Am*, August 1977.

34. Quoted in Garry Wills, "Nixon, Italian Style," *La Parola dal Popolo*, March/April 1975.

35. Marco Ciolli, "Exploiting the Italian Image," *Attenzione*, September 1979.

36. ABC-TV, Bay Area, California, 5 September 2006.

37. Ciolli, "Exploiting the Italian Image."

IV.
ROOTS

16 LA FAMIGLIA: AN ETHNO-CLASS EXPERIENCE

Decades ago in the northeast corner of Manhattan, in what is still known as East Harlem, there existed a congestion of dingy tenements and brownstones wherein resided one of the largest Italian working-class populations outside of Italy itself. The backyards were a forest of clotheslines, poles, and fences. The cellars, with their rickety wooden steps and iron banisters, opened directly onto the sidewalks. On warm days the streets were a focus of lively activity, with people coming and going or lounging on stoops and chatting. Small groups of men engaged in animated conversations, while children played ball in the streets or raced about wildly.

On certain days horse-drawn carts offered a lush variety of fruits and vegetables trucked in from Jersey and Long Island farms. The cries of the vendors were of a Southern Italian cadence unspoiled by a half-century in the new land. Women sat at window sills with elbows planted on pillows, occasionally calling down to acquaintances or yelling at the children. There was always something of interest going on in the streets but rarely anything of special importance except life itself.

It was in this East Harlem of 1933 that I made a fitful entrance into the world. My birth was a cesarean because, as my mother explained years later: "You didn't want to come out. You were stubborn even then." Since she suffered from a congenital heart disease, there was some question as to whether either of us would survive the blessed event. In those days, during a dangerous birth, a doctor might crush the baby's head in order to remove it from the womb and avoid fatal injury to the mother, a procedure the Catholic Church strenuously opposed. The Church's position was to let nature take its course and make no deliberate sacrifice of life. This sometimes meant that the baby came out alive but the mother died, or sometimes both perished. At the last minute the hospital asked my father to grant written permission to have my life sacrificed were it to prove necessary to save his wife. Obeying his heart instead of the Church, my father readily agreed. As it turned out, they decided on a cesarean section, a risky operation in 1933 for a woman with a heart condition. Happily, both of us came through.

To talk of my family I would have to begin with my grandparents who came from the impoverished lands of Southern Italy (as did most of the Italians in America), bringing with them all the strengths and limitations of their people. They were frugal, hardworking, biologically fertile—and distrustful of anyone who lived more than a few doors away.

One grandmother had thirteen children of whom only seven survived, and the other had fourteen with only nine survivors. This was the traditional pattern of high fertility and high mortality carried over from the old country. Given the burdens of repeated childbirth, both my grandmothers died years before my grandfathers. Their children, however, adopted the American style of smaller families. Having discovered birth control and urban living and trying to survive the Great Depression, they rarely had more than two or three children. The image of the large Italian family is an anachronism that hardened into a stereotype.

My father's mother, Grandma Marietta, was a living portrait of her generation: a short squat woman who toiled endlessly in the home. She shared the common lot of Italian peasant women: endless cooking, cleaning, and tending to the family, with a fatalistic submergence of self. "*Che pu fare?*" ("What can you do?") was the common expression of the elderly women. Given their domestic confinement, they learned but a few words of English even after decades of living in New York. They accepted suffering as a daily experience, rather than as something extraordinary. They suffered while mending and washing clothes in their kitchens, or standing over hot stoves; they suffered while climbing tenement stairs, or tending to the children or sitting alone at the windows; and they suffered while praying to their saints in church and burying their dead. Most of them went through life dressed in black in an uninterrupted state of mourning for one or another kin.

Marietta often cast her eyes up toward the kitchen ceiling and muttered supplications to Saint Anthony of the Light Fixture. She lived in fear of *u mal'occhio*, the evil eye. When younger members of the family fell ill, it was because someone had given them *u mal'occhio*. Like a high priestess she would sit by my sickbed and drive away the evil eye, making signs of the cross on my forehead, mixing oil and water in a small dish and uttering incantations that were a combination of witchcraft and Catholicism. Witchcraft was once the people's religion, having been in Southern Italy many centuries before Catholicism and having never quite left. The incantations seemed to work, for sooner or later I always recovered.

Some of the first-generation Italians were extreme in their pre-occupation with the evil eye. I remember as late as the 1950s a few of the late-arriving postwar immigrants would put an open pair of scissors, with one blade deliberately broken, on top of the television set so that no one appearing on the screen could send *u mal'occhio* into their living rooms. As we now know, the contaminations of television are not warded off that easily.

My mother's mother, Grandma Concetta, was something of an exception to this picture of the Italian woman. Endowed with a strong personality and a vital intelligence, she turned to the only respectable profession open to rural Italian women in the late nineteenth century: she became a midwife, a skill she learned in Italy and brought with her to New York. In those days midwives did more than deliver babies. They advised families on the care of children, diagnosed and treated illnesses with herbs, dietary prescriptions, heat applications, and other natural remedies that were said to work with far less destruction and sometimes more efficacy than the expensive chemicalized drugs pushed by the medical and pharmaceutical industries of today. She died at the age of sixty, a few years before I was born. I knew her only from the testimony of others and from a few faded photographs of a woman who gazed into the camera with a friendliness and gentle strength.

The men of my grandfathers' generation had toiled like beasts of burden in the old country, trapped in a grinding poverty, victimized by landlords, tax collectors, and military press gangs. Having fled to the crowded tenements of New York, they found they had a little more to live on but sometimes less to live for. My mother's father, Vincenzo, came to the United States from Calabria in 1887. He spent his working days in East Harlem carrying 100-pound bags of coal up tenement stairs, a profession that left him permanently stooped over. My father's father, Giuseppe, arrived in 1909. A landless peasant who had worked for a large estate near Gravina, outside Bari, he was fleeing military conscription. Giuseppe worked as a ditchdigger and day laborer in New York, managing to raise an enormous family on subsistence wages.

The Italian immigrant laborers were the paragons of the humble, thrifty toilers whom some people like to point to when lecturing the poor on how to suffer in silence and survive on almost nothing. In truth, the immigrants were not all that compliant—at least not originally. In fact, they had taken the extraordinary measure of uprooting themselves from their homelands in order to escape the dreadful oppression of the Old World. Rather than suffer in silence, they voted with their feet. We may think of them as the virtuous poor (although in their day they were denounced as the "swarthy hordes"), but they saw themselves as lifelong victims who were somewhat less victimized in the new land than in the old. Now they worked only twelve hours a day instead of fourteen and were better able to feed their children.

Still, in their hearts, many of the first generation men nursed a sentimental attachment to Italy. As the years wore on "the old country" for them became Paradise Lost, while the new land often seemed heartless, money-mad, and filled with the kind of lures and corruption that distanced children from their parents. They felt little patriotic devotion. What kept them in the United States were the loaves and fishes, not the stars and stripes.

The immigrant men drank wine made in their own cellars, and smoked those deliciously sweet and strong Italian stogies (to which I became temporarily addicted in my adulthood). They congregated in neighborhood clubs, barber shops, and the backrooms of stores to play cards, drink, and converse. They exercised a dominant presence in the home, yet left most domestic affairs including all the toil of child rearing to the women. Religion was also left to the women. The immigrant males might feel some sort of attachment to the saints and the church but few attended mass regularly and some openly disliked the priests. In the literal sense of the word, they were "anticlerical," suspicious of clergymen who did not work for a living but lived off other people's labor, and who did not marry but spent all their time around women and children in church.

The Italians who came to the United States during the great migrations at the turn of the century, like other groups before and since, were treated as unwelcome strangers. Considered incapable of becoming properly Americanized, they endured various forms of discrimination. Like other ethnic groups that have felt the sting of discrimination, many of the immigrants developed a late-blooming compensatory nationalism, becoming more nationalistic regarding Italy while in the new country than when they had lived "on the other side." Certainly that was true of Grandpa Giuseppe. For many, Mussolini appeared on the world stage in 1922 as something of a redeemer. Through his exploits in Africa and by "standing up" to other European powers, Mussolini won "respect" for Italy and for Italians everywhere—or so many of the immigrant men imagined.

"When Mussolini came along," an elderly Italian once told me, "they stopped calling us 'wop.'" The statement is woefully inaccurate. The admiration expressed by the U.S. conservative establishment and the mainstream press for Mussolini did not generate a new respect for immigrants in America. If anything it bespoke a low regard for them. U.S. plutocrats thought no better of ordinary Italians than they did of their own American workers. To them, the Italian was a vice-ridden ne'er-do-well, a disorderly bumpkin lacking in Calvinist virtues, just the sort of person most in need of a dictator's firm hand.

The second generation—that is, the American-born children of the immigrants—usually spoke of Mussolini with scorn and derision, especially after the United States entered World War II. I recall bitter arguments in my grandfather's house between the older and younger men. (With one or two exceptions, the women seldom voiced opinions on such matters.) As the war progressed and Mussolini showed himself to be nothing more than Hitler's acolyte, the old men tended to grow silent about him. But in their hearts, I believe, they never bore him much ill-feeling.

The military performance of Italy's legions in the war proved something of an embarrassment to those who had been anticipating Benito's version of the Second Coming of the Roman Empire. The ordinary recruits in the Italian army had no desire to fight *il Duce*'s battles. Rather they manifested a decided inclination to flee or surrender the moment they realized the other side was using live ammunition. One of my uncles gleefully told the story of how the entire Italian army landed one evening in Brooklyn to invade the Navy Yard, only to be routed and driven into the sea by the nightshift maintenance crew. Grandpa was not amused by that story. When Italy switched sides and joined the Allies in the middle of the war, there was much relief and satisfaction among the American-born and probably even among many of the immigrants.

Contrary to what we have heard, immigrant Italians were not particularly loving toward their children. They sent their young ones to work at an early age and expropriated their earnings. For most of the adults there was little opportunity to face the world with ease and tenderness. Of course, infants and toddlers were hugged, kissed, and loved profusely, but as the children got older it would have been an embarrassment, and in any case was not the custom, to treat them with much overt affection. Besides, there were so many of them, so many to feed or to bury, each new child being either an additional burden or an early tragedy but seldom an unmitigated joy.

"La famiglia, la famiglia," was the incantation of the old Italians. The family, always the family: be loyal to it, obey it, stick with it. This intense attachment to the family was not peculiar to Italians but was, and still is, a common characteristic of almost any poor rural people—be it in the Philippines, Nigeria, India, or Appalachia. More than anything the family was one's defense against starvation, the *padrone*, the magistrates, strangers, and rival families. As in any survival unit, its strictures were often severe and its loyalties intense. And betrayals were not easily forgiven.

The Italian family could also be a terrible battleground within itself. "Nobody can hate like brothers," the saying goes, especially brothers (and sisters) who had a hard childhood ruled over by immigrant parents who themselves saw life as a series of impending catastrophes. I remember the many squabbles, grudges, and hurt feelings that passed between my father, his brothers and sisters and their respective spouses. The series of shifting alliances and realignments among them resembled the Balkan politics of an earlier era. Years later, as the siblings put the deprivations and insecurities of the immigrant family behind them, and mellowed with age and prosperity and the advent of children and grandchildren of their own, they tended to get along much better with each other. It was a good example of how structural relations of the larger society influence personal relations.

I enjoyed the nourishing embrace of the big family gatherings, the outings at the beach, the picnics, parties and holiday dinners. The Italian holiday feast was a celebration of abundance with its endless platters of tasty, well-seasoned foods. I wonder if those marathon meals were a kind of ritual performed by people who had lived too long in the shadows of want and hunger, a way of telling themselves that at least on certain days the good life was theirs. Whether or not there was any larger meaning to them, the dinners were enjoyed for themselves.

I have an especially fond memory of my maternal grandfather, Vincenzo, a stooped, toothless, unimposing old man who was my closest ally in early life. During his last years, finding himself relegated to the edges of the adult world, he entered wholeheartedly into my world, playing cards with me, taking me for walks around the block, watching with undisguised delight as I acted out my highly dramatized cowboy and Indian games. He always took my side and despite his infirmity was sometimes able to rescue me from the discipline of my parents—which is the God-given function of grandparents.

Years before, when Vincenzo was still a youngster in his late seventies and a widower, he was discovered to have a girlfriend, a woman of about fifty-five years. She would steal into the house when no one was home and climb into bed with him. When family members discovered this tryst, they were outraged. My relatives denounced the woman as a whore of the worse sort, whose intent was to drive Grandpa to an early grave by overexerting his heart. (He died at age eighty-seven.) The poor lonely woman dared not see Vincenzo anymore; and poor Grandpa, after being scolded like a child, was kept under a sort of house arrest. In those days the idea that elderly parents might have sexual desires caused a furious embarrassment among their children.

After passing a certain age, Italian grandfathers were frequently made captives by their sons, daughters, older nieces and nephews, who all competed to put the old man under their protective custody. If a car came too close for comfort while the grandfather was crossing the street, as might happen to any pedestrian, the family would try to keep him from taking unaccompanied strolls, convinced that he could no longer judge traffic. If he misplaced his hat or scarf, as might anyone, he would be deemed unable to care for his personal effects. At the beach, if an Italian grandfather waded into the water much above his knees, one or another of his self-appointed guardians could be seen jumping up and down on the shore, waving frantically at him and shouting: "Papa's gonna drown! Somebody get him!" I read somewhere that this phenomenon of grandfather captivity still exists in parts of Italy.

I saw the protective custody game repeated with my paternal grandfather, Giuseppe, who in his later years presided in silence at the head of the table during holiday meals, a titular chieftain whose power had slipped away to his sons and sons-in-law who now earned the money and commanded their own households. While a certain deference was still paid him because of his age, more often he found himself, much to his annoyance, a victim of overprotection—which is a sure sign of powerlessness.

Years later in 1956, when an adult, I had occasion to have a few long talks with him and discovered that he was a most intelligent and engaging man—although he did have a number of opinions that were strange for that time, namely that country air was better for one's health than city air, canned foods were of little nutritional value, and physical exertion was better than sitting around doing nothing. Giuseppe also believed that doctors and hospitals could be dangerous to one's survival, automobiles were the ruination of cities, and too much emphasis was placed on money and material things. We treated such views as quaintly old-fashioned, having no idea that grandpa was merely ahead of his time.

After my birth the doctors warned my mother that with her con-genital heart condition another pregnancy would be fatal. So I went through life as an only child. My mother tended to spoil me, for which she was criticized by her older sisters. More than once she mentioned how sorry she was that I had no brothers and sis-ters to play with, and she encouraged my playmates to come spend as much time as they wanted at our house. But I entertained no regrets about being an only child, for why would I want to share my lovely mother with some other little brat?

My father played a more distant role than my mother, as was the usual way in Italian working-class families—and in just about any other family where the division of labor is drawn along gen-der lines. He labored long hours for meager sums, sometimes two jobs at a time. Born in Italy, he was transported to this country at the age of five. He did poorly in school because of the burdens the immigrant family imposes on its firstborn son. When he was only ten years old, his day went something like this: up at 6 a.m., work on his father's ice truck until 8 a.m., then to school, then back to work from 3 p.m. to 7 p.m. to complete a thirteen-hour day. On Saturdays he worked from 6 a.m. to midnight, an eighteen-hour day. On Sunday he labored eight hours, from 6 a.m. to 2 p.m.—that was supposed to be a half-day.

My father understandably blamed his poor academic perform-ance on his work burdens. As he put it: "I was too damn tired to learn to read and write." His fatigue often overcame him and he would fall asleep in class. He dropped out of school at age four-teen to work full time. Almost sixty years later, shortly before his death, I talked to him about his youthful days and recorded his thoughts. The things he remembered most were the toil, the humiliation of not being able to speak English, and the abuse he received from teachers. There was one bright spot, as he tells it:

"The only teacher that cared about me was Miss Booth because she saw me carry ice a few times on 110th Street and she asked, 'How come you're carrying ice at your age?' I said, 'I got to work. My father can't afford a man. There's seven of us at home to feed.' So she saw I wasn't really a bad kid. She saw I was no good in school really on account of I had to work. Miss Booth, she got me to wash the blackboard. Anything she wanted I did because she showed she cared about me."

In his adult life, my father's friends were all men. Cross-gender friendships were not a common thing in those days. The women in a man's life consisted of his mother, his wife, his sisters, and other female relatives. He might know various women in the neighborhood and stop and chat with them briefly but it would have been considered inappropriate to let things develop further. To illustrate the patriarchal mentality of my father's world I might recall the time he informed me in troubled tones that Uncle Americo, while drunk one night, had started beating his wife, Aunt Fanny (my mother's sister). Americo's son, my cousin Eddy, forcibly intervened and wrestled his father to the floor. What shocked my father was not Americo's behavior but Eddy's. "I don't care what happens," he concluded, "a son should never raise a hand to his father"—a pronouncement that left me wondering what I would have done had I been in Eddy's place.

Hovering over us was the Great Depression, a mysterious force that explained why there was never enough money, why my father was away working all the time, why I couldn't have this or that new toy. I remember during one unusually difficult period my mother bought a small steak and cooked it for me as a special treat. She sat watching intently as every morsel disappeared into my mouth. When I offered her a piece she declined, saying she wasn't hungry. Only years later did I realize with a pang that she very much had wanted some.

None of my relatives talked of "careers"; I don't think the word was in vogue among us. But everyone talked about jobs—or the fear of being without one. A high school education was considered an unusual accomplishment, and the one uncle who had graduated high school was considered something of a celebrity. My mother's dream was that I would someday get a high school diploma, for then all doors would be open to me. As she said, I would be able to "dress nice every day not just Sundays" and "work in an office," a fate that sounded worse than death to a spirited street boy.

Toward the end of World War II the struggle for survival eased a bit. My father got steady work driving his uncle's bread truck and my mother found a job in a neighborhood dress shop, toiling at a sewing machine all day. I pledged to her that someday I would earn lots of money so that she would never have to set foot in that sweatshop again, a vow that heartened her more because of its expression of concern than because she believed she would live to see the day. As it happened, when I was seventeen she died at age forty-three, still employed by the same shop.

During my childhood I would wonder about the world beyond East Harlem, about the strange inhabitants of downtown Manhattan, tall, pink-faced, Anglo-Protestants who pronounced all their r's, patronized the Broadway theater, and traveled to Europe for purposes other than to locate relatives. I would think of other equally exotic peoples and unexplored worlds with anticipation. This "intoxication of experiences yet to come" left me with the feeling that East Harlem was not my final destination in life.

When I was about twelve or thirteen I chanced upon a copy of *Life* magazine that contained an article describing East Harlem as "a slum inhabited by beggar-poor Negroes, Puerto Ricans, and Italians," words that stung me and stuck in my memory. Slum or not, most of the Italians, including all my relatives, abandoned East Harlem in the late 1950s, moving to what sociologists call "second settlement areas," leaving the old neighborhood to the growing numbers of Puerto Rican immigrants. The money the Italians had saved during the war years and post-war period became the down-payment passage to the mass-produced housing tracts of Long Island, Staten Island, and New Jersey, where as proud homeowners they could live a life that approximated the middle-class suburban one they saw in the movies.

But the new lifestyle had a downside to it. One uncle, who used to have huge parties for friends and relatives in his home on Third Avenue, complete with mandolins, accordions, and popular and operatic songs—drawn from the amateur talents of the guests themselves—now discovered that no one came to visit him on the outer edge of Queens. An aunt of mine, who had lived all her life within shouting distance of at least three of her sisters, tearfully told my mother how lonely she was way out in Staten Island.

In time, I went off to graduate school and saw far less of my extended family, as they did of each other. Years later in 1968 I got a call from my cousin Anthony asking me to attend a family reunion. It took place in Anthony's home in Queens, attended by a crowd of cousins and their fourth-generation children, the latter being youngsters whom I was meeting for the first time and for whom East Harlem was nothing more than a geographical expression, if that.

Time had brought its changes. The women wore coiffured hair-dos and stylish clothes, and the men looked heavier. There was much talk about recent vacations and a slide show of Anthony's travels to Europe, and a magnificent buffet of Italian foods that made the slide show worth sitting through. And there were a lot of invitations to "come visit us." Much to my disappointment the older surviving aunts and uncles had decided to stay away because this was an affair for the younger people, an act of age segregation that would have been unthinkable in earlier times. In all, we spent a pleasant evening joking and catching up on things. It was decided we should get together more often. But we never did have another reunion.

In the late 1970s I began to have recurring dreams, one every few months or so, continuing for a period of years. Unlike the recurring dreams portrayed in movies (in which the exact same footage is run and rerun), the particulars and fixtures of each dream in real life—or real sleep—differ, but the underlying theme is the same. In each dream I found myself living in a lovely apartment; sometimes it had spiral stairwells and bare brick walls and sometimes lavish wood paneling and fireplaces, but it always turned out to be a renovation of 304 East 118th Street, the old brownstone in East Harlem where I had spent most of my early life.

We might think of recurring dreams as nightmarish, but these were accompanied by sensations of relief and yearning. The life past was being recaptured and renovated by the life now accomplished. The slum was being gentrified. The working-class Italian youth and the professional-class American academic were to live under the same roof. I had come home to two worlds apart. Never quite at home in either, I would now have the best of both. Once I understood the message, the dreams stopped.

17 BREAD STORY: THE BLESSINGS OF PRIVATE ENTERPRISE

Years ago, my father drove a delivery truck for the Italian bakery owned by his uncle Torino. When Zi Torino returned to Italy in 1956, my father took over the entire business. The bread he made was the same bread that had been made in Gravina, Italy, for generations. After a whole day standing, it was fresh as ever, the crust having grown hard and crisp while the inside remained soft, solid, and moist. People used to say that our bread was a meal in itself.

The secret of the bread had been brought by my Zi Torino all the way from the Mediterranean to Manhattan, down into the tenement basement where he had installed wooden vats and tables. The bakers were two dark wiry men, *paesani di Gravina*, who rhythmically and endlessly pounded their powdery white hands into the dough, molding the bread with strength and finesse. Zi Torino and then my father after him, used time and care in preparing their bread, letting the dough sit and rise naturally, turning it over twice a night, using no chemicals and only the best quality unbleached flour. The bread was baked slowly and perfectly in an old brick oven built into the basement wall by Zi Torino in 1907, an oven that had secrets of its own.

Often during my college days, I would assist my father in loading the bread truck at 5:00 on Saturday mornings. We delivered in the Bronx to Italian families whose appreciation for good bread was one of the satisfactions of our labor. My father's business remained small but steady. Customers, acquired slowly by word of mouth, remained with us forever. He would engage them in friendly conversations as he went along his route, taking nine hours to do seven hours of work. He could tell me more than I wanted to know about their family histories.

In time, some groceries, restaurants, and supermarkets started placing orders with us, causing us to expand our production. My father seemed pleased by the growth in his business. But after some months, one of his new clients, the Jerome Avenue Supermarket did the unexpected. The supermarket's manager informed my father that one of the big companies, Wonder Bread, was going into the "specialty line" and was offering to take over the Italian bread account. As an inducement to the supermarket, Wonder Bread was promising a free introductory offer of two-hundred loaves. With that peculiar kind of generosity often found in merchants and bosses, the supermarket manager offered to reject the bid and keep our account if only we would match Wonder Bread's offer at least in part, say a hundred loaves.

"Their bread is paper compared to mine," my father protested. Indeed, our joke was: the reason they call it Wonder Bread is because after tasting it, you wonder if it's bread. But his artisan's pride proved no match for the merchant's manipulations, and he agreed to deliver a hundred free loaves, twenty-five a day, in order to keep the supermarket account, all the while cursing the manager under his breath. In the business world, this arrangement is referred to as a "deal" or an "agreement." To us it seemed more like extortion.

In response to "deals" of this sort, my father developed certain tricks of his own. By artfully flashing his hands across the tops of the delivery boxes he would short count loaves right under the noses of the store managers, in the case of the Jerome Avenue Supermarket, even loaves that they finally started paying for again. "Five and five across, that's twenty-five, Pete," he would point out, when in fact it was only twenty-three. We would load 550 loaves for the morning run and he would sell 575. Not since the Sermon on the Mount had the loaves so increased.

"Pop," I said to him after one of his more daring performances, "You're becoming a thief."

"Kid," he said, "It's no sin to steal from them that steal from you." [*Individual competition in the pursuit of private gain brings out the best of our creative energies and thereby maximizes our productive contributions and advances the well being of the entire society*. Economics 101]

I left for a few years to go to graduate school, only to return home in 1959 without a penny in my pocket. I asked my father to support me for a semester so that I could finish writing my dissertation. In return, I offered to work a few days a week on the bread truck. My father agreed to this but he wondered how he would explain to friends and neighbors that his son was twenty-six years old and still without full-time employment.

"Kid, how long can you keep going to school and what for?" he asked. "All those books," he would warn me, "are bad for your eyes and bad for your mind."

"Well," I said, "I'm getting a Ph.D." To this he made no response. So I put in a few days a week of hard labor on the truck. Nor did he complain. In fact, he needed the help and liked having me around (as he told my stepmother who told me).

When the bakers asked him how come, at the age of twenty-six, I was working only part-time, he said: "He's getting a Ph.D." From then on they called me "professor," a term that was applied with playful sarcasm. It was their way of indicating that they were not as impressed with my intellectual efforts as some people might be.

On the day my dissertation was accepted and I knew I was to receive my Ph.D., I proudly informed my father. He nodded and said, "That's good." Then he asked me if I wanted to become a full-time partner in the bread business working with him on the truck every day. With all the education out of the way, now maybe I would be ready to do some real work.

I almost said yes.

One day the health inspectors came by and insisted we could not leave the bread naked in stores in open display boxes, exposed to passers-by who might wish to touch or fondle the loaves with their germ-ridden fingers. No telling what kind of infected predators might chance into a supermarket to fondle bread. So my father and I were required to seal each loaf in a plastic bag, thus increasing our production costs, adding hours to our labor, and causing us to handle the bread twice as much with our germ-carrying fingers. But now it looked and tasted like modern bread because the bags kept the moisture in, and the loaves would get gummy in their own humidity inside their antiseptic plastic skins instead of forming a crisp, tasty crust in the open air.

Then some of the bigger companies began in earnest to challenge our restaurant and store trade, underselling us with an inferior quality "Italian bread." At about this time the price of flour went up. Then the son of the landlord from whom Zi Torino had first rented the bakery premises over a half century before raised our rent substantially.

"When it rains it pours," my father said. So he tried to reduce costs by giving the dough more air and water and spending less time on the preparation. The bakers shook their heads and went on making the imitation product for the plastic bags.

"Pop," I complained, "the bread doesn't taste as good as it used to. It's more like what the Americans make."

"What's the difference? They still eat it, don't they?" he said with a tight face.

But no matter what he did, things became more difficult. Some of our old family customers complained about the change in the quality of the bread and began to drop their accounts. And a couple of the big stores decided it was more profitable to carry the commercial brands.

Not long after, my father disbanded the bakery and went to work driving a cab for one of the big taxi fleets in New York City. In all the years that followed, he never mentioned the bread business again.

18 MY STRANGE VALUES

Since rather early in life I have been at odds with some of the conventional values of this society. For instance, I remember the men in my youth who used to talk about cars—and I do mean men. Women rarely even drove cars in those days, let alone held forth about them. The men would compare different auto makes and performances and tell stories about their experiences with cars much the way men in earlier times must have talked about horses. Misfit that I was, I thought such conversations were boring because I never found automobiles to be cool or enticing. I always loathed their noise and stink and pollution—and still do. And I lament the pitiless highway carnage they deliver upon us, not to mention the burden of having to get the car paid for, registered, insured, serviced, repaired, fueled, parked, and dragged through perpetual traffic jams.

To this day I detest the endless auto ads on television that portray cars as devilishly dashing and self-enhancing, whipping fearlessly around mountainous curves at irresponsible speeds. Is there something wrong with me and my values that I am so out of step with the omnipresent "car culture"? I want high-speed monorails, like they have in Japan and some other countries, that can carry millions of people all over the country without injury and in great comfort, with far less expense and minimal environmental damage. At the very least, now that I know about them, I want electric cars that do not pollute, that are simple to maintain and economical to use. Electricity, after all, is the most efficient and cleanest energy source when extracted from solar and wind energy. On this issue I am in step with growing numbers of other drivers. There are millions of us who are no longer, or never were, in love with the automobile, who treated it as nothing more than an expensive necessity and an ecological disaster (including the hybrids). But you would never know it from looking at the endless auto ads on television.

There are other weird things about my values. As I approached adulthood I had no desire to devote my life to making large sums of money. I was never interested in the extravagant material products that money can buy. Nor was I interested in the kind of job that would pay the kind of money needed to buy all those material products. Long before it became fashionable among some people in the late 1960s to drop out of the rat race, I never even wanted to toe the starting line.

In my salad days there was much talk in the country about "succeeding." I attended DeWitt Clinton High School in the Bronx, where a career counselor told us it was important to succeed. I watched Hollywood movies about people fighting like dogs to success. What success consisted of was not always precisely put, but it was understood that it had something to do with making it to some place called "the top," a very elevated and rewarding perch either in the business world or in a profession of some sort. My high school yearbook featured a statement by our class president. I don't recall anything he wrote except the last exclamatory line: "We will succeed!" I do remember the feeling of distaste I experienced upon reading that declaration. Speak for yourself, student prexy. The idea that my life should be taken up with fighting my way up the greasy pole filled me with dismay. What I wanted to do was something creative, something that might help the world and make it a better place, although in 1950 I knew not what that might be.

What I really lusted after was knowledge and understanding of the world. What had happened over the centuries? What was going on in the far reaches of this and other societies? What meaning, if any, did life have? Maybe that is why I became a social science professor and researcher. As such I cannot say I found the final answer to those sorts of questions.

While not sharing the preoccupation that some people had with monetary gain, I certainly did want to have enough money to get by. Coming from a poor family I understood that without sufficient funds, an individual in this dollar-driven society is consigned to a life of constant anxiety, dreadful deprivation, and dangerous vulnerability. Indeed I spent a number of years in just such straits, having been red-baited out of my college-teaching profession and left to survive on my writing and public speaking. Given my uncompromising and unpopular political views, and my unwillingness to self-censor and say less than I believed, I was destined to make do without a stable and secure professional position. I did however pick up an occasional teaching gig here and there, which after awhile was all I wanted or needed.

I think there are a lot of people like me who do not glorify vast wealth as some kind of great accomplishment but who do want to live with some degree of comfort and security. Now in my grey-ing years I resent the idea of having to try to sock away substantial sums because there is no completely adequate public system of human services and retirement support in this free-mar-ket society. Eventually I will have to rely, in part, on my own savings to survive. The poverty income from Social Security just is not enough. And if I get sick, I will have no health insurance other than Medicare which does not cover everything and might even-tually be taken away from us by the free-marketeers. This is the way the social system is organized, forcing many of us into mak-ing "choices" that are not of our own devising.

Here is yet another "strange" thing about my values: I never liked having to exercise authority over people. There are those who are enthralled with playing the kingpin and wielding organi-zational power. I never felt comfortable in that role, even though I am considered a strong personality who can project ideas and feelings. When I do take the spotlight it is to speak about urgent political matters. I try to be a speaker who makes himself an instrument for projecting a message of social justice. This is differ-ent from using the message as an instrument to project and elevate the speaker, which is what too many in public life seem to do.

Whenever I have found someone kowtowing to me or deferring in some way for reasons having to do with that person's needs or fears, I have not liked it. I taught at the college level for many years, and one of the nicest things I ever heard a student say to me was that I had a "democratic personality." She was referring to the way I was acting as faculty advisor to the student newspa-per, encouraging the students to explore issues and make their own decisions, and supporting them when the dean started breathing censorship down their necks.

Lest there be any misunderstanding, I am not trying to pass

myself off as St. Francis of Assisi. I have my share of personal faults, including a hot temper on infrequent occasions. But in the socio-political realm I don't like power for power's sake. I dislike powermongers because they attempt to inflate themselves by diminishing others, and they have no dedication to social justice. Being hungry for power and privilege, they shine up to the top circles, ready to serve the high and mighty as a way of advancing themselves, crawling and clawing their way up the social pyramid. It might be called the Henry Kissinger Way of Life.

It was always an especially exciting thing for me to witness those occasions when people took things responsibly into their own hands in collective and communal actions, working together more or less as equals. I remember during the Vietnam antiwar movement watching young people organize to elect peace delegates to the Democratic Party state convention in Connecticut. I felt so deeply thrilled at how they planned for the tasks that needed to be done and acted in coordinated fashion with an unstudied dignity, with such intelligence and quiet dedication to carry out a successfully orchestrated electoral campaign.

On other occasions I saw antiwar protesters stand against state troopers with courage and spontaneous solidarity. What a beautiful and electrifying experience that always is for me, seeing people come into themselves, creating their own democratic impact, for one bright and shining moment taking control of their own destiny.

This gets back to another essential value. I never wanted to live a life that was dedicated only to my self-advantage. If this makes me a "do-gooder," I can only ask, why is "do-gooder" a pejorative term in the mouths of some? There are only two alternatives to doing good: (a) doing evil, usually by serving the commands of others who do evil, and (b) doing nothing, living only for oneself in a narrowly atomized hustling way, which also makes life easier for those who do evil.

Then there is my feeling about the environment. A half century ago, I used to be considered a little weird the way I worried about what was in my food and water. Long before it became fashionable, I felt concerned about how pollution might affect my personal health and everyone else's.

Moreover, I felt a connection to the environment. I was born and raised in East Harlem, an Italian working-class neighborhood at that time. I was a street kid with no opportunity to cultivate a sensitivity to the natural environment because there was so little of it in New York City. But I do remember journeying into the countryside or to the seashore on occasion, and how I felt something come alive in me. How beautiful the natural world seemed to me, even though I was and still am thoroughly addicted to the livelier city life and could never give up urban living for a rustic existence.

We should recall what the level of environmental consciousness was a half century ago. When I was a young man in the 1950s, I would sometimes complain about the quality of the air in the city. People would smile patronizingly and say "What are you a fresh-air fiend?" Such was the quaint and monumentally ignorant expression of that day: "fresh air fiend."

During the Vietnam War many of us were torn up about the death and destruction being delivered upon Indochina by U.S. forces. On one occasion I saw a slide show of how U.S. planes and helicopters had sprayed tons of Agent Orange across the Vietnamese countryside, how a rich soil and fecund foliage were turned into a toxic moonscape. In this show there were no mangled bodies or burned villages, just ecocide, a bleached poison hardpan where once there had been living nature. It left me with a knot in my stomach and a weight on my heart. It was one of the most wrenching antiwar presentations I had ever seen.

Those who feel perfectly free to use Agent Orange in order to win a war are the same ones who, in times of peace, believe they have a right to what remains of the Earth's natural resources to use as they wish, transforming living nature into commodities, and commodities into dead capital. We hear the reactionaries dilate about all the fine values for which they stand. Endlessly they go on about personal values, family values, religious values, patriotic values, old-fashioned values of honesty and clean living. Yet their ranks are plagued with illicit sexual scandals, unlawful scams, untrammeled mendacity, massive corruption, and corporate grand thefts. They plunder the public treasure while posing as holier-than-thou patriots. Unfortunately, many beleaguered working folks—who need to believe that something in their world is right and trustworthy—give uncritical allegiance to these misleaders.

Opportunistic, hypocritical valuemongers are no more honest and virtuous than anyone else. In many instances, they are far worse than the worst of us. They perpetrate monumental deceptions and crimes that most of us would never even imagine. They tirelessly tarnish their critics for being self-indulgent liberals and libertines who lack upstanding values. But the truth is, if you are a progressive person, rather than devoting yourself to plunder and privilege, you have values for peace and justice, for fair play, and environmental sustainability, for communal caring and power sharing.

Everyone has values, but ours are much better than theirs, not only because our values stand for far, far better things, but also because we really try to live by them, as much as we can.

V.

A GUIDE TO
CONCEPTS
AND ISMS

19 TECHNOLOGY AND MONEY: THE MYTH OF NEUTRALITY

I recently heard a television network official assert that technology is inherently neither good nor bad; it can be used for helping or harming society. He voiced this notion with such authoritative insistence that one would think he was the first to have thought of it. In fact, many people hold to this view, and they are just as mistaken as he.

Only when one speaks hypothetically does technology achieve neutrality: "It could be used for good or it could be used for evil." Such unspecified references to how it *could* be used overlook the reality of how it actually and regularly *is* used. The truth is, technology is "neutral" only when conceived in the abstract, divorced from the social context in which it develops. But since it actually develops *only* in a social context and since its application is always purposive, then we must ask, *Cui bono?* Who benefits? And at whose expense?

Technology in the present social order is used mostly to advance the interests of the higher circles. New advances in technology are not neutral things; they sometimes impact upon us,

177

our communities, and our environment in hurtful and regressive ways. Consider a recent example of how technology has been used to maximize corporate earnings. Monsanto Company spent $500 million to develop bovine growth hormone (BGH), a "wonder drug" that induces cows to produce abnormally high amounts of milk. The drug is causing serious illnesses and greater health maintenance costs for dairy herds, and increased feeding needs and animal waste runoffs that further damage the environment. The cows suffer from infection and malnutrition and must be given even more than the usual ration of antibiotics, all of which gets into the milk we consume. The long-term effects of BGH are not known, but it is suspected of having carcinogenic effects.

The increased milk production induced by BGH is costing taxpayers $100 million a year in additional federal surplus purchases, mostly benefiting a few giant dairy producers and, of course, Monsanto. So here is technology used for "good" (increased production of a food) having predictably bad results for the cows, the environment, the federal budget, and perhaps millions of consumers.

The same can be said of all of the genetically modified seeds and crops marketed by Monsanto and other such companies: they benefit a few giant producers, drive small farmers into destitution, undermine the natural diversity of products, and will likely cause problems for those who regularly ingest the Frankenfoods that are produced.

Developed within an existing social order that is dominated by big government in the service of big business, modern technology takes a form that perforce favors the well-placed few over the general populace. Today much technical research and development is devoted to creating weapons of destruction and instruments of surveillance and control. When over 75 percent of all research and development is financed in whole or part by the Pentagon, then it is time to stop prattling about technology as a neutral instrumentality and see how it takes form and definition in a context of money and power that gives every advantage to the special interests of the military-industrial complex, the profit-gouging defense industry, and state agencies of control, coercion, and surveillance. Meanwhile, the rest of us, the ordinary taxpayers, pony up the funds to pay for it all, while suffering the consequences.

The same myth of neutral instrumentality is applied to money itself. When I studied economics in school I was taught that money was "a medium of exchange." Such a nice neutral-sounding definition hides a host of troublesome realities. In fact, money circulates within a particular social context. Like technology, money has a feedback effect of its own, advantaging the already advantaged.

Money creates a way of liquefying and mobilizing wealth, expanding the impact of its power. With mobility comes greater opportunities for accumulation and concentration of riches. Before money, wealth could only be accumulated as realty (land and edifices), livestock, horses, gems, furs, finery, spices, and the like. The advent of precious metals was the first great step to a mobile form of wealth that allowed for greater fluidity and accumulation. As any banker can tell you, money is not just a means of exchange but itself is a source of wealth and accretion, and not just a source but the ultimate end of all corporate production and transactions.

With the growth of wealth and the emergence of a moneyed class there comes a greater concentration and command over technology by that class. In a word, big money finances big technology. No wonder that technology, in turn, is developed with an eye to enriching and making the world safe for those who have the money.

What if, instead of defining money in that benign and neutral way, as "a medium of exchange," we defined it as "an instrument for the mobility and accumulation of capital and the concentration of economic power"? That would give us a whole new slant on life. Money allows for a level of investment and accretion previously unknown.

Again, hypothetically speaking, money is just an instrument of exchange that "could" be used for good or bad, for medicine or murder. And to be sure, in everyday life we do use it often for good things like food and shelter. But looking at the larger picture, money best serves those who have immense amounts of it and who use it to accumulate power in order to accumulate still more money.

One could go on with other specific cultural artifacts and institutional arrangements: guns, vehicles, the military, education, and even what is called "culture." Rather than mouthing the truism that these things can be used for good or bad, it is more useful to recognize that such instrumentalities do not exist as abstractions but gather definition only within the context of a social order. Thus the instrumentality not only has all the potential biases and distortions of that order but it contributes distortions and injustices of its own, bringing still more empowerment and efficacy to those who least need it.

It is not very helpful to say that technology or money can be used for good or bad. What we have to determine is why potentially beneficial things like technology and money most often are applied with such ill effect. But that would bring us to a radical analysis of the politico-economic system itself, a subject that is avoided like the plague even by most of those investigators who denounce the symptomatic abuses of that system.

20 FALSE CONSCIOUSNESS

Some observers hold that people often pursue goals that do not really serve their best interests. But others maintain that when making such an assertion we are presuming to know better than the people themselves what is best for them. To avoid superimposing one's own ideological expectations on others, one should be a neutral observer, not an elitist social engineer; hence, whatever policy or social condition people define as being in their best interest at any given time should be accepted as such—so the argument goes.

This "neutral" position, however, rests on an unrealistic and deliberately one-dimensional view of the way people arrive at their beliefs. It denies the incontrovertible fact that awareness about issues and events is often subject to control and manipulation. In judging what is in their own interest, individuals are influenced by many factors, including the impact of dominant social forces greater than themselves. In C. Wright Mill's words: "What people are interested in is not always what is to their interest; the troubles they are aware of are not always the ones that beset them. . . . It is not only that [people] can be unconscious of their situations; they are often falsely conscious of them."

For example, if the U.S. public manifests no mobilized opposition to the existing social order or some major aspect of it, this is treated as evidence of a freely developed national consensus. What is ruled out a priori is the possibility of a manipulated consensus, a controlled communication universe in which certain opinions are given generous play and others—such as many of the contrary notions found in this book—are systematically ignored, suppressed, or misrepresented.

To deny the possibility of false consciousness is to assume there has been no indoctrination, no socialization to conventional values, and no suppression of information and dissenting opinion. In fact there exists a whole array of powers that help prefigure how we see and define our own interests and options.

If no overt conflict exists between rulers and ruled, this may be because of one or more of the following reasons:

Consensus satisfaction: Citizens are content with things because their real interests are being served by their rulers.

Apathy and lack of perception: People are indifferent to political matters. Preoccupied with other things, they do not see the link between issues of the polity and their own well-being.

Discouragement and fear: People are dissatisfied but acquiesce reluctantly because they do not see the possibility of change or they fear that change will only make things worse or they dread the repression that will be delivered upon them if they try to confront the powers that be.

False consciousness: People accept the status quo out of lack of awareness that viable alternatives exist and out of ignorance as to how their rulers are violating their professed interests or out of ignorance of how they themselves are being harmed by what they think are their interests.

Those who are enamored with the existing order of things would have us believe that of the above possibilities only the first three, relating to consensus, apathy, and fear, are conditions of consciousness that can be empirically studied, because they are supposedly the only ones that exist.

In fact, there exist two kinds of false consciousness. First, there are the instances in which people pursue policy preferences that are actually at odds with their interests—as they themselves define those interests. For instance, there are low-income citizens who want to maximize their disposable income but then favor a regressive sales tax over a progressive income tax because of a misunderstanding—repeatedly propagated in TV ads financed by the opponents of the progressive income tax—of the relative effects of each tax on their pocketbooks. The sales tax actually falls proportionately more heavily upon them than does the progressive income tax, and costs them far more in dollars. A limited level of information or a certain amount of misinformation leads people to pursue policy choices that go directly against their "self-defined" interests.

In the second instance of false consciousness, the way people define their interests in the first place may itself work against their well-being. Thus, they may think that supporting the actions of U.S. troops in Vietnam or Panama or Iraq or wherever may be furthering their interest in maintaining the United States as the world's leading superpower and keeping them safe from terrorists. But the superpower nation-state, with its huge arms expenditures, heavy taxes, gigantic national debt, neglected domestic services, and environmental devastation—along with the death and destruction it delivers upon other peoples and the culture of violence and statist autocracy it propagates at home—may actually be creating more enemies rather than less, while lowering rather than enhancing the security and quality of people's lives and the nation's vitality.

To give a less complicated example, there are people who think the system of private health care, ever so costly it may be, is best for them. They have been told, and they believe, that a socialized health program or a national insurance program would produce medical care that is inferior, "bureaucratic," and more costly. Here again such opinions are well fertilized by the powers that be, in this case the private health care industry. But the truth is that in nations with *public* health care, the costs are less, the coverage is comprehensive, and the care is far less nightmarish than what is encountered by so many in our present system.

In short, it is possible to demonstrate that (a) many people support positions or political forces that violate their own *professed* interests, and (b) many people profess interests that violate their actual well-being. Their stated preferences may themselves be a product of a socio-political system that works against their interests. To know what their interests are, they need access to accurate information about the policy world and how it affects them.

The rejection of false consciousness as being an ideological and elitist superimposition leads mainstream social scientists and other opinion makers to the conclusion that no distinction should be made between *perceptions* of interest on the one hand, and what might be called *real* or *objective* interest on the other. Any preference expressed by any individual must be accepted as his or her real interest. (Does this apply to teenagers as well?) This position makes no distinction between our perceived interests (which might be ill-informed and self-defeating) and our real interests (which might be difficult to perceive because of a lack of accurate, honest, and readily accessible information). To reject the concept of false consciousness as elitist is to ignore the fact that one's awareness of one's own interests and one's political consciousness in general may be stunted or distorted by misinformation, disinformation, years of manipulated socialization, and a narrow but highly visible mainstream political agenda that rules out feasible alternatives. It is really not too much to say that people can be misled.

The reduction of interest to a subjective state of mind leads us not to a more rigorous empiricism but to a tautology: "people act as they are motivated to act" becomes "people always act in their own interest." Whatever individuals are motivated to do or select or pursue or believe, or not do and not believe, is taken as being in their interest because, by definition, their interest *is* their motivational condition.

The point, then, is that without making judgments about people's beliefs we can still inquire as to how they came to their preferences rather than treat these preferences as an irreducible and unchallengeable given. For instance, Americans are not congenitally endowed with loyalty to a particular social order that propagates competitiveness, consumerism, militarism, economic inequality, and environmental devastation. The definition they give to their interests—by selecting officeholders who *are* dedicated to such a social order—is shaped almost entirely by the social forces determining their universe of discourse, all sorts of forces acting well beyond their awareness, especially when the so-called impartial information being circulated is actually profoundly biased and manipulative in favor of moneyed interests.

One can see instances of false consciousness all about us. There are people with legitimate grievances as employees, taxpayers, and consumers who direct their wrath against welfare mothers but not against corporate plunderers of the public purse, against the inner-city poor but not the outer-city superrich, against human services that are needed by the community rather than regressive tax systems that favor the affluent. In their confusion they are ably assisted by conservative commentators and hate-talk hosts who provide ready-made explanations for their real problems, who attack victims instead of victimizers, denouncing "liberal elites," feminists, gays, minorities, and the poor. Thus the legitimate grievances of millions are deliberately and with much strenuous effort directed against irrelevant foes.

Does false consciousness exist? It certainly does and in mass-marketed quantities. It is the mainstay of the conservative reactionism of the last three decades. Without it, those at the top, who profess a devotion to our interests while serving only their own, would be in serious trouble indeed.

21 LEFT, RIGHT, AND THE "EXTREME MODERATES"

The terms "right" and "left" are seldom specifically defined by policymakers or media commentators—and with good reason. To explicate the politico-economic content of leftist governments and movements is to reveal their egalitarian and humane goals, making it much harder to demonize them. The "left," as I would define it, encompasses those individuals, organizations, and governments that advocate equitable redistributive policies benefiting the many and infringing upon the privileged interests of the wealthy few.

The right-wingers are also involved in redistributive politics, but the distribution goes the other way, in an upward direction. In almost every country, including our own, rightist groups, parties or governments pursue policies that primarily benefit those who receive the bulk of their income from investments and property, at the expense of those who live off wages, salaries, fees, and pensions. That is what defines and distinguishes the right from the left.

What is called the political right consists of *conservatives*, many of whom are dedicated to *free-market capitalism*, the unregulated laissez-faire variety that places private investment ahead of all other social considerations. Conservative ideology maintains that rich and poor get pretty much what they deserve; people are poor not because of inadequate wages and lack of economic opportunity but because they are lazy, profligate, or incapable. The conservative keystone to individual rights is the enjoyment of property (moneyed) rights, especially the right to make a profit off other people's labor and enjoy the privileged conditions of a favored class.

Conservatives blame our troubles on what billionaire Steve Forbes called the "arrogance, insularity, [and] the government-knows-best mentality" in Washington, D.C. Everything works better in the private sector than in the public sector, they maintain. Most conservative ideologues today might better be classified as *reactionaries*, having an agenda not designed merely to protect their present privileges but to expand them, rolling back all the progressive gains made over the last century. They want to do away with most government regulation and taxation of business, along with environmental and consumer protections, minimum-wage laws, unemployment compensation, job-safety regulations, and injury-compensation laws. They assure us that private charity can take care of needy and hungry people, and that there is no need for government handouts. On that last point, it should be noted, the superrich donate a far smaller proportion of their income to private charities than people of more modest means.[1]

Conservatives seem to think that everything would be fine if government were reduced to a bare minimum. Government is not the solution, it is the problem, they say. In actual practice, however, they are for or against government handouts depending on whose hand is out. They want to cut human services to low- and middle-income groups, but they vigorously support gargantuan government subsidies and bailouts for large corporate enterprises. They admonish American workers to work harder for less and have not a concern about the increase in economic hardship for working people.

Conservatives and reactionaries also support strong government measures to restrict dissent and regulate our private lives and personal morals, as with anti-abortion laws and bans on gay marriage. Most of them are big supporters of mammoth military budgets and the U.S. global empire, which they seem to equate with "Americanism." Yet many of them managed to avoid military service, preferring to let others do the fighting and dying. Such was the case with President George W. Bush, Vice President Dick Cheney, Congressman Tom Delay, commentator Rush Limbaugh, and scores of other prominent right-wing leaders and pundits.[2]

Not all conservatives and reactionaries are affluent. Many people of rather modest means, are conservative about "family values." They want government to deny equal rights to homosexuals, impose the death penalty more vigorously, propagate the superpatriotic virtues, and take stronger measures against street crime, issues about which they feel liberals are dangerously deficient. As one newspaper columnist writes, they think that government has a prime responsibility to protect "their right to kill themselves with guns, booze, and tobacco" but a "minimal responsibility to protect their right to a job, a home, an education or a meal."[3] Conservative politicians talk about "upholding values," but they make no effort to uphold values by rooting out corruption in the business world or protecting the environment or lending material support to working families.

The same conservatives who say they want government to "stop trying to run our lives" also demand that government regulate our personal morals, keep us under surveillance, and deny us the right to habeas corpus, open dissent, antiwar demonstrations, and safe and legal abortions. They want government to put God back into public life, require prayers in our schools, subsidize religious education, and shove their particular notion of Jesus down our throats at every opportunity. They blame the country's ills on secular immorality, homosexuality, feminism, "liberal elites," and the loss of family values. TV evangelist and erstwhile Republican presidential hopeful Pat Robertson charged feminism with hatching diabolical and even murderous plots against family, marriage, and capitalism.[4] The religious right supports conservative causes. In turn, superrich conservatives help finance the religious right.

Toward the center of the political spectrum we find the *moderates*, also known as the *centrists,* exemplified by former president Bill Clinton. Like the conservatives, the centrists accept the capitalist system and its basic values but they think social problems should be rectified by piecemeal reforms and regulatory policies. Along with conservatives, many centrists support "free trade" and globalization, claiming that it will benefit not just corporations but everyone. They pushed for the elimination of family assistance ("welfare"), and regularly vote in Congress for big subsidies to private business and big military spending bills. They often back military interventions abroad if convinced that the White House is advancing the cause of peace and democracy—as with the massive 78-day U.S. bombing of women, children, and men in Yugoslavia in 1999, and the interventions in Afghanistan and Iraq (withdrawing their support in the latter instance when Iraq proved more costly than anticipated).

A shade to the left of the centrists are the *liberals* who see a need for improving public services and environmental protections. They support minimum-wage laws, unemployment insurance, and other wage supports, along with Social Security, nutritional aid for needy children, occupational safety, and the like. They say they are for protection of individual rights and against government surveillance of law-abiding political groups, yet in Congress (where most of them are affiliated with the Democratic Party), they sometimes have supported repressive measures and have gone along with cuts in programs for the needy. Some of them also have voted for subsidies and tax breaks for business. At other times they have opposed the reactionary rollback of human services, the undermining of labor unions, and shredding of environmental protections.

Further along is the political left: the progressives, social democrats, democratic socialists, and issue-oriented Marxists. (There is also a more ideologically oriented component of the left composed mostly of Trotskyists, anarchists, anarcho-syndicalists, "libertarian socialists" and others who will not figure in this discussion given their small numbers and intense sectarian immersion. What they all have in common is an obsessional anti-communism, a dedication to fighting imaginary hordes of "Stalinists" whom they see everywhere, and with denouncing existing communist nations and parties. In this they resemble many centrists, social democrats, and liberals.)

The issue-oriented progressive left wants to replace or substantially modify the corporate free-market system, putting some large corporations and utilities under public ownership, and smaller businesses under cooperative worker ownership when possible. Some left progressives would settle for a social democracy—as might be found in Sweden, Denmark, Finland, and a few other countries—with strong labor unions and firm controls on corporate business to safeguard the public interest and the environment. A democratically responsive government, progressives insist, has an important role to play in protecting the environment, advancing education, providing jobs for everyone able to work, along with occupational safety, secure retirement, and affordable medical care, education, and housing. In sum, a left-progressive government would spend far less on the military and on business subsidies and far more improving the social wage and the quality of life.

There remains a problem with this alignment of left, right, and center. It has to do with the tendency to ascribe "moderation" to those on the center, and "extremism" indiscriminately to those on the "far left" and "far right," based on an inclination to conflate spatial relations with moral meanings. Labels such as "left," "center," and "right" refer to the political spectrum. They are metaphoric spatial terms used to signify one's position on social, political, and economic issues. By virtue of its linear nature, the political spectrum can be extended at both ends to allow for limitless left-wing and right-wing extremes. The extreme, by definition, is the "utmost part, utmost limit."

It follows that an "extreme center" is a contradiction in terms, the extremes of the center being nothing more than the beginnings of the moderate left and moderate right.

But "extreme" has another meaning, a behavioral one that evokes an image of intransigence and violence. In news reports and common parlance, this second meaning is blended with the first and then ascribed to the left and right, but by definition never to the center.

By the same token, "moderate" has a purely quantitative meaning, as in a "moderate amount" or "moderate placement." However "moderate" also connotes "fair-mindedness" and "not given to excess." Again, the two meanings are conflated, and the political center is said to be occupied by moderates who, by definition, cannot be excessive or immoderate.

Other laudable concepts are associated with centrist moderation. Political moderates in various countries are described as defenders of *stability*. But whose stability? For whose benefit? At whose expense? Centrist moderates are "pragmatic," "undogmatic," and "free of ideology," a judgment made by ignoring, say, Chile, where the Christian Democratic centrists supported the fascist overthrow of a democratic government because, like most centrists, they were far more afraid of those to the left of them, even a democratically elected coalition of leftists, than they were of the militarists to the right who tore up the Chilean constitution and murdered thousands.

As our unexamined political vocabulary would have it, the moderate centrists can do no evil, while the immoderate extremists can do no good. In truth, those who occupy the mainstream center are capable of immoderate, brutal actions. It wasn't fascist extremists who pursued a massively destructive war in Indochina. It was the "best and the brightest" of the political center, the extremists of the center, the moderate extremists, if you will. These same moderates supported the overthrow of popular governments in Guatemala, Indonesia, Iran, and Chile, and helped install fascist military regimes in their stead.

It wasn't the leftists or rightists who waged a war against Yugoslavia, with its repeated bombings of civilian populations and its military assistance to ex-Nazi Croatian and Muslim Bosnian separatists.[5] It was that paragon of centrism Bill Clinton and all the centrists and moderate liberals who stood shoulder to shoulder with him and with NATO and the CIA (along with a gaggle of those anarchists and Trotskists I mentioned earlier who convinced themselves that the destruction of the Yugoslavian social democracy was a blow against Stalinist communism).

The crucial point is that those who occupy the extremes of the political spectrum (in accordance with beliefs about changing the politico-economic order) are not necessarily extremists in the pejorative or moral sense. We might ask what is so extremist about landless peasants and destitute laborers in countries such as El Salvador taking up arms against death squads and starvation? What is so moderate about governments that maintain such repressive conditions? A glance at the many miseries of the Third World should tell us that extremism, in the worst sense of the word, is embedded in the prevailing "moderate" stability.

Our understanding of politics should allow us to distinguish between racists and anti-racists, between those on the "far left" who work with low-income ethnic minorities and those on the "far right" who want to exterminate low-income ethnic minorities. But the presumptive label of "extremism" imposed by centrists is designed to blur just such essential distinctions. Indeed, the French go so far as to fashion a slogan, *les extrêmes se touche*; the extremes extend so far that they "touch," that is, they resemble each other and end up doing the same things. That is a rare thing if ever it does happen. At opposite ends of the political spectrum, the extremes stand for quite markedly different socio-political worlds.

The question of who is and who isn't extremist in the moral sense, then, is not to be settled by resorting to a linear political spectrum. Different varieties of extreme moderates or centrists have long been in power. In collaboration with the rightists, they have given us Vietnam, Watergate, global counterinsurgency, gargantuan military budgets, dirty wars in Iraq and Afghanistan, a regressive tax burden, huge corporate subsidies, and the promise of a rigorous repression of dissent—all in the name of security, stability, patriotism, religion, family, and other such things. Look then at what they do, not at how they are labeled.

22 STATE VS. GOVERNMENT

We might best think of the American polity (like any other polity) as a dual system of government and state. The *government* deals with visible officeholders, pressure-group politics, and popular demands. It provides the representative cloak and whatever substance of democratic rule that has been won through generations of mass struggle. In contrast, the *state* has little if anything to do with popular rule or public policy as such. It is the ultimate coercive instrument of class power. Max Weber wrote that the state's essential trait, its irreducible feature, is its monopoly over the legitimate uses of force—"legitimate" in that they are legally sanctioned by the duly constituted authorities.

To fulfill its role as protector of existing order, the state often circumvents the democratic restraints that exist within government. The late FBI chief J. Edgar Hoover noted in a 1970 interview that "justice is merely incidental to law and order." And, as Hoover made clear by his actions, the real goal of law and order is to protect the dominant social order.

Roughly speaking, the difference between government and state is the difference between the city council and the police, between Congress and the armed forces. The government mediates public policy. The state orchestrates coercion and control, both overtly and covertly. However, this is a conceptual distinction between what are really empirically overlapping phenomena. The overlap is especially evident in regard to the executive, which is both the center of government policy and the purveyor of state power.

The conceptual distinction between state and government allows us to understand why taking office in government seldom guarantees full access to the instruments of state power. When Salvador Allende, a Popular Unity candidate dedicated to democratic egalitarian reforms, was elected president of Chile in 1971, he took over the reins of government and was able to initiate some popular policies. But he could never gain control of the state apparatus, that is, the military, the police, the intelligence services, the courts, and the fundamental organic law that rigged the whole system in favor of wealth and corporate property. When Allende began to develop a reform program for the benefit of the common populace and against class privilege, the Chilean military, abetted by the White House and the CIA, seized power and murdered thousands of his supporters, destroying not only Allende's government but the democracy that produced it.[6]

In Nicaragua, after the Sandinistas lost the 1990 election to a right-centrist coalition, the army and police remained in their hands. However, in contrast to the Chilean military, which was backed by the immense power of the United States, the Nicaraguan military was the target of that same power and was unable to keep the government on its revolutionary course. Sandinista police and military were seriously defunded by a U.S.-backed government.

Capitalist countries with ostensibly democratic governments often manifest a markedly undemocratic state power. In the United States, not just conservatives but Cold War liberals have used the FBI to suppress anticapitalists and other dissidents in the interest of state security and often in violation of the U.S. Constitution. In 1947, President Harry Truman created the Central Intelligence Agency to gather and coordinate foreign intelligence. As ex-Senator George McGovern noted "Almost from the beginning, the CIA engaged not only in the collection of intelligence information, but also in covert operations which involved rigging elections and manipulating labor unions abroad, carrying on paramilitary operations, overturning governments, assassinating foreign officials, protecting former Nazis and lying to Congress."[7]

With its secrecy, laundering of funds, drug trafficking, and often unlawful use of violence, the national security state stands close to organized crime. State agencies sometimes find it convenient to collude with underworld elements. Anthony Summers found that the FBI retained close links with organized crime. Former CIA-operative Robert Morrow, along with others, discovered that the CIA too was cozy with the mob. And over the years, several congressional investigative committees uncovered links between the CIA and the narcotics trade.[8]

In other Western democracies, secret paramilitary forces of neofascist persuasion (the most widely publicized being Operation Gladio in Italy) were created by NATO, to act as resistance forces should anticapitalist revolutionaries take over their countries. Meantime, these secret units were involved in terrorist attacks against the legal left. They helped prop up a fascist regime in Portugal, participated in the Turkish military coups of 1971 and 1980, and the 1967 coup in Greece. They drew up plans to assassinate social democratic leaders in Germany and stage "preemptive" attacks against socialist and communist organizations in Greece and Italy. They formed secret communication networks and drew up detention lists of political opponents to be rounded up in various countries.

These crypto-fascist operations "flowed from NATO's unwillingness to distinguish between a Soviet invasion and a victory at the polls by local communist parties."[9] As far as NATO was concerned there was not much distinction between losing Europe to Soviet tanks or to peaceful ballots. Indeed, the latter prospect seemed more likely. The Soviet tanks could not roll without risking a nuclear conflagration, but through the ballot box the anticapitalists might take over whole countries without firing a shot. One is reminded of Secretary of State Henry Kissinger's comment, supporting the overthrow of Chilean democracy: "I don't see why we need to stand by and watch a country go communist [that is, voting for Allende's coalition government] because of the irresponsibility of its own people."

In the United States, various right-wing groups with well-armed paramilitary camps and secret armies flourish unmolested by the Justice Department, which does not find them in violation of any law. Were they *anticapitalist* armed groups, they would likely be attacked by federal and local police and their members killed, as happened to the Black Panther Party in various parts of the country in the late 1960s and early 1970s.

Today, conservative theorists represent themselves as favoring laissez-faire policies; the less government the better. In practice, however, the "free market" system is rooted in state power. Every private corporation in America is publicly chartered, made a legal entity by the state, with ownership rights and privileges protected by the laws, courts, police, and army.

While conservative elites want less *government* control, they usually want more *state* power to contain the egalitarian effects of democracy. They want strong, intrusive, statist action to maintain the prerogatives and privileges of corporate America. They prefer a state that restricts access to information about its own activities, takes repressive measures against dissidents, and in other ways acts punitively not toward the abusers of state power but toward their challengers.

Conservative propaganda that is intended for mass consumption implicitly distinguishes between government and state. It invites people to see government as their biggest problem, while at the same time, encouraging an idolatrous admiration for the state, its flag and other patriotic symbols and rituals, and the visible instruments of its power, such as the armed forces.

The executive, be it monarch, prime minister, or president, usually stands closer to state functions than does the legislature. Some European systems have a prime minister, who deals with legislative and budgetary agendas and other governmental affairs, and a president, who is commander in chief of the armed forces and head of state—a duality that gives unspoken embodiment to the distinction between government and state. In the U.S. system, the executive combines the functions of prime minister and president, of government and state, of party leader and constitutional monarch.

In Italy, from 1969 to 1980, high-ranking elements in military and civilian intelligence agencies, along with secret and highly placed neofascist groups, embarked upon a campaign of terror and sabotage known as the "strategy of tension," involving a series of kidnappings, assassinations, and bombing massacres (*i stragi*), including the explosion that killed 85 people and injured some 200 in the Bologna train station in August 1980. This terrorism was directed against the growing popularity of the democratic parliamentary left, and was designed to "combat by any means

necessary the electoral gains of the Italian Communist Party."
Deeply implicated in this campaign, the CIA refused to cooperate
with an Italian parliamentary commission investigating *i stragi* in
1995. Of special interest is that the rightist terrorists understood
the importance of a strong executive in maintaining state control.
Their professed objective, according to the commission, was to create enough terror to destabilize the multiparty social democracy
and replace it with an authoritarian "presidential republic," or, in
any case, "a stronger and more stable executive."[10]

Marx himself grasped the special role played by the executive
in the maintenance of state power and class supremacy. He noted
that the president of the Second Republic in France represented
the entire nation rather than a particular district. The National
Assembly exhibits in its individual representatives "the manifold
aspects of society," but it is the president who is "the elect of the
nation," an embodiment of the nation-state.[11]

Marx is often misquoted as having said that the state is the
executive committee of the bourgeoisie. Actually, in *The Communist Manifesto*, he and Engels wrote that "the executive of the
modern State is but a committee for managing the common
affairs of the whole bourgeoisie." Thus they recognized the systemic class function of the executive. They also implicitly
acknowledged that bourgeois government in toto is not a solid
unit. Parts of it can become an arena of struggle. This is true even
within the executive branch itself. Thus, the U.S. Department of
Health and Human Services and the Department of Housing and
Urban Development usually deal with constituencies and interests
that differ from those components of the executive represented by
the Department of Defense, or the Departments of Treasury and
Commerce.

Nesting within the executive is that most virulent purveyor of state power: the *national security state*, an informal configuration that usually includes the Executive Office of the White House, special White House planning committees, the sixteen intelligence agencies, the Pentagon, Joint Chiefs of Staff, director of national intelligence, National Security Council, and other such units engaged in surveillance, suppression, covert action, and forceful interventions abroad and at home. The president operates effectively as head of the national security state as long as he stays within the parameters of its primary dedication—which is to advance the interests of corporate investors and protect the overall global capital accumulation process.

In 1977, President Carter tried to appoint Theodore Sorenson as director of the CIA. Sorenson, a high-profile liberal, had been a conscientious objector and had filed affidavits defending Daniel Ellsberg and Anthony Russo for their role in releasing the Pentagon Papers. Conservative Republicans on the Senate Select Committee on Intelligence, along with Democrats like chairperson Daniel Inouye, opposed Sorenson. They said his association with a law firm that dealt with countries in which the CIA had a great deal of influence might cause a "conflict of interest." They questioned his use of classified documents when writing a book and raised a number of other rather unconvincing complaints. It was later reported that the real concern of some senators was that "the CIA director should be a more hardline conservative figure than Mr. Sorenson."[12] Officials in the CIA itself quietly made known their opposition and Sorenson's candidacy was withdrawn.

After John Kennedy assumed presidential office in 1961, CIA director Allen Dulles regularly withheld information from the White House regarding various covert operations. When Kennedy replaced Dulles with John McCone, the agency began withholding information from McCone. Placed at the head of the CIA in order to help control it, McCone was never able to penetrate to the deeper operations of the agency.

This does not mean that the CIA is a power unto itself. It is an instrument that serves the enduring interests of the plutocracy. ("Plutocracy" refers to rule by the wealthy or to rulers who favor wealthy interests.) In 2004 this became clear when the White House under Bush Jr. stripped the top leadership of the CIA, blamed it for the administration's own misjudgments about Iraq and appointed a National Director of Intelligence to preside over all the various intelligence agencies. Having been thoroughly drubbed by the White House, a number of top members of the CIA meekly left office in quick succession. Ultimate power does not rest with the CIA but with the class for which it works.

When the presidency is controlled by a liberal who might depart from the prime path of global corporate supremacy, the CIA can be expected to oppose and even sabotage the administration. When the presidency is controlled by the ascendant ultra-conservative elements of the plutocratic class as in the Bush Jr. administration, then the CIA's role is still the same, to serve the interests of global corporate supremacy, even if it must fall on its sword to do so.

A president working closely with the national security state and unequivocally for corporate hegemony usually can operate outside the laws of democratic governance with impunity. Thus President Reagan violated international law by engaging in an unprovoked war of aggression against Grenada. He violated the U.S. Constitution when he refused to spend monies allocated by Congress for various human services. He and other members of his administration refused to hand over information when specific actions of theirs were investigated by Congress. By presidential order, he overruled statutory restrictions on the CIA's surveillance of domestic organizations and activities—even though a presidential order does not supersede an act of Congress. His intervention against Nicaragua was ruled by the World Court, in a 13-to-1 decision, to be a violation of international law, but Congress did nothing to call him to account. He was up to his ears in the Iran-Contra conspiracy but was never called before any investigative committee while in office. One could build a similar record with just about every other president in recent decades. In its unpunished, illegal acts, the executive demonstrates the autocratic nature of the state.

With enough agitation and publicity, government sometimes is able to put the state under public scrutiny and rein it in—a bit. During the late seventies, House and Senate committees investigated some of the CIA's unsavory operations, and laid down restrictive guidelines for the FBI. But the Iran-Contra hearings of 1987 reveal the damage-control function of most official inquiries. As representatives of popular sovereignty, the Joint Select Committee of Congress investigating the Iran-Contra conspiracy had to reassure the public that these unlawful, unconstitutional doings would be exposed and punished. However, the process of legitimation through rectification is a two-edged sword. It must go far enough to demonstrate that the system is self-cleansing, but not so far as to destabilize the executive power. So the same congressional investigators who professed a determination to get to the bottom of Iran-Contra were also repeatedly reminding us that "this country needs a successful presidency," meaning that after the scandals of Watergate and President Nixon's downfall, they had better not uncover too much and risk further damage to executive legitimacy.

In sum, the Iran-Contra investigation was both an exposé and a cover-up, unearthing wrongdoing at the subordinate level—to show that the system is self-correcting—while leaving President Reagan and the immense powers of his office largely untouched.

Congressional intelligence committees are usually occupied by members of both parties who identify closely with the needs of the national security state. The Bush Sr. administration was reportedly stunned by the appointment of five liberals to the House Intelligence Committee (of twenty or so members) by a Democratically controlled House. By registering its disapproval, the administration was saying in effect that the committee has a distinctive relationship to the state and that there should be a special ideological test for its members.

Lawmakers who fail the state's ideological test but who occupy key legislative positions run certain risks. When Jim Wright (D-TX), became Speaker of the House of Representatives, he began raising critical questions about CIA covert actions against Nicaragua. Because the Speaker of the House was not someone who could easily be ignored, his charges received press coverage. Indeed, he was taken seriously enough to be attacked editorially by the *Washington Post* and the *New York Times* for his comments on Nicaragua. At the time, I began to wonder aloud if Wright might have a mysterious fatal accident or just die suddenly of natural causes. But nowadays there sometimes is a neater way of getting rid of troublesome officeholders. The Republican-controlled Justice Department did a thorough background check on Wright and found questionable financial dealings—not too difficult to do in regard to most politicians who are ever in need of campaign funds. He allegedly had accepted improper financial gifts from a Texas developer and a publisher. Wright quickly resigned.

Next in line to be Speaker was Tom Foley of Washington State, who could be counted on never to raise troublesome questions about the doings of the national security state. Critics of the national security state are a minority within Congress. Generally, congressional leaders are complicit with the state and with their own disempowerment. Members serving on intelligence committees rarely fulfill their oversight function. They do not ask too many questions about secret operations and dirty tricks.

During the Iran-Contra hearings, Rep. Jack Brooks (D-TX), taking his investigative functions seriously, asked Lieutenant Colonel Oliver North if there was any truth to the story that he had helped draft a secret plan, code-named, to suspend the Constitution and impose martial law in the United States "in the event of emergency." A stunned expression appeared on North's face and the committee chair, the predictable Senator Daniel Inouye, stopped Brooks in his tracks, declaring in stern tones "I believe the question touches upon a highly sensitive and classified area. So may I request that you not touch upon that, sir." Brooks attempted to continue but Inouye again cut him off. It was a tense moment. The chair was making it clear that the state was not to be too closely policed.

The national security state has largely succeeded in removing much of its activities from democratic oversight. Intelligence agencies have secret budgets that are explicitly in violation of Article I, Section 9, which reads in part: "No Money shall be drawn from the Treasury but in Consequence of Appropriations made by Law. And a regular Statement and Account of the Receipts and Expenditures of all public Money shall be published from time to time." There are no published statements of expenditures for the intelligence community, guessed to be between $35 billion and $50 billion a year. Its appropriations are hidden in other parts of the budget and are unknown even to most members of Congress who vote on the funds.

Sometimes the state's determination to set itself above and outside the Constitution is not done secretly but expressed overtly, as on the eve of war during the 1990–1991 Gulf crisis when Secretary of State James Baker publicly stated, "We feel no obligation to go to Congress for a declaration of war," and President Bush Sr. announced he would commit troops to combat even if he got not a single supporting vote in Congress. Rather than being censored for such a lawless declaration and for acting as if the army were his personal force, Bush was hailed in the media for his "strong leadership."

One is reminded of Teddy Roosevelt's boast almost a century ago regarding his imperialist intervention in Panama: "I took the Canal Zone and let Congress debate." The danger of the executive is that it executes. Unlike the legislature or the courts it has its hands on the daily levers of command and enforceable action.

Having said that the national security state is removed from the democratic process, I do not wish to imply that it is removed from our lives. In fact, it reaches deeply into various areas of society. Consider organized labor. In collaboration with the national security state, the AFL-CIO leadership has sponsored organizations like the American Institute for Free Labor Development (AIFLD) in Latin America, along with similar ones in Africa and Asia, dedicated to building collaborationist, anticommunist unions that undermine the more militant leftist ones.

The national security state exercises an influence over the corporate media. The CIA owns numerous news organizations, publishing houses, and wire services abroad, which produce disinformation that makes its way back to the states. In the United States, the CIA has actively trained "Red squads" of local police in methods of surveillance and infiltration. The narcotics traffic has been supported in part by elements in the CIA and various local police forces with the inevitable effect, and probably actual intent, of disorganizing and demoralizing the inner-city masses and discouraging militant community movements from emerging.[13]

Executive usurpation is visible also in Eastern Europe, where the people of former communist nations now are able to savor the draconian joys of the capitalist paradise. The political democracy that had been used to overthrow communism soon became something of a hindrance for capitalist restoration. So democracy itself needed to be diluted or circumvented in order that the "democratic reforms"—that is, the transition to free-market capitalism—be fully effected. Not surprisingly the presidents of various Eastern European states such as Hungary, Poland, the Czech Republic, and Russia, have repeatedly chosen state over government, calling for the right to rule by executive ukase. In Russia, President Boris Yeltsin used force and violence to tear up the constitution, suppress the democratically elected parliament and provincial councils, monopolize the media, kill over a thousand people and arrest thousands more—all in the name of saving democracy.[14] The new government instituted by Yeltsin granted sweeping powers to the executive.

The U.S. Constitution contains provisions that apply directly to state functions, for instance, the power to organize and arm the militia and call it forth to "suppress Insurrections." Article I, Section 9 of the Constitution says that the writ of habeas corpus, intended to defend individuals from arbitrary arrest, can be suspended during national emergencies and insurrections. A presidential edict is sufficient for that purpose. In effect, the Constitution provides for its own suspension on behalf of executive-state absolutism. In recent years Congress has proven most accommodating in that endeavor, passing all sorts of repressive laws, from the Patriot Act to the Military Commissions Act, giving the executive state a host of undemocratic and unconstitutional powers.

When capitalism is in crisis, the capitalist state escalates its repression, from attacking the people's standard of living to attacking the democratic rights that might allow them to defend that standard of living. Democracy uneasily rides the tiger of capitalism. People with immense wealth and overweening power will resort to every conceivable means to secure their interests— the state being the most important weapon in their furious undertaking.

23 DEMOCRACY VS. CAPITALISM

It will disappoint some people to hear this, but in fact there is no one grand, secret, power elite governing this country. But there are numerous coteries of corporate and governmental elites who communicate and coordinate across various policy realms. And behind their special interests are the common overall interests of the moneyed class. Many of the stronger corporate groups tend to predominate in their particular spheres of interest, more or less unmolested by other elites, which is not to say that disputes never arise between plutocratic interests.

Business exerts an overall influence as a system of social power, a way of organizing capital, employment, and large-scale production. Because big business controls much of the nation's economy, government perforce enters into a uniquely intimate relationship with it. The health of the economy is treated by policymakers as a necessary condition for the health of the nation, and since it happens that the economy is mostly in the hands of large corporate interests, then presumably government's service to the public is best accomplished by service to those interests. The goals of business (high profits, cheap labor, expanding markets, and easy access to natural resources) become the goals of government. The "national interest" becomes identified with the systemic needs of corporate capitalism at home and abroad. In order to keep the peace, business may occasionally accept reforms and regulations it does not like, but ultimately government cannot ignore business's own raison d'être, which is the limitless accumulation of wealth.

Wealth, in turn, is the most crucial power resource in public life. It creates a pervasive political advantage, and affords ready access to other resources such as organization, skilled personnel, mass visibility, media ownership, outreach capacity, and the like. So wealth is used to attain power, and power is applied to secure and increase wealth.

Government involvement in the U.S. economy represents not socialism (as that term is normally understood by socialists) but *state-supported capitalism*, not the communization of private wealth but the privatization of the commonwealth. This development has brought a great deal of government involvement, but of a kind that revolves largely around bolstering the profit system, not limiting or replacing it.

In capitalist countries, government generally (a) nationalizes sick and unprofitable industries ("lemon socialism") and (b) privatizes profitable public ones—in both cases for the benefit of big corporate investors.

Examples of (a): In 1986, in what amounted to a bailout of private investors, the social democratic government in Spain nationalized vast private holdings to avert their collapse. After bringing them back to health with generous nourishment from the public treasury, they were sold back to private companies at bargain prices. The same was done with Conrail in the United States: run into insolvency by private profiteers, brought back to health by generous infusions of public funds, only to be sold off again to private investors.

Some examples of (b), the privatization of prosperous state enterprises: A conservative Greek government privatized publicly-owned companies such as the telecommunications system, which had been reporting continuous profits for several years. In similar fashion, any number of industries in the United States were developed and capitalized by the government at great public expense, then handed over to private companies to be marketed for private profit.

When a government takes over a private enterprise, it usually gives full compensation to the owners. The investors who once owned the private stocks now own public bonds and collect the interest on these bonds. The wealth of the enterprise shifts from stocks to bonds. While ownership is now nominally public, the income still flows into private pockets. What the public owns in this case is a huge bonded debt—with all the risks and losses and none of the profits.

Defenders of the existing system assert that the history of "democratic capitalism" has been one of gradual reform. To be sure, important reforms have been won by working people. To the extent that the present economic order has anything humane and civil about it, it is because millions of people struggled to advance their living standard and their rights as citizens. It is somewhat ironic to credit capitalism with the genius of gradual reform when most reforms through history have been vehemently and sometimes violently resisted by the capitalist class and were won only after prolonged and bitter contest. It is doubly ironic to credit capitalism with being reformist when most of the problems needing reform have been caused or intensified by the capitalist plutocracy.[15]

Furthermore, the corporation does not exist for social reconstruction but for private gain. Corporations cannot build low-rent houses, feed the poor, clean up the environment, or offer higher education to any qualified modest-income person—unless government gives them lucrative contracts to do so. Even then their major concern would be to squeeze as much profit out of the program as possible.

How can we speak of the U.S. politico-economic system as being a product of the democratic will? What democratic mandate directed the government to give away more money every year to the top 1 percent of the population in interest payments on public bonds than are spent on services to the bottom 20 percent? When was the public last consulted on interest rates and agribusiness subsidies? When did the public insist on having unsafe overpriced medications, and genetically altered foods, and hormone-ridden meat and milk, and federal agencies that protect rather than punish the companies marketing such things? When did the American people urge that utility companies be allowed to overcharge consumers billions of dollars? When did the voice of the people clamor for unsafe work conditions in mines, factories, and on farms, and for recycling radioactive metals into consumer products and industrial sludge into agricultural topsoil? How often have the people demonstrated for multibillion-dollar tax breaks for the superrich, and privatization of Social Security, and cutbacks in student aid? When did they demand a multibillion-dollar space shuttle program that damages the ozone layer and leaves us more burdened by taxes and deprived of necessary services, along with an unworkable multi-billion-dollar outer-space missile program that would only increase the dangers of nuclear confrontation if it ever did work? When did the populace insist that the laws of the land be over-ruled by international, nonelective, anonymous, "free-trade" panels in service to transnational corporations?

What democratic will decreed that we destroy the Cambodian and Laotian countrysides between 1969 and 1971 in bombing campaigns conducted without the consent or even the knowledge of Congress and the public? When did public opinion demand that we wage a mercenary war of attrition against Nicaragua, or attack Grenada, Panama, Somalia, Yugoslavia, Afghanistan, Iraq, and Haiti, slaughtering tens of thousands in the doing; or support wars against popular forces in El Salvador, Guatemala, Angola, Mozambique, the Western Sahara, and East Timor? Far from giv-ing our consent, we ordinary people have had to struggle to find out what is going on.

The ruling class has several ways of expropriating the earnings of the people. First and foremost, as *workers,* people receive only a portion of the value their labor power creates. The rest goes to the owners of capital.

Second, as *consumers*, people are victimized by monopoly prac-tices that force them to spend more for less. They are confronted with exploitative forms of involuntary consumption, as when rel-atively inexpensive mass-transit systems are eliminated to create a greater dependency on automobiles, or low-rent apartments are converted to high-priced condominiums, or a utility company doubles its prices after deregulation.

Third, as *taxpayers*, working people have had to shoulder an ever larger portion of the tax burden, while corporate America and the superrich pay less and less. Indeed, the dramatic decline in taxes on business and the superrich has been a major cause of growth in the federal debt. The debt itself is a source of investment and income for the moneyed class (via government bonds) and an additional tax burden on the populace.

Fourth, as *citizens* the people endure a lower quality of life. Hidden diseconomies are repeatedly foisted onto them by private business, as when a chemical company contaminates a community's air or groundwater with its toxic wastes, or when the very survival of the planet is threatened by global warming.

The reigning system of power and wealth, with its attendant abuses and injustices, activates a resistance from workers, consumers, community groups, and taxpayers—who are usually one and the same people. There exists, then, not only class oppression but class struggle. Popular struggle in the United States ebbs and flows but never ceases. Moved by a combination of anger and hope, ordinary people have organized, agitated, demonstrated, and engaged in electoral challenges, civil disobedience, strikes, sit-ins, takeovers, boycotts, and sometimes violent clashes with the authorities—for socio-economic betterment at home and peace abroad. Against the heaviest odds, dissenters have suffered many defeats but won some important victories, forcibly extracting concessions and imposing reforms upon resistant rulers.

Democracy is something more than a set of political procedures. To be worthy of its name, democracy should produce outcomes that advance the well-being of the people. The struggle for *political* democracy—the right to vote, assemble, petition, and dissent—has been largely propelled by a desire to be in a better position to fight for one's socioeconomic interests. In a word, the struggle for political democracy has been an inherent part of the struggle against plutocracy, a struggle for *social* and *economic* democracy.

Through the nineteenth and twentieth centuries, the moneyed classes resisted the expansion of democratic rights, be it universal suffrage, abolitionism, civil liberties, or affirmative action. They knew that the growth of popular rights would only strengthen popular forces and impose limits on elite privileges. They instinctively understood, even if they seldom publicly articulated it, that it is not socialism that subverts democracy, but democracy that subverts capitalism.

The reactionary agenda successfully advanced in recent years has been designed to take us back to 1900 or thereabouts. Wages are held down by forcing people to compete more intensely for work on terms favorable to management. This is done with speedups, downgrading, layoffs, the threat of plant closings, and union busting. In addition, owners eliminate jobs through mechanization and moving to cheaper labor markets overseas. They have sought to roll back child-labor laws, lower the employable age for some jobs, bring in unregulated numbers of immigrants, and raise the retirement age, further increasing the number of workers competing for jobs.

Another way to depress wages is to eliminate alternative sources of working-class support. The historical process of creating people willing to work for subsistence wages entailed driving them off the land and into the factories, denying them access to farms and to the game, fuel, and fruits of the commons. Divorced from this sustenance, the peasant reluctantly metamorphosed into the proletarian.

Today, unemployment benefits and other forms of public assistance are reduced in order to deny alternative sources of income. When public jobs are eliminated there are more people competing for employment in the private sector. When jobs are scarce, people are compelled to work harder for less. Conservatives seek to lower the minimum wage for youth and resist attempts to equalize wages and job opportunities for women and minorities, thus keeping women, youth, and minorities as the traditionally underpaid "reserve army of labor," used throughout history to lower the floor on wages and keep the workforce divided and poorly organized. Racism is especially useful when channeling the economic fears and anger of Whites away from employers and toward out-groups who are seen as competitors for scarce jobs, education, and housing.

A century ago the working populace lived in hovels and toiled twelve to fourteen hours a day for poverty wages under gruesome conditions. Their children more often went to work than to school. But with decades of struggle, working people were able to better their lot. By the 1970s millions of them were working eight-hour days, had job seniority, paid vacations, time-and-half overtime, company medical insurance, and adequate retirement pensions; many lived in decent housing and even could pay a mortgage on a home of their own, while their kids went to public school and some even to public universities. Along with this came improvements in occupational safety, consumer safety, and health care.

More for the general populace, however, meant less for the privileged few. By the 1970s it looked like this country might end up as a quasi-egalitarian social democracy unless something was done about it. As Paul Volcker said when he was chair of the Federal Reserve in 1980, "The standard of living of the average American has to decline."[16]

Decline it has. Over the last two decades the reactionary rollback has brought an increase in poverty and homelessness, substandard housing and substandard schools, longer work days with no overtime pay, less job security, wage and benefit cutbacks, a growing tax burden increasingly shifted onto the backs of the lower and middle classes, fewer if any paid vacation days, less affordable health care, privatization of public services, disappearance of already insufficient pensions, drastic cuts in disability assistance and family support, and serious dilution of occupational safety regulations and consumer and environmental protections.

Democracy becomes a problem for the plutocracy not when it fails to work but when it works too well helping the populace to move toward a more equitable and favorable social order, narrowing the gap however modestly between the superrich and the rest of us. So democracy must be diluted and subverted, smothered with disinformation and media puffery, with rigged electoral contests and with large sectors of the public disfranchised, bringing faux victories to the more reactionary candidates. At the same time, the right of labor to organize and strike has come under persistent attack by courts and legislatures. Federal security agencies and local police repress community activists and attack their right to protest.

The state is the single most important instrument that corporate America has at its command. The power to use police and military force, the power of eminent domain, the power to tax and legislate, to use public funds for private profit, float limitless credit, mobilize highly emotive symbols of loyalty and legitimacy, and suppress political dissidence—such resources of state give corporate America a durability it could never provide for itself. The state also functions to stabilize relations among the giant enterprises themselves. Historically, "firms in an oligopolistic industry often turn to the federal government to do for them what they cannot do for themselves—namely, enforce obedience to the rules of their own cartel."[17]

The state is also the place where different ruling factions struggle over how best to keep the system afloat. The more liberal and centrist elements argue that those at the top of the social pyramid should give a little in order to keep a lot. If conservative goals are too successful, if wages and buying power are cut back too far and production increased too much, then the contradictions of the free market intensify. Profits may be maintained and even increased for a time through various financial contrivances, but overcapacity and overproduction lead to economic recession. Unemployment grows, markets shrink, discontent deepens, and small and not so small businesses perish. The corporate capitalist system begins to devour itself.

As the pyramid increasingly trembles from reactionary victories, some of the less myopic occupants of the apex develop a new appreciation for the base that sustains them. They advocate granting concessions to those below. But the more reactionary free-marketeers will have none of that. Instead they press ever forward with their backward agenda. If demand slumps and the pie expands only slightly or not at all, that is quite all right as long as the slice going to the moneyed class continues to grow. If profits are going up, then the economy is "doing well"—even if the working public is falling behind in real wages and living conditions, as happened during much of 2001–2007.

The state has two roles that have been readily recognized by political thinkers as varied as Adam Smith and Karl Marx. First, it must provide those services that cannot be developed entirely through private sources: a national defense, a dependable currency, postal service, roads, ports, canals and the like. Second, the state protects the moneyed and propertied interests from the have-nots; this is the capitalist class-control function we have been discussing in this and the previous selection.

But there is a third function of the capitalist state not usually mentioned. It consists of preventing the capitalist system from devouring itself. We have witnessed how this self-destruction might happen in places like Argentina during the 1990s when free marketeers stripped enterprises for massive profits, leaving the entire economy in shambles. Then in the United States there was the multi-billion-dollar plunder and theft perpetrated against the investor class itself by corporate conspirators in Enron, World-Com, Harkin, and a dozen other companies. Instead of making money by going through the trouble of manufacturing and selling products, the corporate predators dip directly into the money streams of the system itself, using every subterfuge and fraud in the doing.

I would suggest that a major difference between the Democratic and Republican parties is that the Democrats recognize this third state function and the Republicans—or their more militantly reactionary wing—refuse to be bothered about it. Indeed some of their key players, for instance, Bush Jr., Dick Cheney, and Ken Lay, were directly involved in the plunder that turned rich successful enterprises into sheer wreckage in order that a few might pocket billions in ill-gotten gains.

The state best protects the existing class structure by enlisting the loyalty and support of the populace. This is accomplished by keeping an appearance of popular rule and neutrality in regard to class interests, and by playing on the public's patriotic pride and fear, conjuring up images of cataclysmic attack by foreign forces, domestic subversives, communists, and now Islamic terrorists.

Having discerned that "American democracy" as professed by

establishment opinion makers is something of a sham, some people incorrectly dismiss the democratic rights won by popular forces as being of little account. But these democratic rights and the organized strength of democratic forces are, at present, all we have to keep reactionary rulers from imposing a dictatorial final solution, a draconian rule to secure the unlimited dominance of capital over labor. Marx anticipated that class struggle would bring the overthrow of capitalism. Short of that, class struggle constrains and alters the capitalist state, so that the government itself, or portions of it, become a contested arena.

The vast inequality in economic power remains a threat to whatever little democracy we have. More than half a century ago Supreme Court Justice Louis Brandeis commented, "We can have democracy in this country, or we can have great wealth concentrated in the hands of a few, but we can't have both." And some years earlier, the German sociologist Max Weber wrote: "The question is: How are freedom and democracy in the long run at all possible under the domination of highly developed capitalism?"[18] That question is still with us. As the contradiction between the egalitarian expectations of democracy and the demoralizing realities of the free market sharpens, the state must act more repressively to protect the existing class inequities.

Why doesn't the capitalist class in the United States resort to fascist rule? It would make things easier: no organized dissent, no environmental or occupational protections to worry about, no elections or labor unions. In a country like the United States, the success of a dictatorial solution would depend on whether the ruling class could stuff the democratic genie back into the bottle. Ruling elites are restrained in their autocratic impulses by the fear that they might not get away with it, that the people and the enlisted ranks of the armed forces would not go along. Given secure and growing profit margins, elites generally prefer a "democracy for the few" to an outright dictatorship. Rather than relying exclusively on the club and the gun, bourgeois democracy employs a co-optive, legitimating power—which is ruling-class power at its most hypocritical and most effective. By playing these contradictory roles of protector of capital and "servant of the people," the state best fulfills its fundamental class control function.

Finally, it should be noted that much of what has been said of the state applies also to the law, the bureaucracy, the political parties, the legislators, the universities, the professions, and the media. In order to best fulfill their class-control functions yet keep their credibility, these players must maintain the appearance of neutrality and autonomy. To foster that appearance, they must occasionally exercise some critical independence and autonomy from the state and from corporate America. They sometimes save a few decisions for the people, and take minimally corrective measures to counter some of the many egregious transgressions against democratic interests. As insufficient and hypocritical as these concessions are, they still sometimes lead to substantive gains in the struggle for social democracy.

24 SOCIALISM TODAY?

The structural problems of capitalism are not likely to solve themselves. What is needed, some say, is public ownership of the major means of production and public ownership of the moneyed power itself—in other words, some ample measure of *socialism*. But can socialism work? Is it not just a dream in theory

and a nightmare in practice? Can the government produce anything of worth?

Indeed it can. Private industries such as railroads, satellite
communication, aeronautics, the Internet, and nuclear power
exist today only because the government funded the research and
technological development, and provided most of the risk capital.
The great scientific achievements of numerous universities and
government laboratories during and after World War II were the
fruits of federal planning and not-for-profit public funding. We
already have some socialized services and, when sufficiently
funded, they work quite well and less expensively than private
ones. Our roads and some utilities are publicly owned and sustained, as are our bridges, ports, and airports. In a few states so
are liquor stores, which yearly generate hundreds of millions of
dollars in state revenues.

There are credit unions and a few privately owned banks like
the Community Bank of the Bay (Northern California) whose primary purpose is to make loans to low- and middle-income
communities. We need public banks that can be capitalized with
state funds and with labor-union pensions that are now handled
by private banks. The Bank of North Dakota is the only one
wholly owned by a state. In earlier times it helped farmers who
were being taken advantage of by grain monopolies and private
banks. Today, the Bank of North Dakota is still an important
source of reasonable credit for farmers, small businesses, local
governments, and college students. Other states have considered
creating state banks, but private banking interests have blocked
enactment.

Often unnoticed is the "third sector" of the economy, consisting of more than 30,000 worker-run producer cooperatives and
thousands of consumer cooperatives, 13,000 credit unions, nearly

100 cooperative banks, and more than 100 cooperative insurance companies, plus about 5,000 housing co-ops, 1,200 rural utility co-ops, and 115 telecommunication and cable co-ops. Employees own a majority of the stock in at least 1,000 companies.[19] Labor unions in the construction industry have used pension funds to build low-cost housing and to start unionized, employee-owned contracting firms.

There are also the examples of "lemon socialism," in which governments in capitalist countries have taken over ailing private industries and nursed them back to health, testimony to the comparative capacities of private and public capital. In France immediately after World War II, the government nationalized banks, railways, and natural resources in a successful attempt to speed up reconstruction. France's telephone, gas, and electric companies were also public monopolies. Public ownership in that country brought such marvels as the high-speed TGV train. The publicly owned railroads in France and most of western Europe work far better than the privately owned ones in the United States.

The state and municipal universities and community colleges in the United States are public and therefore "socialist" (shocking news to some of the students who attend them). Of these some are among the very best institutions of higher learning in the country. Publicly owned utilities in this country are better managed than investor-owned ones; and since they do not have to produce huge salaries for their CEOs and big profits for stockholders, their rates are lower and they put millions in profits back into the public budget, saving the taxpayers money. Then there is the British National Health Service, which costs 50 percent less than our private system yet guarantees more basic care for the medically needy. Even though a Tory government during the

1980s imposed budget cuts in an attempt to undermine the public system, a majority of Britons still want to keep their socialized health service.

Free-marketeers in various countries do what they can to defund public services and eventually privatize them.[20] Privatization is a bonanza for rich stockholders but a misfortune for workers and consumers. The privatization of postal services in New Zealand brought a tidy profit for investors, wage and benefit cuts for postal workers, and a closing of more than a third of the country's post offices. Likewise, the privatization of telephone and gas utilities in Great Britain resulted in dramatically higher management salaries, soaring rates, and inferior service. The problem for private investors is that public ownership *does* work, at least in regard to certain services. A growing and popular not-for-profit public sector is a danger to the free-market system.

Most socialists are not against personal-use private property, such as a home. And some are not even against small businesses in the service sector. Nor are most against moderate income differentials or special rewards to persons who make outstanding contributions to society. Nor are they against having an industry produce a profit, as long as it is put back into the budget to answer the needs of society. Not just the costs but also the benefits of the economy should be socialized.

There is no guarantee that a socialized economy will always succeed. The state-owned economies of Eastern Europe and the former Soviet Union suffered ultimately fatal distortions in their development because of the backlog of poverty and want in the societies they inherited; years of capitalist encirclement, embargo, invasion, devastating wars, and costly arms buildup; poor incentive systems, and a lack of administrative initiative and technological innovation;

and a repressive political rule that allowed little critical feedback while fostering stagnation and elitism. Despite all that, the former communist states did transform impoverished countries into relatively advanced societies. Whatever their mistakes and political crimes, they achieved—in countries that were never as rich as ours—what U.S. free-market capitalism cannot and has no intention of accomplishing: adequate food, housing, and clothing for all; economic security in old age; free medical care; free education at all levels; and a guaranteed income. Today by overwhelming majorities, people in Russia and other parts of Eastern Europe say that life was better under communism than under the present free-market system.[21]

American socialism cannot be modeled on the former Soviet Union, China, Cuba, or other countries with different historical, economic, and cultural developments. But these countries ought to be examined so that we might learn from their accomplishments, problems, failures, and crimes. Our goal should be an egalitarian, communitarian, environmentally conscious, democratic socialism, with a variety of participatory and productive forms.

What is needed to bring about fundamental change is a mass movement that can project both the desirability of an alternative system and the great necessity for change in a social democratic direction. There is much evidence indicating that Americans are well ahead of political leaders in their willingness to embrace new alternatives, including consumer and worker cooperatives and public ownership of some industries and services. With time and struggle, we might hope that people will become increasingly intolerant of the inequitable free-market plutocracy and will move toward a profoundly democratic solution. Perhaps then the day will come, as it came in social orders of the past, when those who seem invincible will be shaken from their pinnacles.

There is nothing sacred about the existing system. All economic and political institutions are contrivances that should serve the interests of the people. When they fail to do so, they should be replaced by something more responsive, more just, and more democratic. Marx said this, and so did Jefferson. It is a revolutionary doctrine, and very much an American one.

NOTES

1. *New York Times*, 22 August 1996.
2. See the discussion in Michael Parenti, *Superpatriotism* (City Lights, 2004) 111–132.
3. Frank Scott, editorial in *Coastal Post* (Marin County, California), 1 February 1996.
4. Robertson quoted in *Nation*, 10 January 2000. See also Thomas Frank, *What's the Matter with Kansas? How Conservatives Won the Heart of America* (Henry Holt, 2004).
5. See selection 31, "The Rational Destruction of Yugoslavia."
6. For a discussion of how events in Allende's Chile have been misrepresented in the United States, see Michael Parenti, Inventing Reality, 2nd ed. (Wadsworth/Thomson, 1993), 143–147.
7. McGovern quoted in *Parade*, 9 August 1987.
8. Anthony Summers, *Official and Confidential* (Putnam, 1993); Robert Morrow, *Firsthand Knowledge* (S.P.I. Books, 1993); Pete Brewton, *The Mafia, CIA & George Bush* (S.P.I. Books, 1992); Peter Dale Scott and Jonathan Marshall, *Cocaine Politics* (University of California Press, 1991).
9. Ben Lowe, in *Guardian*, 5 December 1990.
10. *La Repubblica*, 9 April 1995; *Corriere della Sera*, 27 and 28 March, 12 April and 29 May 1995.
11. Karl Marx, *The Eighteenth Brumaire of Louis Bonaparte* (various editions).
12. *New York Times*, 18 January 1977.
13. See Gary Webb, *Dark Alliance: The CIA, the Contras, and the Crack Cocaine Explosion* (Seven Stories Press, 1998).
14. Michael Parenti, "Yeltsin's Coup and the Media's Alchemy," in Michael Parenti, *Dirty Truths* (City Lights, 1996), 133–140.
15. Once again, in case the reader missed it in the last selection, "plutocracy" refers to rule by the wealthy or to rulers who favor the wealthy interests.
16. *Washington Post*, 9 March 1980.

17. Frank Kofsky, *Harry S. Truman and the War Scare of 1948* (St. Martin's Press, 1993), 190.

18. Brandeis quoted in David McGowan, *Derailing Democracy* (Common Courage, 2000), 42; Weber in H. H. Gerth and C. Wright Mills (eds.), *From Max Weber: Essays in Sociology* (Oxford University Press, 1958).

19. Christopher Gunn and Hazel Dayton Gunn, *Reclaiming Capital: Democratic Initiatives and Community Development* (Cornell University Press, 1991).

20. See for instance, Tor Wennerberg, "Undermining the Welfare State in Sweden," *Z Magazine*, June 1995.

21. See selection 30, "The Free Market Paradise Liberates Communist Europe"

VI.
MONEY, CLASS, AND CULTURE

25 CAPITAL AND LABOR, AN OLD STORY

Most people who talk and write about the U.S. political system never mention corporate capitalism. But the capitalist economy has an overbearing impact upon political and social life. It deserves our critical attention.

To begin, one should distinguish between those who own the wealth of society, and those who must work for a living. The very rich families and individuals who compose the *owning class*, live mostly off investments: stocks bonds, rents, and other property income. Their employees live mostly off wages, salaries, and fees. The distinction between owners and employees is blurred somewhat by the range of incomes within both classes. "Owners" refer both to the fabulously wealthy stockholders of giant corporations and the struggling proprietors of small stores. But the latter hardly qualify as part of the *corporate* owning class. Among the victims of big business is small business itself. Small businesses are just so many squirrels dancing among the elephants. And squirrels that dance among elephants have a notoriously low life expectancy. Every year over 30,000 small enterprises go out of business in the United States.

Among the employee class, too, there is much diversity. Along with factory and service workers there are professionals and executives who in income, education, and lifestyle tend to be identified as "middle" or "upper-middle" class. Company managers and executives are employees whose task is to extract more value-producing performance from other employees. And some top business executives, corporate lawyers, and entertainment and sports figures enjoy such huge incomes as to be able eventually to live off their investments, in effect becoming members of the owning class.

You are a member of the owning class when your income is immense and comes mostly from the labor of other people, that is, when others work for you, either in a company you own, or by creating the wealth that allows your investments to give you a handsome return. The secret to wealth usually is not to work hard but to have others work hard for you. This explains why workers who spend their lives toiling in factories or offices retire with little or no wealth to speak of, while owners who never set foot in the factory or firm can amass considerable fortunes. The ultimate purpose of a business is not to perform public services or produce goods as such, but to make as large a profit as possible for the investor.

Adam Smith, considered one of the founding theorists of capitalism, noted in 1776, "Labor . . . is alone the ultimate and real standard by which the value of all commodities can at all times and places be estimated and compared. It is their real price; money is their nominal price only."[1] What transforms a tree into a profitable commodity such as paper or furniture is the labor that goes into harvesting the timber, cutting the lumber, and manufacturing, shipping, advertising, and selling the product.

Workers' wages represent only a portion of the wealth created by their labor. The average private-sector employee works two hours for herself or himself and six or more hours for the boss.

The portion that goes to the owner is what Marx called "surplus value," the source of the owner's wealth. Capitalists themselves have a similar concept: "value added in manufacture." In 2000, workers employed in manufacturing alone produced at least $1.64 trillion in value added, as reported by the U.S. Census Bureau, for which they were paid $363 billion in wages, or less than one-fourth of the value created by their labor. Workers employed by Intel and Exxon received only about one-ninth of the value added, and in industries such as cigarettes and pharmaceuticals, the worker's share was a mere one-twentieth. In the last half century, the overall average rate of value added (the portion going to the owner) in the United States more than doubled, far above the exploitation rate of other industrialized countries.[2] Workers endure an exploitation of their labor as certainly as do slaves and serfs. The slave obviously toils for the enrichment of the master and receives only a bare subsistence in return. James Madison told a visitor shortly after the American Revolution that he made $257 a year on every slave he owned and spent only $12 or $13 for the slave's keep. Slavery is a very profitable system (which explains why it still exists in many parts of the world). Sharecroppers who must give a third or half their crop to the landowner are also obviously exploited. Under capitalism, however, the portion taken from the worker is not visible. Workers are simply paid substantially less than the value they create. Indeed, the only reason they are hired is to make money off their labor. If wages did represent the total value created by labor (after expenses and improvements), there would be no surplus value, no profits for the owner, no great fortunes for those who do not labor.

The value distributed to the owners is apart from workers' wages or even executives' salaries; it consists of profits—the money one makes *when not working*. The author of a book, for instance, does not make profits on his book; he earns a recompense (fancily misnamed "royalties") for the labor of writing it. Likewise, editors, proofreaders, printers, and salespersons all contribute labor that adds to the value of the book (usually). Profit on the book goes to those who own the publishing house and who contribute nothing to the book's marketable value. The sums going to owners are aptly called *unearned* income on tax reports.

While corporations are often called "producers," the truth is that they produce nothing. They are organizational devices for the exploitation of labor and accumulation of capital. The real producers are those who apply their brawn, brains, and talents to the creation of goods and services. The primacy of labor was noted in 1861 by President Abraham Lincoln in his first annual message to Congress: "Labor is prior to, and independent of, capital. Capital is only the fruit of labor, and could never have existed if labor had not first existed. Labor is the superior of capital, and deserves much the higher consideration." Lincoln's words went largely unheeded.

Capitalists like to say they are "putting their money to work," but money as such does not work. What they really mean is that they using their money to put human labor to work, paying workers less in wages than they produce in value, thereby siphoning off more profit for themselves. That's how money "grows." Capital annexes living labor in order to convert itself into goods and services that will produce still more capital.[3] All of Rockefeller's capital could not build a house or a machine or even a toothpick; only human labor can do that. Of itself, capital cannot produce anything. It is the thing that is produced by labor.

Persons of great wealth can get quite annoyed when it is pointed out that they do not work. Since many of them equate work with whatever activity they happen to pursue, they do not see themselves as parasitic idlers. When asked, they will tell of their endeavors: serving with a charity organization or on a church or museum board of directors; running for public office; studying art, photography, or ceramics; writing a personal memoir; raising horses; preparing for a long sailing expedition up the coast, an exploration in Indonesia, or a shopping trip to Paris or London; or going on a spiritual retreat or to a health spa to work on their personal development.

Some wealthy individuals actually do work in the more usual sense. They pursue professions and occupy managerial posts—but it is out of personal choice, not economic necessity. Such labor would seem to entitle them to a fair recompense, not an immense fortune. Some prominent tycoons, whose names regularly appear in the press, manage vast financial empires. But the workday they put in, no matter how arduous, does not explain the source of their immense wealth nor the pace at which it accumulates. The far greater portion of their money still comes from the acquisition of assets that directly or indirectly engage the labor of others. This perpetual transference of value is the less conspicuous part of their otherwise highly publicized careers.

The power of the wealthy business class is like that of no other group in our society. The giant corporations control the rate of technological development and availability of livelihoods. They relegate whole communities to destitution when they export their industries overseas to cheaper labor markets. They devour environmental resources, stripping our forests and toxifying the land, water, and air. They command an enormous surplus wealth while helping to create and perpetuate conditions of scarcity for millions of people at home and abroad. And they usually enjoy a predominating voice in the media and the highest councils of government.

That they can reach so deeply into our society and culture

while incurring relatively little critical attention is itself a measure of their ideological hegemony.

26 WEALTH, ADDICTION, AND POVERTY

In order that a select few might live in great opulence, millions of people work hard for an entire lifetime, never completely free from financial insecurity, and at great cost to the quality of their lives. The complaint made against this social arrangement is not that the very rich have so much more than the rest of us but that their superabundance and endless accumulation comes at the expense of everyone and everything else, including our communities and our environment.

Furthermore, the absence of money is what makes the have-nots and have-littles relatively powerless, depriving them of access to wider publics and severely limiting their influence over political life. As the gap between the corporate rich and the general populace grows, the opportunities for popular rule diminish.

One does not have to be destitute and jobless to experience the stress and scarcity of a corporate economy. Even people with fairly well-paying jobs can face cutbacks in pay, speedups, loss of seniority, layoffs, loss of health insurance and other benefits, runaway housing and medical costs, and persistent debt. Economic insecurity and income inequality have increased considerably since 1978. Real wages (wages adjusted for inflation) have remained flat or have declined; labor unions are fewer and weaker; still greater subsidies and giveaways go to corporate America as the public sector increasingly supports the private sector; and massive cuts in taxes go to the superrich.

This picture is at variance with the accepted "trickle-down" ideology of modern capitalism which says that as the economy booms, and investments and profits increase, so do wages and general prosperity. As the pie gets bigger, we all get a larger slice. "A rising tide lifts all boats," the saying goes. But in these days of reactionary ascendancy, a rising tide lifts all yachts and drowns many people.

In certain respects the political economy really is zero sum. No rent control means higher rents, more for the landlords, and less disposable income for the renters. Wage cuts for the workers means more for the owners. Conversely, more for the workers means less for the owners. Every dollar the employer has to spend on such annoying things as wages, benefits, occupational safety, and environmental protection, is one less dollar pocketed as profits.

The corporate ideology maintains that capitalism creates prosperity not poverty; just look at the prosperity of capitalist North America and capitalist Western Europe. But that is a very selective view of capitalism. I would argue the reverse: class wealth creates poverty. Put aside the fact that in the United States there are millions who live in hardship and serious want, let us look elsewhere. Quite simply, *most of the world is capitalist and getting more capitalist, yet most of the world is poor and getting poorer.* Capitalism works best in the poor countries, where wages are low, regulations and human services are paltry, and unions are weak or nonexistent; the result is that profit margins are higher than ever. Look at *capitalist* countries like Indonesia, Nigeria, Mexico, the Philippines, Haiti, Thailand, El Salvador, and so many others—all so capitalist and all so poor. Their populations get still poorer while a handful of transnational corporate investors get ever richer off them.

What is the imperative that propels wealthy individuals and their powerful financial organizations? In large part it is the desire, even the necessity, to accumulate still more wealth. "Accumulate, accumulate, accumulate," as Marx put it. Why? Those who have billions of dollars, who have more money than they know what to do with, why would they want still more and more? There are several reasons:

First, wealth can become addictive. Fortune whets the appetite for more fortune. There is no end to the amount of money one might desire to accumulate, giving oneself over to the *auri sacra fames*, the cursed hunger for gold, the desire to possess more wealth than can be consumed in a thousand lifetimes of limitless indulgence.

Wealth buys every comfort and privilege that is available, elevating the possessor to the highest social stratosphere, an expression of the aggrandizing self, leaving one feeling almost invulnerable to time and mortality. Wealth is an extension of one's existence beyond the grave. There is little desire to see your fortune dispensed or scattered after you depart from this world. Years ago a comedian wisecracked: "If I can't take it with me, I'm not going." The comment touches a real sentiment. If you can't take it with you, the next best thing is to keep it going after you're gone. The thought of breaking up one's estate into, say, four smaller parts for one's four offspring becomes painful. Worse, it is dangerous to the family's standing. If one great family fortune is reduced to four relatively modest holdings, the family slips in social standing.

So there was invented the custom of *primogeniture*: the oldest son inherited the entire estate and kept it intact. The other sons had to make do with going into the upper echelons of the military, the church, or the diplomatic corps. The daughters were married off to other families of fortune whenever possible. Failing that, they were sent to the nunnery or left to live out their dreary days in the lonely comforts of the family manor. Such is the addictive nature of wealth, keeping *all* of it together, always adding to it, never subtracting. The family wealth is immortalized in order to secure the family name and fortune—though not necessarily the well-being of all family members.

In modern times things do not always work that neatly. Great fortunes can sometimes breed fractious family dynasties, as siblings and other relatives contest for a cut of the inheritance in messy clashes that spill into public view, a far cry from the older practice of primogeniture.

Another reason for the relentless accumulation of wealth is less psychological and more systemic. Even in today's monopolistic oligopoly where a few corporate giants dominate each field of commerce and mergers are the rule, capitalism is still a potentially insecure system for the capitalist (as well as for everyone else). Markets change, new competitors with new technologies enter the fray, suppliers turn elsewhere, consumer tastes prove transient, investments backfire.

The competitive investment system requires constant expansion, from local to regional to national to international scope. The companies that grow are the ones most likely to survive. In 2006 Wal-Mart, the world's largest retailer, reportedly was going to build a chain of five hundred outlets in China. "For Wal-Mart, China represents an opportunity to tap a vast and fast-growing market abroad at a time when the company's sales are lagging elsewhere and it has run into obstacles to expansion at home."[4] In short, even the very biggest of corporations never feels perfectly secure unless they are accumulating in still greater quantities.

Of course there are exceptions. Some small companies with specialized markets and devoted clientele do well enough without perpetual growth. Still, global mergers and expansion are the general pattern. To remain in one place usually is to lose ground, not just relatively but absolutely, as competitors gain an edge that some day might prove fatal if carried too far.

In addition, one's accumulated wealth is rarely totally safe. It might get expropriated or plundered by other forces: revolution, insurrection, invasion, natural disaster. Or it might be lost through devaluation, inflation, overproduction, insider looting, market crash, or some other failure to realize its value. The safest way to remain very rich is to get still richer, coming out on top, never on bottom. Given this rat race, the tendency is for wealth to be pursued without moral restraint. Like any addiction, or any systemic imperative, money is pursued in that singleminded way, with a disregard for what is right or wrong, just or unjust, helpful or harmful to others.

If the workforces of the world are being downsized and wages are stagnating, where will purchasing power come from? Who will buy all the goods and services produced by overworked and underpaid employees? This question is often asked. The elites are cutting their own throats, the argument goes, and sooner or later they will have to reverse their policies as consumption diminishes. Indeed, a major preoccupation of the financial sector is *overcapacity*. There is overcapacity in Brazil, Indonesia, Japan, the United States, and numerous other countries. This is a real problem that capitalism chronically faces. But there are several mitigating factors.

First, though people may be working for proportionately lower real wages in the United States, more of them are working. Despite all the downsizing, millions of new but poorer paying jobs are being created every year. In many households, the collective family wage has been maintained because the male breadwinner (who might now have a poorer paying job) has been joined in the job market by his wife and one or two of the older children. Instead of going off to school or getting their own living quarters, the offspring stay at home because it is affordable, get a job, and contribute to the household income.

Second, we not only have the two- and three-job family but the two- and three-job person. People are working longer hours. Economists say that the average workweek is close to record levels. Overtime is more common, although time-and-a-half pay for overtime is becoming less common. In states like Texas, white-collar salaried workers in many firms are expected to stay well into the evening, come to the office on weekends, and put in an eighty-hour week if asked to do so. Workers are still buying things but they have to work harder and longer to do so. Of course, if you have to work harder to stay in the same place, you are not staying in the same place. In fact, you are losing ground, giving more of your life energy and labor power, but getting back relatively less in return.

Third, for the big-ticket items—durable-use goods like cars, refrigerators, and homes—there is installment buying. The consumer debt is climbing precipitously. Those with lots of extra money need to do something with it, so they lend it to those in need—at a price. Here is an area of poverty that is also a source of profit for rich creditors.

Fourth, the government keeps the economy going by massive deficit spending, a large chunk of which goes to the military. To make up for these deficits, the government borrows from rich financial interests at home and abroad. The accumulation of these yearly deficits is what we call the national debt, amounting to upwards of $9 *trillion* as of the end of 2006. Over the last two decades, the U.S. national debt has skyrocketed by 120 percent or so, mostly driven by conservative presidents: Ronald Reagan, George H. W. Bush, and his son, George W. Bush. The U.S. national debt is larger than the national debts of all Third World nations combined.

Conservatives like a big deficit because it represents an upward transfer of income from those who are eventually held responsible to pay it (the general public) to those who hold the notes on the debt (rich creditors). A massive national debt is a way of privatizing the public treasury. The bigger the debt, the larger the portion of the federal budget that finds its way back into the coffers of private creditors, as the government continues to borrow from those it should be taxing.

Fifth, demand is increasing among the very rich. Even during recent recession years, the sales of highly expensive jewelry, antiques, artwork, executive apartments, mansions, vacation homes, yachts, luxury cars, and fabulous excursions abroad boomed among upper-class clientele.

Sixth, there probably will always be some sort of middle-class consumption. In the United States there are some ten million professionals, upper and middle corporate managers and government bureaucrats, small investors, and small but successful entrepreneurs who do well enough. Even in a country like India, with a vast impoverished population of a billion people, there are some 80 million who might be designated as middle class, a consumer market much larger than the entire consumer population of most industrialized European nations.

Seventh, it should be noted that the present forced rollback in the United States started from a relatively high level of consumer abundance. With downsizing, the pie may expand at a slower rate or even get a little smaller, but if the plutocrats at the top keep getting larger and larger slices, they are not much troubled about sluggish demand.

The poor shall always be with us, says the Bible. Indeed, that will be so—as long as the superrich also are with us. For wealth and poverty do not just exist in an unfortunate but innocent juxtaposition. They endure in a close dynamic interrelationship. Wealth creates poverty and relies on it for its own continued existence. Without slaves how could the slaveholder live in the lavish style to which he is accustomed? Without serfs or overworked peasants, how could the lord be to the manor born? Without the working poor, how could the leisurely rich make do? With no underprivileged, who would be privileged? As Gilbert and Sullivan said, "If everybody is somebody, then nobody is anybody."

Economic downturns, or what is popularly known as "hard times," are not unmitigated gloom, at least not for the giant transnational corporations. During recessions, smaller competitors are weeded out, unions are weakened and often broken, and a reserve supply of unemployed workers grows in number, further helping to depress wages. And depressed wages increase profit margins. In recessions, profits rise faster than wages; indeed, in the severer slumps, wages are not likely to rise at all.

The idea that all Americans experience good and bad times together should be put to rest. Even as the economy declines, rich investors grow richer by grabbing a still bigger slice of whatever exists. During recent recessions, corporate profits rose to record levels, as companies squeezed more output from each employee while paying less in wages and benefits.

Former Secretary of the Treasury Nicholas Brady once remarked that recessions are "not the end of the world" and "no big deal."[5] Certainly not for Brady, who rested comfortably on a handsome fortune, and certainly not for his wealthy associates, who welcomed the opportunity to acquire bankrupted holdings at giveaway prices. Brady and friends understood that the comfort and prosperity of the superrich require an abundant supply of those who, spurred by the lash of necessity, toil as servants on rich estates, tend the country club grounds, serve the banquet luncheons, work the mines, mills, fields, and offices, performing a hundred thankless and sometimes health damaging tasks for paltry wages so that Brady and company can live in the style to which they are accustomed.

Worse still, poverty is not just a material condition. It is not just about income levels, consumption patterns, and employability—as some middle-class economists seem to think. For those who have known it firsthand, poverty is an encompassing oppression. It permeates and muddies all other life experiences. Not having enough money for food or rent; not having a place to live, sleep, and bathe; not being able to get needed medical care; these are not just material hardships, they are conditions that stress the soul and damage the spirit. And in an increasingly industrialized and urbanized society organized around high consumption and high prices, the poor find even less opportunity to create pockets of sustenance and survival.

Although they are getting ever wealthier, today's superrich are paying fewer taxes, if any at all, while the poor see their limited resources cut back further and their hopes grow dimmer. With free-market globalization, the same pattern emerges abroad. Poverty is spreading as wealth accumulates in ever greater concentrations. Again, it is no coincidence. Wealth battens on poverty.

In most instances, working people are not the authors of their own oppression but victims of the inequities and iniquities of corporate coteries whose consuming need for more and more accumulation creates the tragedies of history, big and small, personal and global.

27 MONOPOLY CULTURE AND SOCIAL LEGITIMACY

In the realm of governance, the economically dominant class is also the politically dominant. Lest this assertion be dismissed as a tired Marxist shibboleth, we should note that throughout much of the seventeenth, eighteenth and early nineteenth centuries, leading bourgeois theorists and philosophers saw the linkage between wealth and political hegemony, and readily accepted it as a necessary and desirable social feature. The English political philosopher John Locke wrote in 1689: "The great and chief end of Men's uniting into Commonwealths and putting themselves under Government, is the Preservation of their Property."[6] Adam Smith wrote in 1776: "The necessity of civil government grows up with the acquisition of valuable property." And "till there be property there can be no government, the very end of which is to secure wealth, and to defend the rich from the poor." Civil authority, Smith went on, "is in reality instituted for the defense of the rich against the poor, or of those who have some property against those who have none at all."[7] (Parenthetically we might remind ourselves that from ancient Athens to today the historic purpose of *democratic* government has been the reverse, to protect the poor from the rich.)

The framers of the U.S. Constitution understood the class nature of the state. In 1787, while ostensibly cobbling together a representative republic, they repeatedly asserted that an essential purpose of governance was to resist the "leveling tendencies of the masses" and to secure the interests of affluent property holders against the competing demands of small farmers, artisans, and debtors. In short, they wanted a stronger state in order to defend the haves from the have-nots.[8] In *Federalist* No. 10, James Madison wrote that "the most common and durable source" of divisions and conflict within a polity "has been the various and unequal distribution of property [wealth]. Those who hold and those who are without property have ever formed distinct interests in society" and "the first object of government" is "the protection of different and unequal faculties of acquiring property," so that those who possess great wealth are not hampered in any way by those who do not. That is not the only function of government, according to Madison, but it is "the first object."

The state power of the dominant economic class, however, never stands alone. A class that relies solely on the state's police and military to maintain its rule is never really secure. As Napoleon once said, one can do anything with bayonets except sit on them. Behind the state is a whole supporting network of doctrines, values, myths, and institutions that are not normally thought of as political. The state, as Antonio Gramsci noted, is "only the outer ditch behind which there [stands] a powerful system of fortresses and earthworks."[9] These auxiliary institutions help create the ideology that transforms a ruling-class interest into a "general interest," justifying existing class relations as the only natural and optimal—albeit not perfect—societal arrangements. Hence, along with monopoly capital we have monopoly culture. In other words, modern corporate capitalism is not just an economic system but an entire social order.

Ideologically conventional observers resist such a notion of ruling-class cultural hegemony. They see social institutions as autonomous and neutral configurations, largely independent of any linkage to business power and the state. They treat culture as something distinctly separate from—and even competitive with—politics. They talk about keeping our social institutions free of the taint of political ideologies.

A closer look reveals that cultural institutions such as the media, publishing houses, professional sports, entertainment enterprises, and most hospitals are not merely influenced by business ideology but are themselves profit-making corporate conglomerates. Furthermore, *nonprofit* cultural institutions like schools, museums, scientific and research associations, foundations and universities are tied by purchase and persuasion, by charter and power, to capitalist-class interests, ruled much like the profit-making ones—by boards of directors (or trustees or regents), drawn mostly from the corporate business class or from the ranks of loyal acolytes in the employ of that class. These boards have final say over the institution's system of rewards and punishments, its budget and personnel, its investments and purposes. They exercise power either by occupying the top positions or hiring and firing those who do. Their power to change the institution's management if it fails to perform as they desire is what gives them control over operations.

The boards of directors exercise authority not by popular demand but by state charter. Incorporated by the state, they can call upon the courts and police to enforce their decisions against the competing claims of staff, clients, or other constituents. These boards are unaccountable to the institution's rank and file or the general public, whose lives they might affect with their decisions. "When the state acts to protect [corporate] authority, it does so through the property system; that is, it recognizes the corporation as the private property of some determinate group of [persons] and it protects their right to do, within legal limits, what they please with their property."[10] Yet, institutions so ruled are said to be the mainstay of democratic pluralism.

In a word, social institutions are controlled by the more active members of the business class in what amounts to a system of interlocking and often interchanging directorates. We know of more than one business leader who not only presides over a bank or corporation but has served as a cabinet member in Washington, is a regent of a large university, a trustee of a civic art center, and at one time or another a member of the board of a major newspaper, a church, a foundation, or a television network. This pattern became evident by the latter part of the nineteenth century as capitalism came to maturity and capitalists moved to achieve a cultural hegemony that would be useful to their economic dominance. As one historian describes it:

> In short order the railroad presidents, copper barons, the big dry-goods merchants and the steel masters became Senators, ruling the highest councils of the national government . . . but they also became in even greater number lay leaders of churches, trustees of universities, partners or owners of newspapers or press services and figures of fashionable, cultured society. And through all these channels they labored to advance their policies and principles.[11]

With command over organizational structure, personnel, and budget, the owners and trustees pretty much call the tune. They may not be able to exercise perfect control over every note that is played but employees who stray too far from the score, who create too much cacophony, eventually find themselves without pay or position. Along with the punishments there are the rewards for compliance—the grants, fellowships, commissioned studies, honorary awards, special programs, promotions, top appointments, conference invitations, fat lecture fees, junkets, and other such career enticements.

Cultural dominance provides a number of payoffs for the plutocrats:

First, cultural institutions such as the media, and the health and entertainment industries are a major source of capital accumulation. Capitalists are involved in them because they make lots of money from them.

Second, nonprofit institutions such as universities, professional schools and research centers provide the kind of services and trained personnel that business does not want to pay for itself. When capitalists realized they needed literate, punctual and compliant machinists, they then favored public schools. When they needed lawyers, engineers and managers, they approved of professional and technical schools. The substantial public funds used to sustain these institutions represent an indirect public subsidy to the private sector.

Third, these institutions are crucial instruments of ideological and class control, socializing people into values that are functional to the existing system, while suppressing perspectives that are not.

Fourth, not only through propaganda and socialization but also through "good works," or the appearance of such, do plutocrats achieve hegemonic legitimacy. The ruthless industrialist becomes the generous philanthropist; the expropriator becomes "a leader of society," a trustee of our social and cultural needs. This was a conscious policy on the part of some moneyed leaders.[12] To appreciative American audiences Mobil Corporation was for years better known as the sponsor of *Masterpiece Theater* than as the heartless exploiter of oil workers in the Middle East and elsewhere. Cornell, Johns Hopkins, Clark, Duke, Vanderbilt, Tulane and Stanford are no longer ruthless tycoons but prestigious universities. And Carnegie is remembered not for the workers he starved and attacked, but for his Hall, his Institute, and his Endowment.

The primary goal of capitalist cultural dominance is not to provide us with nice concerts and museums but to give capitalism's exploitative reality a benign gloss and providential appearance so that people learn to accept and admire the "stewardship" of the owning class. So some say, "More for the rich means more for the rest of us because they create the jobs we need" and, "they do a lot of other good things for society."

In fact, some of their undertakings do have beneficial spinoffs. This brings us back to Antonio Gramsci's insights about how hegemony works to induce the people to consent in their own oppression. Gramsci noted that the capitalist class achieves hegemony not only by propagating the self-serving values, attitudes and beliefs but by actually performing vital social functions that have diffuse benefits. Railroads and highways may enrich the magnates, but they also provide transportation for much of the public. Private hospitals are for-profits not for people, but people who can afford them do get treated. The law is a class instrument, but it must also to some degree be concerned with public safety.

Gramsci notes that if a ruling class fails to keep up the appearance of being concerned for the public interest at least some of the time, its legitimacy will decline, its cultural and national hegemony will falter and its power will shrink back to its police and military capacity, leaving it with a more overtly repressive but ultimately less secure rule.[13]

The struggle for democratic change is long and difficult, but progressive victories are not impossible. The ruling class rules, but not quite in the way it wants. Its socializing agencies do not work with perfect effect. To maintain popular acceptance and democratic appearances it must lie, distort, and try to hide its oppression and unjust privileges. Occasionally it even must make concessions to popular demands.

In time, the legitimating ideology propagated by the plutocracy becomes a two-edged sword. Hypocrisies that rulers mouth about "democracy" and "fair play" are more than just the tribute vice pays to virtue. Such standards put limitations on ruling-class oppression once the public takes them seriously and fights for them. Legitimacy cuts both ways within cultural institutions. The danger with calling the oligarchic university a "democratic institution" is that students and faculty may take the assertion seriously and demand the right to ideological diversity and self-governance.

In sum, monopoly culture, like monopoly economy, suffers from internal contradictions. It can invent and control just so much of reality. Its socialization is imperfect and not without vulnerabilities. It cannot rest absolutely secure because it does not serve the people, yet it must pretend that it does. Its legitimating deceptions are soft spots of vulnerability, through which democratic forces can sometimes press for greater gains.

An understanding of monopoly culture shows us how difficult it is to fight capitalism on its own turf, but sometimes it is the only turf available. At the same time, we must continue to create alternatives to monopoly culture—alternative media, films, art, schools, and scholarship. But such a "counterculture" must be grounded in an alternative politics so that it confronts rather than evades the realities of class power and avoids devolving into cultural exotica and inner migration. It is easier to shock the plutocracy with cultural deviance than to defeat it with mass revolutionary organization.

The struggle for democracy is, among other things, a struggle to win back the entire cultural and social life of the people, so that someday we can say this land is our land, and so too this art and science, this learning and healing, this prayer and song, this peace and happiness.

28 THE FLIGHT FROM CLASS

Writers of varying political persuasions, including some who consider themselves to be on the left, maintain that *class* is a concept that is no longer preeminently relevant to understanding what is happening in society. Class is dismissed out of hand as an outworn Marxist notion. At a conference at Brown University years ago, I heard the anarchist Murray Bookchin assert, "There are no classes, only people."

Dissident ideas become all the more difficult to express when there are no acceptable words to express them. With the C-word out of the way, it is then easy to dispose of other "irrelevant" concepts such as class privilege, class interest, class power, class exploitation, class conflict, and class struggle.

When acknowledged at all, the concept of class is treated as nothing more than an occupational status, an educational or income level, or a social lifestyle. Thus reduced to a set of demographic traits, one's class affiliation certainly can seem to have a relatively low political salience, less significant than, say, race, gender, sexual orientation, or other components of "identity politics." Society itself is perceived as little more than a pluralistic configuration of status groups, having nothing to do with the dynamics of wealth and power. In this way have many observers perfected the art of looking at class in capitalist society without ever having to look at capitalism itself.

But class, as used by those who are awake to broader social dynamics, has another meaning: it describes an interrelationship. Classes get their definition from each other. One cannot think of a class as just existing unto itself. There can be no slaveholders without slaves, no lords without serfs, no capitalists without workers. The crucial axis of the relationship, however, is not between the two classes as such but pertains to the relationship each class has to the means of production, to ownership (or nonownership) of the land, industry, and wealth of society, and to the exploitative nature of the process of production and capital accumulation.

This defining relationship involves a conflict of material interests between those who own and those who work for those who own. Class gets its significance from the process of surplus extraction. The relationship between master and slave, lord and serf, boss and worker is essentially an exploitative one, involving the constant transfer of value from those who labor (but do not own) to those who own (but do not labor). This explains how some people can get ever richer without working or with doing only a fraction of the work that enriches them, while others toil hard for an entire lifetime only to end up with little or nothing.

Those who occupy the higher perches of wealth and power are keenly aware of their favored position. While they occasionally differ among themselves on specific issues, they exhibit a workable cohesion when it comes to protecting the overall class system of corporate power, property, privilege, and profit. At the same time, they are careful to discourage public awareness of the class power they wield. They avoid the C-word, especially when used in reference to themselves as in "owning class," "upper class," or "moneyed class." And they like it least when the politically active elements of the owning class are called the "ruling class," or plutocracy. This country's superrich owning class labors hard to engineer the impression that it does not possess the lion's share of wealth and investment, and does not exercise a vastly disproportionate influence over the affairs of the nation. Such an unwillingness to discuss class power is not symptomatic of a lack of class consciousness, quite the opposite.

Conservative ideologies justify existing socio-economic inequities as inevitable outcomes of largely innate human proclivities. But if the very rich are just naturally superior to the rest of us, why must they be provided with so many artificial privileges under the law, so many government protections, services, bailouts, subsidies, and other special considerations—at our expense? Their "naturally superior talents" include unprincipled and illegal subterfuges such as price-fixing, stock manipulation, insider trading, fraud, tax evasion, unfair competition, bribery, rigged laws, ecological spoliation, labor-contract violations, harmful products, and unsafe work conditions. One might expect naturally superior people not to act in such morally inferior ways. Differences in talent and capacity as might exist between individuals do not excuse the endemic venality, rapacity, hypocrisy, and crimes.

The idea that wealth is constantly being transferred from the labor of many into the accounts of the few is widely at variance with the established notion that the relationship between rich and poor, owner and worker, is not exploitative but symbiotic. The question "Where would workers be without the company?" is more likely to be asked than "Where would the company be without workers?" Worker and owner are supposedly engaged in a mutually beneficial "teamwork." Such class collaboration is presumed beneficial to all. Conversely, class strife is seen as harmful to all.

Even among persons normally identified as progressive, one finds a reluctance to deal with the reality of capitalist class-power. Sometimes the dismissal of the C-word is quite categorical. At a meeting in New York in 1986 I heard the sociologist Stanley Aronowitz exclaim, "When I hear the word 'class' I just yawn." Through the whole evening he never used the term "Marxist" without preceding it with the loaded adjective "orthodox," as if by definition Marxism was a set of rigid dogmatic beliefs, and not a fruitful mode of inquiry.

Aronowitz's self-appointed task is, in his words, "to interrogate Marxists' habitual separation of political economy and culture and to make a contribution to their articulation, even reunification."[14] But his dismissive boredom with the term "class" and his energetic bludgeoning of something he calls "orthodox Marxism" would suggest that he is more interested in replacing class analysis with cultural explanations than in linking class and culture. While claiming that the two concepts are complimentary, he seems to treat them as adversarial.

Aronowitz was one of several people who edited *Social Text*, a journal devoted to articles that specialize in impenetrable verbiage and niggling academic one-upmanship, supposedly representative of a field called "cultural studies," whose primary function seems to be to deny the importance and centrality of class power. (That the journal's writings are seldom connected to the real world was demonstrated in 1996 by physicist Alan Sokal, himself a leftist, who wrote a parody and submitted it to *Social Text*. Sokal's piece was laden with bloated but trendy hypertheorized jargon and many footnoted references to the likes of Jacques Derrida and Aronowitz himself. It purported to be an "epistemic exposition" of "recent developments in quantum gravity" and "the space-time manifold" and "foundational conceptual categories of prior science" that have "become problematized and relativized" with "profound implications for the content of a future post-modern and liberatory science." Various *Social Text* editors, including Aronowitz, read and accepted the piece as a serious contribution. After they published it, Sokal revealed that it was little more than fabricated gibberish and hot air that "wasn't obliged to respect any standards of evidence or logic." In effect, he demonstrated that the journal's editors were themselves so profoundly immersed in pretentiously inflated, obscurantist, and incomprehensible discourse as to be unable to distinguish a genuine intellectual effort from a silly hoax. Aronowitz responded by calling Sokal "ill-read and half-educated."[15])

Another left academic, Ronald Aronson, claims that classes in capitalist society have become "less polarized" and class exploitation is not an urgent issue nowadays because labor unions "have achieved power to protect their members and affect social policy."[16] This at a time when many unions were being destroyed, real wages were slumping, the income gap was wider than in decades, and the number of people living in poverty throughout the capitalist world was (and still is) growing at a faster rate than the world's population.

The left anti-class theorists say we are giving too much attention to class. Who exactly is doing that? Surveying the mainstream academic publications, radical journals, and socialist scholars conferences, one is hard put to find much class analysis of any kind. Far from giving too much attention to class power, most of these theorists have yet to discover the subject. While perpetually pummeling a rather minuscule Marxist left, they would have us think they are doing courageous battle against hordes of

Marxists who dominate intellectual discourse in this country—yet another hallucination they share with conservatives.

Almost any allusion to class is likely to elicit a negative response from academics. Years ago, in a discussion with Harold Isaacs, a faculty member at MIT, I suggested that much of what we define as "ethnic" is really representative of a common class experience, so that in many respects, urban working-class ethnic groups manifest, along with distinctly different traits, many *similar* ones because of their being similarly situated in the class structure. Having arrived at this hypothesis after years of work in ethnic studies, I thought it was worthy of further consideration. But Isaacs was not happy to hear it. "Well, if you want to fall back on a *Marxist* viewpoint, you can," he said. His response puzzled me. Like any red-blooded American social scientist, I was at that time blithely ignorant of what Marxists might be saying about ethnicity or most other subjects. Yet the mere idea that class should be taken into account was enough for him to equate my suggestion with Marxism. To be sure, there is nothing inherently wrong in having one's views thought of as Marxist. What is wrong is the habit of immediately rejecting an idea as deficient or dogmatic because it has been labeled "Marxist."

To support their view that class struggle is passé, the left anti-class theorists repeatedly assert that there is not going to be a workers' revolution in the United States in the foreseeable future. (I heard this sentiment expressed at three different panels during what purported to be a "Gramsci conference" at Amherst, Massachusetts, in April 1987.) Even if we agree with this prognosis, we still might wonder how it becomes grounds for rejecting class analysis and seeing class struggle as of no import. The feminist revolution that was going to transform our entire patriarchal society has thus far not materialized, yet no progressive person takes this to mean that sexism is a chimera or that gender-related struggles are of no great moment. That workers in the United States are not throwing up barricades does not mean class conflict is a myth. In present-day society, such struggle permeates almost all workplace activities. Management constantly wages class war using court injunctions, anti-labor laws, lobbying, tax cuts for the superrich, police repression, union busting, contract violations, sweatshops, dishonest clocking of time, forced and unpaid overtime, safety violations, speedups, harassment and firing of resistant workers, cutbacks in wages and benefits, layoffs, plant closings, outsourcing to cheaper labor markets, and pilfering pension funds.

Workers fight back—when they can—with union organizing, strikes, slowdowns and other job actions, boycotts, public demonstrations, legal appeals, electoral struggle, coordinated absenteeism, and workplace sabotage. "The class struggle is never absent, right down to an argument over whether a worker has spent too long in the lavatory, or whether they have the right to go the lavatory if they wish."[17]

Class power may not be the only factor, but it is an important one in setting the political agenda, selecting leaders, determining public budgets, silencing dissenters, and funding scientific research. Class is a major determinant in how people gain access to higher education, how health care is distributed, how the environment is (mis)treated, how the elderly try to survive, how women and people of color are dealt with, and how religion, news, entertainment, art, and sports are marketed.

Left anti-class theorists like the hyper-theorizing Chantal Mouffe define the working class as composed only of industrial proletarians. This definition excludes farm workers, service workers, and white-collar employees. It enables the anti-class theorists to see the working class as on the way out, declining in numbers and importance. When I once observed that the Nicaraguan Revolution was a "working-class victory," Mouffe vehemently objected, stating that the Nicaraguan Revolution was "a popular uprising." But who is the populace? Was the Sandinista victory carried out by a leisure class? By a small professional class? In Nicaragua and other countries, a popular uprising and a working-class uprising are much the same thing.

A grasp of class reality vastly superior to Chantal Mouffe's was evidenced by George Rohal, a supermarket manager in Weirton, West Virginia, and the son of a steelworker. Rohal commented, "All classes are really working classes. Very few people sit back and just collect income. Anyone drawing any type of salary or a weekly paycheck is a working-class person."[18] This might not be true of the very top corporate CEOs, whose huge salaries are well complemented by enormous investment earnings and whose wealth and organizational command positions give them an inescapable identity with the owning class, yet Rohal's comment contains a core insight. Having never read the anti-class theorists and mainstream social scientists, he is able to see that class is a *relationship to ownership* and not just a demographic characteristic.

By the 1980s "the retreat from class" became something of a stampede, most notably in countries like France and the United States. For those who sought to be *au courant*, class oppression and class struggle now seemed terribly passé. During the seventies and eighties, the anti-class theorists set sail for seemingly more inviting ports, announcing that the future belonged to the Greens, the feminists, the gays, the political culturalists—or even the free market and the ideological right. Few people wanted to associate with a loser, and class struggle seemed like a loser.

Various "left" theorists devoted yet more time to Marxist bashing. Anyone who still thought that class was of primary importance was labeled a diehard Marxist, guilty of "economism"[19] and "reductionism" and unable to keep up with the "post-Marxist," "post-structuralist," "post-industrialist," "postmodernist," and even "post-capitalist" times.

Explaining why, like so many other French intellectuals, she shifted away from Marxism and from studying working-class history, Michelle Perrot remarked: "After the war, the working class was highly visible; we believed that it was the vanguard. To do working-class history was one way of being an intellectual."[20] A revealing admission by Perrot. She did not side with the working class because of the inherent question of economic justice, but because "the working class was highly visible," and an identity with the class was largely a means to another end, that of being a certified intellectual. And now, when the working class is perceived as "declining in importance," the anti-class theorists move on to matters more deserving of their attention, announcing the advent of a post-something-or-other era, and marketing a new line of threadbare ideas. The intellectual life resembles the fashion industry in more ways than one.

Rather than treating class, race, culture, and gender as mutually exclusive and competitive concepts, we need to see how they interact, often with compound effect. The resurgence of racism is not proof that class realities are thereby less important. Indeed just the opposite. Racial and ethnic divisions are often incited as a way of retarding class consciousness and unity.

Consider the way the left anti-class theorists have misused Antonio Gramsci, an Italian Communist Party leader and intellectual of the 1920s. Gramsci made much of the fact that cultural hegemony was one of the ways the bourgeoisie maintained itself and buttressed state power. In emphasizing the importance of cultural hegemony, he did not mean to downplay the significance or centrality of class. Quite the contrary, he was showing how culture was a force instrumental to class struggle. Gramsci would have been appalled at those theorists who try to use his work as a weapon against Marxism, since he himself was a Marxist-Leninist.

When Marxists and other social critics argue that the class dimension is of primary importance, they are being neither reductionist nor "economistic," for they continue to recognize the multifaceted nature of social phenomena. That all human activity has a material base does not mean that all human activity is reduced to material motives but that it is all anchored within the overall structure of politico-economic power.

While all things cannot and should not be reduced to class, class does penetrate so much of our social experience. An economically dominant class is able to hold sway over other social institutions and cultural forces in society—albeit not in all matters for all time. The capitalist class is dominant but not omnipotent. One of the prime conditions of that class's hegemony is the ability to mute and blur class awareness. In this they have plenty of allies across the political spectrum.

NOTES

1. Adam Smith, *An Inquiry into the Nature and Causes of the Wealth of Nations* (Modern Library, 1937), 33.

2. See Victor Perlo's columns in *People's Weekly World*, 31 May 1997, and 1 August 1998; and Paul Lawrence, "Capitalism is Organized Crime," *The People*, September/October 2003.

3. For the classic statement on capitalism, see Karl Marx, *Capital*, vol. 1, available in various editions; see also Marx's *A Contribution to the Critique of Political Economy* (International Publishers, 1970).

4. *New York Times*, 17 October 2006.

5. Brady quoted in Lewis Lapham, "Notebook," *Harper's* 26 April 1995.

6. John Locke, *Treatise of Civil Government* (Appelton-Century-Croft, 1937), 82.
7. Adam Smith, *An Inquiry into the Nature and Causes of the Wealth of Nations* (Encyclopedia Britannica, 1952), 309, 311.
8. See Michael Parenti, *Democracy for the Few*, 8th ed. (Wadsworth/Thomson, 2007), chapter 4.
9. Antonio Gramsci, *Selections from the Prison Notebooks*, edited by Quinton Hoare and Geoffrey Nowell-Smith (International Publishers, 1971), 238.
10. Michael Walzer, "Civil Disobedience and Corporate Authority," in Philip Green and Sanford Levinson (eds.), *Power and Community* (Pantheon, 1969), 226.
11. Matthew Josephson, *The Robber Barons* (Harcourt Brace and World, 1962), 317.
12. E. Richard Brown, *Rockefeller Medicine Men* (University of California Press, 1960), 13–59.
13. Gramsci, *Selections from the Prison Notebooks*; also Edward Greer, "Antonio Gramsci and 'Legal Hegemony'," in David Kairys, ed., *The Politics of Law* (Pantheon, 1982), 306.
14. Stanley Aronowitz, "Alan Sokal's 'Transgression,'" *Dissent*, Winter 1997.
15. *New York Times*, 18 May 1996; and also Aronowitz, "Alan Sokal's Transgression."
16. Ronald Aronson, *After Marxism* (Guilford Press, 1994).
17. John Downing, *The MediaMachine* (London: Pluto Press, 1980), p. 18.
18. *New York Times*, April 24, 1978.
19. "Economism" was originally a term used by Lenin to criticize those who thought that the class struggle was entirely encapsulated in the trade union movement. It is now used by anti-Leninists and anti-Marxists to criticize those who see economic factors as of prime importance.
20. "New Subjects, New Social Commitments: An Interview with Michelle Perrot," *Radical History Review* 37, 1987, 27.

VII.
DOING THE WORLD

29 IMPERIALISM FOR BEGINNERS

Imperialism has been the most powerful force in world history over the last four or five centuries, carving up whole continents while oppressing indigenous peoples and obliterating entire communities. Yet, it is seldom accorded any serious attention by our academics, media commentators, or political leaders. When not ignored outright, the subject of imperialism has been sanitized, so that empires become "commonwealths," and colonies become "territories" or "dominions" (or, as in the case of Puerto Rico, "commonwealths" too). Imperialist military interventions become matters of "national defense," "national security," and maintaining "stability" in one or another region. Here I want to look at imperialism for what it really is.

By "imperialism" I mean the process whereby the dominant politico-economic interests of one nation expropriate for their own enrichment the land, labor, raw materials, and markets of another people.

The earliest victims of Western European imperialism were other Europeans. Some 800 years ago, Ireland became the first colony of what later became known as the British Empire. A part of Ireland still remains under British occupation. Other early Caucasian victims included the Eastern Europeans. The people Emperor Charlemagne worked to death in his mines in the early part of the ninth century were Slavs. So frequent and prolonged was the enslavement of Eastern Europeans that "Slav" became synonymous with servitude. The word "slave" derives from "Slav." Eastern Europe was an early source of raw materials, cheap labor, and capital accumulation, having become wholly dependent upon Western manufactures by the seventeenth century.

A particularly pernicious example of intra-European imperialism was the Nazi aggression during World War II, which gave the German business cartels and the Nazi state an opportunity to plunder the resources and exploit the labor of occupied Europe, including the slave labor of concentration camps.

The preponderant thrust of the European, North American, and Japanese imperial powers has been directed against Africa, Asia, and Latin America. By the nineteenth century, they saw the Third World as not only a source of raw materials and slaves but a market for manufactured goods. By the twentieth century, the industrial nations were exporting not only goods but capital, in the form of machinery, technology, investments, and loans.

Of the various notions about imperialism circulating today in the United States, the dominant view is that it does not exist. Imperialism is not recognized as a legitimate concept, certainly not in regard to the United States. One may speak of "Soviet imperialism" or "nineteenth-century British imperialism" but not of *U.S.* imperialism. A graduate student in political science at most universities in this country would not be granted the opportunity to research U.S. imperialism, on the grounds that such an undertaking would be ideologically driven and therefore not scholarly. While many people throughout the world charge the United States with being an imperialist power, in this country persons who talk of U.S. imperialism are usually judged to be mouthing "leftist" or "hate-America" blather.

Imperialism is older than capitalism. The Persian, Macedonian, Roman, and Mongol empires all existed centuries before the Rothschilds and Rockefellers. Emperors and conquistadors were interested mostly in plunder and tribute, gold and glory. Capitalist imperialism differs from these earlier forms in the way it invests in other countries, penetrates cultural and political life, and integrates the overseas economies into an international system of profit accumulation.

Given its expansionist nature, corporate capitalism has little inclination to stay home. Almost 150 years ago, Marx and Engels described a bourgeoisie that "chases over the whole surface of the globe. It must nestle everywhere, settle everywhere, establish connections everywhere. . . . It creates a world after its own image."[1] Indigenous communities and folk cultures are replaced by mass-market, mass-media societies. Cooperative lands are supplanted by agribusiness factory farms, villages give way to desolate shanty towns, and autonomous regions are forcibly wedded to centralized autocracies and international markets.

Consider one of a thousand such instances. Some years ago the *Los Angeles Times* carried a special report on the rainforests of Borneo in the South Pacific. By their own testimony, the people there lived contented lives. They hunted and fished, and raised food in their jungle orchards and groves. But their community was ruthlessly wiped out by a few giant companies that destroyed the rainforest in order to harvest the hardwood for quick profits. Declared "business zones," their lands were turned into ecological disaster areas. Driven from their homesteads, the inhabitants were transformed into disfranchised shantytown dwellers, forced to work for subsistence wages—when fortunate enough to find employment.

North American and European corporations have acquired control of more than three-fourths of the known mineral resources of Asia, Africa, and Latin America. But the pursuit of natural resources is not the only reason for capitalist overseas expansion. There is the additional need to cut production costs and maximize profits by investing in countries with cheaper labor markets. U.S. corporate foreign investment grew 84 percent from 1985 to 1990, the most dramatic increase being in cheap-labor countries, mostly in Asia.

Because of low wages, low taxes, nonexistent work benefits, weak labor unions, and nonexistent occupational and environmental protections, U.S. corporate-profit rates in the Third World are 50 percent greater than in developed countries and have continued to rise dramatically. Citibank, one of the largest U.S. transnationals, earns about 75 percent of its profits from overseas operations. Today some four hundred transnational companies control about 80 percent of the capital assets of the global "free market" and are extending their grasp into the ex-communist countries of Eastern Europe.

Transnationals have developed a global production line. General Motors has factories that produce cars, trucks and a wide range of auto components in Canada, Brazil, Venezuela, Spain, Belgium, the former Yugoslavia, Nigeria, Singapore, Philippines, South Africa, South Korea and a dozen other countries. Such "multiple sourcing" enables GM to ride out strikes in one country by stepping up production in another, playing workers of various nations against each other.

Some writers question whether imperialism is a necessary condition for capitalism, pointing out that most Western capital is invested in Western nations, not in the Third World (but with higher growth rates in the Third World in recent years). If corporations lost all their Third World investments, they argue, many of them could still survive on their European and North American markets. In response, one should note that even in the unlikely event that capitalism could survive without imperialism—it shows no inclination to do so. It manifests no desire to discard its enormously profitable Third World enterprises. Imperialism may not be a necessary condition for investor survival but it seems to be an inherent tendency and a natural outgrowth of advanced capitalism. Imperial relations may not be the only way to pursue profits, but they are a most lucrative way.

Whether imperialism is necessary for capitalism is really not the question. Many things that are not absolutely necessary are still highly desirable, therefore strongly pursued. Overseas investors are strongly attracted to the Third World's cheap labor, rich natural resources, and various other highly profitable conditions. Superprofits may not be necessary for capitalism's survival but survival is not all that capitalists are interested in. Superprofits are strongly preferred to more modest earnings. That there may be no necessity between capitalism and imperialism does not mean there is no compelling linkage.

The same is true of other social dynamics. For instance, wealth does not necessarily have to lead to luxurious living. A higher portion of an owning class's riches could be used for investment rather personal consumption. The very wealthy could survive quite comfortably on more modest sums but that is not how most of them prefer to live. Throughout history, wealthy classes generally have shown a preference for getting the best of everything.

After all, the whole purpose of getting rich off other people's labor is to live well, avoiding all forms of thankless toil and drudgery, enjoying superior opportunities for lavish lifestyles, superior medical care, quality education, travel, recreation, security, leisure, and opportunities for power and prestige. While none of these things are really "necessary," they are fervently clung to by those who possess them—as witnessed by the violent measures endorsed by advantaged classes whenever they feel the threat of an equalizing or leveling democratic force.

The impoverished lands of Asia, Africa, and Latin America are known to us as the "Third World" to distinguish them from the "First World" of industrialized Europe and North America and the now largely defunct "Second World" of communist states. Third World poverty, called "underdevelopment," is treated by most Western observers as an original and inherent historic condition. In fact, the lands of Asia, Africa, and Latin America have long produced great treasures of foods, minerals and other natural resources. That is why the Europeans went through so much trouble to plunder them. One does not go to poor places for self-enrichment. The Third World is rich. Only its people are poor—and they are poor because of the pillage they have endured.

The process of expropriating the natural resources of the Third World began centuries ago. First, the colonizers extracted gold, silver, furs, silks, and spices; then flax, hemp, timber, molasses, sugar, rum, rubber, tobacco, calico, cocoa, coffee, cotton, copper, coal, palm oil, tin, iron, ivory, and ebony; and still later on, oil, zinc, manganese, mercury, platinum, cobalt, bauxite, aluminum, and uranium. Not to be overlooked is that most hellish of all expropriations: the abduction of millions of human beings into slave labor.

Through the centuries of colonization, many self-serving imperialist theories have been spun. I was taught in school that people in tropical lands are slothful and do not work as hard as we denizens of the temperate zone. In fact, the inhabitants of warm climates have performed remarkably productive feats, building magnificent civilizations well before Europe emerged from the Dark Ages. And today, even though they often work long, hard hours for meager sums, the early stereotype of the "lazy native" is still with us. We hear that Third World peoples are culturally retarded in their attitudes, customs, and technical abilities. It is a convenient notion embraced by those who want to depict Western investment as a rescue operation designed to help backward peoples help themselves. This myth of "cultural backwardness" goes back to ancient times, when conquerors used it to justify enslaving indigenous peoples.

What cultural supremacy could by claimed by the Europeans of yore? From the fifteenth to nineteenth centuries Europe certainly was "ahead" of Africa, Asia, and Latin America in a variety of things, such as the number of hangings, murders, and other violent crimes; instances of venereal disease, smallpox, typhoid, tuberculosis, cholera, and other such afflictions; social inequality and poverty (both urban and rural); and frequency of famines, slavery, prostitution, piracy, religious massacres and inquisitions. Those who claim the West has been the most advanced civilization should dwell a bit more on all its achievements.

More seriously, we might note that Europe enjoyed a telling advantage in navigation and armaments. Muskets and cannon, Gatling guns and gunboats, and today missiles, helicopter gunships, and fighter bombers have been the deciding factors when West meets East and North meets South. Superior firepower, not superior culture, has brought the Europeans and Euro-North Americans to positions of global supremacy.

It was said that colonized peoples were biologically less evolved than their colonizers. Their "savagery" and "lower" level of cultural evolution were emblematic of their inferior genetic evolution. Actually in many parts of what is now considered the Third World, people developed impressive skills in architecture, horticulture, crafts, hunting, fishing, midwifery, medicine, and other such things. Their social customs were often more gracious and humane and less autocratic than what was found in Europe at that time. Of course we must not romanticize these indigenous societies, some of which had a number of cruel and unusual practices of their own. But generally, their peoples enjoyed healthier, happier, more leisurely lives than most of Europe's inhabitants.

Other theories enjoy wide currency. We hear that Third World poverty is due to overpopulation, too many people having too many children to feed. Actually, over the last several centuries, many Third World lands have been less densely populated than certain parts of Europe. Furthermore, it is the industrialized nations of the First World, not the poor ones of the Third, that devour some 80 percent of the world's resources and pose the greatest threat to the planet's ecology.

This is not to deny that overpopulation is a real problem for the planet's ecosphere. Limiting population growth in *all* nations would help the global environment but it would not solve the problems of the poor—because overpopulation in itself is not the cause of poverty but one of its effects. The poor tend to have large families because children are a source of family labor and income and usually sole support during old age.

Frances Moore Lappé and Rachel Schurman found that of seventy Third World countries, there were six—China, Sri Lanka, Colombia, Chile, Burma, and Cuba—and the state of Kerala in India that had managed to lower their birth rates by one third.

They enjoyed neither dramatic industrial expansion nor high per capita incomes nor extensive family planning programs.[2] The factors they had in common were public education and health care, a reduction of economic inequality, improvements in women's rights, food subsidies, and in some cases land reform. In other words, fertility rates were lowered not by capitalist investments and economic growth as such but by socio-economic betterment, even of a modest scale, accompanied by the emergence of women's rights.

What is called "underdevelopment" is a set of social relations that has been forcefully imposed on countries. With the advent of the Western colonizers, the peoples of the Third World were set back in their development sometimes for centuries. British imperialism in India provides an instructive example. In 1810, India was exporting more textiles to England than England was exporting to India. By 1830, the trade flow was reversed. The British had put up prohibitive tariff barriers to shut out Indian finished goods and were dumping their commodities in India, a practice backed by British gunboats and military force. Within a matter of years, the great textile centers of Dacca and Madras were turned into ghost towns. The Indians were sent back to the land to raise the cotton used in British textile factories. In effect, India was reduced to being a cow milked by British investors.

By 1850, India's debt had grown to 53 million. From 1850 to 1900, its per capita income dropped by almost two-thirds. The value of the raw materials and commodities that the Indians were obliged to send to Britain during most of the nineteenth century amounted yearly to more than the total income of the sixty million Indian agricultural and industrial workers. British imperialism did two things: first, it ended India's development, then it forcibly underdeveloped that country. The massive poverty we associate with India was not an original historical condition that antedates imperialism.

As with India, so with many other Third World countries: they are not "underdeveloped" but overexploited. The bleeding process that attends Western colonization and investment has created a lower rather than a higher living standard. Referring to what the English colonizers did to the Irish, Friedrich Engels wrote in 1856: "How often have the Irish started out to achieve something, and every time they have been crushed politically and industrially. By consistent oppression they have been artificially converted into an utterly impoverished nation."[3] So with most of the Third World, including China, Egypt, and much of Africa. The Mayan Indians in Guatemala had a more nutritious and varied diet and better conditions of health in the early 16th century before the Europeans arrived than they have today. They had more craftspeople, architects, artisans, and horticulturists than today. What is called underdevelopment is not an original historical condition but a product of imperialism's superexploitation.

Imperialism has created what I call "maldevelopment": modern office buildings and luxury hotels in the capital city instead of housing for the poor, cosmetic surgery clinics for the affluent instead of hospitals for workers, highways that go from the mines and latifundios to the refineries and ports instead of roads in the back country for those who might hope to see a doctor or a teacher.

Wealth is transferred from Third World people to the economic elites of Europe and North America (and later on Japan) by the expropriation of natural resources, the imposition of ruinous taxes and land rents, the payment of poverty wages, and the forced importation of finished goods at highly inflated prices. The colonized country is denied the opportunity to develop its own natural resources, markets, trade, and industrial capacity. Self-sustenance and self-employment are discouraged at every turn.

Hundreds of millions of Third World people now live in destitution in remote villages and congested urban slums, suffering hunger and disease, often because the land they once tilled is now controlled by agribusiness firms who use it for mining or for commercial export crops such as coffee, sugar, and beef, instead of growing beans, rice, and corn for home consumption. Imperialism forces millions of children around the world to live nightmarish lives, with their mental and physical health severely damaged. In countries like Mexico, India, Colombia, and Egypt, children are dragooned into health-shattering, dawn-to-dusk labor on farms and in factories and mines for pennies an hour, with no opportunity for play, schooling, or medical care. In India, 55 million children are pressed into the work force. In the Philippines and Malaysia, corporations have lobbied to drop age restrictions for labor recruitment.

When we say a country is underdeveloped, we are implying that it is backward and retarded in some way, that its people have shown little capacity to achieve and evolve. The negative connotations of "underdeveloped" has caused the United Nations, the *Wall Street Journal*, and parties of contrasting political persuasion to refer to Third World countries as *developing* nations, a term somewhat less insulting than "underdeveloped" but equally misleading.

I prefer to use "Third World" because "developing" still implies that backwardness and poverty were part of an original historic condition and not something imposed by the imperialists. It also falsely suggests that these countries *are* developing when actually their economic conditions are usually worsening.

The dominant theory of the last half century, enunciated repeatedly by writers like Barbara Ward and W. W. Rostow, and afforded wide currency in the United States and other parts of the Western world, maintains that it is up to the rich nations of the North to help uplift the "backward" nations of the South, bringing them technology and teaching them proper work habits. This is an updated version of "the White man's burden," a favorite imperialist fantasy.

The development scenario goes like this: With the introduction of Western investments, the backward economic sectors of the poor nations will release their workers, who then will find more productive employment in the modern sector at higher wages. As capital accumulates, business will reinvest its profits, thus creating still more products, jobs, buying power, and markets. Eventually a more prosperous economy evolves.

This "development theory" or "modernization theory," as it is sometimes called, bears little relation to reality. What has emerged in the Third World is an intensely exploitative form of dependent capitalism. Economic conditions have worsened drastically with the growth of corporate investment. The problem is not poor lands or unproductive populations but self-enriching transnationals.

People in these countries do not need to be taught how to farm. They need the land and the implements to farm. They do not need to be taught how to fish. They need the boats and the nets and access to shore frontage, bays, and oceans. They need industrial plants to cease dumping toxic effusions into the waters. They do not need to be convinced that they should use hygienic standards. They do not need a Peace Corps Volunteer to tell them to boil their water, especially when they cannot afford fuel or have no reliable access to firewood. They need the conditions that will allow them to have clean drinking water and clean clothes and homes. They do not need advice about balanced diets from over-weight North Americans. They usually know what foods best serve their nutritional requirements. They need to be given back their land and labor so that they might work for themselves and feed themselves.

The local economies of the world are increasingly dominated by a network of international corporations that are beholden to parent companies based in North America, Europe and Japan. If there is an integrative globalization, it is happening among the global-investor classes, not among the indigenous Third World economies that are becoming increasingly fragmented from each other and within themselves. In sum, what we have is a world economy that excludes much of the world's people.

Territorial acquisition is no longer the prevailing imperial mode. Compared to the nineteenth and early twentieth centuries, when the European powers carved up the world among themselves, today there is almost no colonial dominion left. Colonel Blimp is dead and buried, replaced by men in business suits. Rather than being directly colonized by the imperial power, the weaker countries have been granted the trappings of sovereignty—while Western finance capital retains control of the lion's share of their profitable resources. This relationship has gone under various names: "informal empire," "colonialism without colonies," "neo-colonialism," and "neo-imperialism."

U.S. political and business leaders were among the earliest practitioners of this new kind of empire, most notably in Cuba at the beginning of the twentieth century. Having forcibly wrested the island from Spain in the war of 1898, they eventually gave Cuba its nominal independence. The Cubans then had their own government, constitution, flag, currency, and security force. But major foreign policy decisions remained in U.S. hands, as did the island's wealth, including its sugar, tobacco, nickel, and tourist industries, and its major imports and exports.

Historically U.S. capitalist interests have been less interested in acquiring more colonies than in acquiring more wealth, preferring to make off with the treasure of other nations without the bother of owning and administering the nations themselves. Under neo-imperialism, the flag stays home, while the dollar goes everywhere.

After World War II, European powers like Britain and France adopted a similar strategy of neo-imperialism. Left financially depleted by years of warfare, and facing intensified popular resistance from within the Third World itself, they reluctantly decided that indirect economic hegemony was less costly and politically more expedient than outright colonial rule. Though the newly established Third World country might be far from completely independent, it usually enjoyed more legitimacy in the eyes of its populace than a foreign colonial power. Furthermore, under neo-imperialism the native government takes up the costs of administering the country while the imperialist interests are free to concentrate on skimming the cream—which is all they really want.

After years of colonialism, the Third World country finds it extremely difficult to extricate itself from the unequal relationship with its former colonizer and impossible to depart from the global capitalist sphere. Those countries that try to make a break are subjected to punishing economic and military treatment by one or another major power, nowadays usually the United States.

The leaders of the new nations may voice revolutionary slogans, yet they find themselves locked into the global corporate orbit, cooperating perforce with the First World nations for investment, trade, and loans. In many instances a *comprador class* was installed as a first condition for independence, that is, a coterie of rulers who cooperate in turning their own country into a client state for foreign interests. A *client state* is one that is open to investments on terms that are decidedly favorable to the foreign investors. In a client state, corporate investors enjoy direct subsidies and land grants, access to raw materials and cheap labor, light or nonexistent taxes, no minimum wage or occupational safety laws, no prohibitions on child labor, and no consumer or environmental protections to speak of. The protective laws that do exist go largely unenforced.

The comprador class is well recompensed for its cooperation. Its leaders enjoy opportunities to line their pockets with the foreign aid sent by the U.S. government. Stability is assured with the establishment of security forces, armed and trained by the United States in the latest technologies of terror and repression.

In all, the Third World is something of a capitalist paradise, offering life as it was in Europe and the United States during the nineteenth century, with a rate of profit vastly higher than what might be earned today in a country with strong social regulations, effective labor unions, and higher wage and work standards.

Still, neo-imperialism carries risks. The achievement of de jure independence eventually fosters expectations of de facto independence. The forms of self-rule incite a desire for the fruits of self-rule. Sometimes a national leader emerges who is a patriot and reformer rather than a comprador collaborator. Therefore, the changeover from colonialism to neocolonialism is not without risks for the imperialists and represents a net gain for popular forces in the world.

30 THE FREE MARKET PARADISE LIBERATES COMMUNIST EUROPE

For decades we were told that the Cold War was a contest between freedom and communism, without any references to capitalism. But with the collapse of communism in Eastern Europe and the Soviet Union, U.S. leaders and news media began to intimate that there was something more on their agenda than just free elections for the former "captive nations"—namely free markets. Of what value was political democracy in the former communist countries, they seemed to be saying, if it allowed for the retention of an economy that was socialistic or even social democratic? So they publicly acknowledged that a goal of U.S. policy was to restore capitalism in the former communist nations.

The propaganda task was to treat capitalism as inseparable from democracy, while ignoring the many undemocratic capitalist regimes from Guatemala to Indonesia to Zaire. However, "capitalism" sounded, well, too capitalistic, so the preferred terms were "free market" and "market economy," labels that sound less capitalistic by appearing to include more of us than just the Fortune 500. Thus President Clinton announced before the United Nations on September 27, 1993: "Our overriding purpose is to expand and strengthen the world's community of *market-based* democracies."[4]

A few years earlier, in 1990, as the Soviet Union was preparing for its fatal plunge into the free-market paradise, Bruce Gelb, head of the United States Information Agency, told a reporter that the Soviets would benefit economically from U.S. business education because "the vipers, the bloodsuckers, the middlemen—that's what needs to be rehabilitated in the Soviet Union. That's what makes our kind of country click!"[5]

Today, the former communist countries and China are clicking away with vipers and bloodsuckers. Thousands of luxury cars have appeared on the streets of Moscow and Prague. Rents and real-estate prices have skyrocketed. Numerous stock exchanges have sprung up in China and Eastern Europe, sixteen in the former USSR alone. And a new and growing class of investors, speculators, and racketeers are wallowing in wealth.[6]

Greater opulence for the few has meant more poverty for the many. As one young female journalist in Russia put it: "Every time someone gets richer, I get poorer."[7] In Russia, the living standard of the average family has fallen almost by half since the market "reforms" took hold.[8] A report from Hungary makes the same point: "While the 'new rich' live in villas with a Mercedes parked in a garage, the number of poor people has been growing."[9]

Under the direction of Western policymakers, the free-market governments in Eastern Europe have eliminated price controls and subsidies for food, housing, transportation, clothing, and utilities. They have cut back on medical benefits and support for public education. They abolished job guarantees, public employment programs, and most benefits. They forbade workplace political activities by labor unions. They have been selling off publicly owned lands, factories, and news media at bargain prices to rich corporate investors. Numerous other industries have been simply shut down. The breakup of farm collectives and cooperatives and the reversion to private farming has caused a 40 percent decline in agricultural productivity in countries like Hungary and East Germany—where collective farming actually had performed as well and often better than the heavily subsidized private farming in the West.

The fundamental laws were changed from a public to private ownership system. There was a massive transfer of public capital into the coffers of private owners, and a sharp increase in crime, corruption, beggary, alcoholism, drug addiction, and prostitution; a dramatic drop in educational levels and literacy standards; and serious deterioration in health care and all other public services. In addition, there has been galloping inflation, and a dramatic rise in environmental devastation, spousal abuse, child abuse, and just about every other social ill.[10]

In countries like Russia and Hungary, as widely reported in the U.S. press, the suicide rate has climbed by 50 percent in a few years. Reductions in fuel service, brought about by rising prices and unpaid bills, have led to a growing number of deaths or serious illnesses among the poor and the elderly during the long winters. Medical personnel in public clinics are now grossly underpaid. Free health clinics are closing. More than ever, hospitals suffer from unsanitary conditions and shortages of disposable syringes, needles, vaccines, and modern equipment. Many hospitals now have no hot water, some no water at all.[11]

The deterioration of immunization programs and health standards has allowed polio to make a serious comeback, along with tuberculosis, cholera, diphtheria, dysentery, and sexually transmitted diseases. Drug addiction has risen sharply. "Russia's hospitals are struggling to treat increasing numbers of addicts with decreasing levels of funding."[12]

There has been a decline in nutritional levels and a sharp increase in stress and illness. Yet the number of visits to doctors has dropped by half because fees are so costly in the newly privatized health care systems. As a result, many illnesses go undetected until they become critical. Russian military officials describe the health of conscripts as "catastrophic." Within the armed forces, suicides and deaths from drug overdoses have risen dramatically.[13]

The overthrow of communism brought rising infant-mortality

and plummeting life-expectancy rates in Russia, Bulgaria, Hungary, Latvia, Moldavia, Romania, Ukraine, Mongolia, and East Germany. One-third of Russian men never live to sixty years of age. In 1992, Russia's birth rate fell below its death rate for the first time since World War II. In 1992 and 1993, East Germans buried two people for every baby born. The death rate rose nearly 20 percent for East German women in their late thirties, and nearly 30 percent for men of the same age.[14]

With the end of subsidized rents, homelessness has skyrocketed. The loss of resident permits deprives the homeless of medical care and other state benefits, such as they are. Dressed in rags and victimized by both mobsters and government militia, thousands of indigents die of cold and hunger on the streets of various cities. In Romania, thousands of homeless children live in sewers and train stations, sniffing glue to numb their hunger, begging and falling prey to various predators.[15]

In Mongolia, hundreds of homeless children live in the sewers of Ulaanbaatar. Before 1990, Mongolia was a prosperous nation that had benefited from Soviet and East European financial assistance and technical aid. Its industrial centers produced leather goods, woolen products, textiles, cement, meat, grain, and timber. "The communist era dramatically improved the quality of life of the people . . . achieving commendable levels of social development through state-sponsored social welfare measures," but free-market privatization and deindustrialization has brought unemployment, mass poverty, and widespread malnutrition to Mongolia.[16]

Unemployment rates have risen as high as 30 percent in countries that once knew full employment under communism. One Polish worker claims that the jobless are pretty much unemployable after age 40. Polish women say economic demise comes earlier for them, since to get a job, as one puts it, "you must be young, childless and have a big bosom."[17] Occupational safety is now almost nonexistent and workplace injuries and deaths have drastically increased. Workers now toil harder and longer for less, often in sweatshop conditions. Teachers, scientists, factory workers, and countless others struggle for months without pay as their employers run out of funds.[18]

Even in the few remaining countries in which communist governments retain ostensible control, such as China and Vietnam, the opening to private investment has contributed to a growing inequality. In China, there are workers who now put in twelve- to sixteen-hour days for subsistence pay, without regularly getting a day off. Those who protest against poor safety and health conditions risk being fired or jailed. The market reforms in China have also brought a return of child labor.[19] "I think this is what happens when you have private companies," says Ms. Peng, a young migrant who has doubts about the new China. "In private companies, you know, the workers don't have rights."[20]

Likewise, as socialist Vietnam opens itself to foreign investment and the free market, "gaps between rich and poor . . . have widened rapidly" and "the quality of education and health care for the poor has deteriorated."[21] Prosperity has come "only to a privileged few in Vietnam" leading to "an emerging class structure that is at odds with the country's professed egalitarian ideals."[22]

Throughout Eastern Europe, unions have been greatly weakened or broken. Sick leave, maternity leave, paid vacations, and other job benefits once taken for granted under communism have been cut or abolished. Worker sanitariums, vacation resorts, health clinics, sports and cultural centers, children's nurseries, daycare centers, and other features that made communist enterprises more than just workplaces, have nearly vanished. Rest homes once reserved for workers have been privatized and redone as casinos, night clubs, and restaurants for the nouveau riche.

One booming employment area—besides prostitution—is business security. Private police and private armies in Russia alone muster some 800,000 men. Another employer of choice for working-class youth is the immense and repressive state apparatus of secret police, surveillance units, and other state paramilitary security forces which are *"now more formidable than that of the Soviet period.* Today, this apparatus is numerically superior to the Armed Forces, better paid and better equipped."[23]

Real income has shrunk by as much as 30 to 40 percent in the ex-communist countries. In 1992 alone, Russia saw its consumer spending drop by 38 percent. (By comparison, during the Great Depression of the 1930s, consumer spending in the United States fell 21 percent over four years.) In both Poland and Bulgaria, an estimated 70 percent now live below or just above the poverty line. In Russia, it is 75 to 85 percent, with a third of the population barely subsisting in absolute economic desperation. In Hungary, which has received most of the Western investment to Eastern Europe, over one-third of the citizens live in abject poverty, and 70 percent of the men hold two or more jobs, working up to 14 hours a day, according to the Ministry of Labor.

After months of not getting paid, coal miners in far eastern Russia were beginning to starve. By August 1996, 10,000 of them had stopped working simply because they were too weak from hunger. With no coal being extracted, the region's power plants began to shut down, threatening an electrical blackout that would further harm the nation's Pacific-coastal industry and trade.[24]

Eastern Europeans are witnessing scenes "that are common-place enough in the West, but are still wrenching here: the old man rummaging through trash barrels for castaway items, the old woman picking through a box of bones at a meat market in search of one with enough gristle to make a thin soup."[25] With their savings and pensions swallowed up by inflation, elderly pensioners crowd the sidewalks of Moscow selling articles of their clothing and other pathetic wares, while enduring harassment by police and thugs.[26] A Russian senior citizen refers to "this poverty, which only a few have escaped" while some "have become wildly rich." [27]

As the people in these former communist countries are now discovering, the "free market" means freedom mostly for those who have money, and a drastic decline in living standards for most everyone else. A leading anti-Soviet academic, Richard Pipes of Harvard, uncomfortably reported in 2004 that, according to recent surveys, four out of five Russian respondents blame "the country's widespread poverty on an unjust economic system," and feel that the inequalities in wealth are "excessive and illegitimate"; 78 percent said that democracy is a façade for a state that is in the grip of rich and powerful cliques; 70 percent want to restrict "private economic activity," and 74 percent regret the demise of the USSR, believing that life was better under communism.[28]

No wonder the newly established "democracies" of Eastern Europe are making moves to repress communist organizations and activities. For example, in October 2006 the Czech government outlawed the Communist Youth Union (KSM). The youth group had been leading a well-organized campaign against the building of U.S. military bases on Czech soil. The campaign included a mass petition drive against the bases and for a public referendum. In the June election, the Communist Party's vice-president and parliament member was viciously beaten by unidentified thugs. Election ballots cast by communist voters were stolen. Around that time, government-sponsored T-shirts sporting the slogan "Fight for peace, Kill a Communist" were widely circulated, even being sold in Czech embassies around the world. The government justified the ban, arguing that the KSM program wants "to replace private ownership of the means of production with public ownership," a position that "is against the constitution and is incompatible with fundamental democratic principles."[29] Once again, the propagators of free-market capitalism equate it with democracy.

In 1986, when the Soviet Union and the other Eastern European communist countries were still in existence, I wrote:

> The U.S. media's encompassing negativity in regard to the Soviet Union might induce some of us to react with an unqualifiedly glowing view of that society. The truth is, in the USSR there exist serious problems of labor productivity, industrialization, urbanization, bureaucracy, corruption, and alcoholism. There are production and distribution bottlenecks, plan failures, consumer scarcities, criminal abuses of power, suppression of dissidents, and expressions of alienation among some persons in the population.[30]

Still I argued that, despite the well-publicized deficiencies, crimes, and injustices, there were positive features about existing communist systems that were worth preserving, such as the free medical care and human services; affordable food, fuel, transportation, and housing; universal literacy; gains in women's rights; free education to the highest level of one's ability; a guaranteed right to a job; free cultural and sporting events, and the like.

But to utter anything that might be halfway positive about existing communist countries has long been an unforgivable ideological sin in the eyes of many U.S. left intellectuals, whose greatest passion was—and still seems to be—anticommunism, a totalistic negative view that borrows heavily from the demonized images propagated by U.S. policymakers and mainstream media.

When the communist governments were overthrown, most such anticommunist left intellectuals enthusiastically welcomed it as a great leap forward, a liberation from what they saw as the Leninist aberration and Stalinist monstrosity. A normally verbose group, these intellectuals—some of them quite prominent and prolific—have had almost nothing to say about the post-communist free-market paradise of Eastern Europe and the former Soviet Union.

31 THE RATIONAL DESTRUCTION OF YUGOSLAVIA

In 1999 the White House, with other NATO countries in tandem, launched round-the-clock aerial attacks against Yugoslavia for seventy-eight days, dropping 20,000 tons of explosives, and killing upwards of three thousand women, children, and men. All this was done out of humanitarian concern for Albanians in Kosovo—or so we were told. Many of the liberals, progressives, and other leftists of various ideological leanings who *opposed* President George W. Bush's destruction of Iraq (rightly so) were the same people who *supported* President Bill Clinton's destruction of Yugoslavia. How strange that they would denounce a war against a dictator and torturer like Saddam Hussein yet support a war against a social democracy like Yugoslavia. Substantial numbers of liberals and other "leftists" were taken in, standing shoulder to shoulder with the White House, NATO, the CIA, the Pentagon, the IMF, and the mainstream media when it came to Yugoslavia.

In the span of a few months, Clinton bombed four countries: Sudan, Afghanistan, Iraq intermittently, and Yugoslavia massively. At the same time, the United States was involved in proxy wars in Angola, Mexico (Chiapas), Colombia, East Timor, and sundry other places. And of course U.S. forces continued to be deployed around the globe, with hundreds of overseas support bases—all in the name of peace, democracy, national security, and humanitarianism.

U.S. leaders have been markedly selective in their "humanitarian" interventions. They have made no moves against the Czech Republic for its mistreatment of the Roma ("gypsies"), or Britain for oppressing the Catholic minority in Northern Ireland, or Israel for its continual repression of Palestinians in the occupied territories, or Turkey for what was done to the Kurds, or Indonesia for the slaughter of over 200,000 East Timorese, or Guatemala to stop the systematic extermination of tens of thousands of Mayan villagers. U.S. leaders not only tolerated such atrocities but were often complicit with the perpetrators—who usually happened to be faithful client-state allies dedicated to helping Washington make the world safe for the Fortune 500. Why then did U.S. leaders suddenly develop such strong "humanitarian" concerns regarding Yugoslavia?

Yugoslavia was built on an idea, namely that the Southern Slavs would not remain weak and divided peoples, squabbling among themselves and easy prey to outside imperial interests. Together they would compose a substantial territory capable of its own self-development. Indeed after World War II, socialist Yugoslavia became a viable nation and something of an economic success. For many years it had a vigorous growth rate, a decent standard of living, free medical care and education, a guaranteed right to a job, one-month vacation with pay, a literacy rate of over 90 percent, and a high life expectancy. Yugoslavia offered its multi-ethnic citizenry affordable public transportation, housing, and utilities, with a not-for-profit economy that was almost entirely publicly owned, although there was a substantial private sector that included some Western corporations.

Whether Yugoslavia thereby qualified as *socialist* in the eyes of all left intellectuals is not the question. It was far too socialistic for U.S. policymakers, not the kind of country that free-market global capitalism would normally tolerate. Still, it had been allowed to exist for 45 years, useful as a nonaligned buffer to the Warsaw Pact nations. But once the Soviet Union and the other communist regimes were dissolved, there was no longer any reason to have to tolerate Yugoslavia.

The dismemberment policy was initiated by Germany, the United States, and other Western powers. Yugoslavia was the one country in Eastern Europe that would not voluntarily abolish its public sector and install a free-market system, the one country that had no interest in joining NATO or the European Union. The U.S. goal was to transform the Yugoslav nation into a cluster of weak, dependent right-wing polities whose natural resources would be completely accessible to multinational corporate exploitation, including the enormous mineral wealth in Kosovo; with an impoverished population constituting a cheap labor pool that would help depress wages in Europe and elsewhere; and whose petroleum, engineering, mining, fertilizer, pharmaceutical, construction, and automobile industries would be dismantled or destroyed outright, thereby offering no further competition with existing Western producers.

U.S. rulers also wanted to abolish Yugoslavia's public-sector services and social programs—just as they want to abolish *our* public-sector services and social programs. The ultimate goal was the privatization and Third Worldization of Yugoslavia, as it is the privatization and Third Worldization of the entire world, including the United States itself. Much of the Yugoslav economy remained in the not-for-profit public sector, including the Trepca mining complex in Kosovo, described in the *New York Times* as "war's glittering prize . . . the most valuable piece of real estate in the Balkans . . . worth at least $5 billion" in rich deposits of coal, lead, zinc, cadmium, gold, and silver.[31]

That U.S. leaders planned to dismember Yugoslavia is not a matter of speculation but of public record. As early as 1984, the Reagan administration issued U.S. National Security Decision Directive 133: "United States Policy towards Yugoslavia," labeled "secret sensitive." It followed closely the objectives laid out in an earlier directive aimed at Eastern Europe, one that called for a "quiet revolution" to overthrow Communist governments while "reintegrating the countries of Eastern Europe into the orbit of the World market."[32]

In November 1990 the Bush Sr. administration managed to persuade Congress to pass the 1991 Foreign Operations Appropriations Act, which provided aid only to the separate republics, not to the Belgrade government, and only to those forces whom Washington defined as "democratic," that is, free-market separatist parties.

In 1992 another blow was delivered. A freeze was imposed on all trade to and from Yugoslavia, bringing recession, hyperinflation, greater unemployment, and the virtual collapse of the health care system. At the same time, the IMF and other foreign creditors mandated that all socially owned firms and worker-managed production units be transformed into private capitalist enterprises.[33]

In February 1999, U.S. officials at Rambouillet made clear their dedication to capitalist restoration. The Rambouillet agreement—actually an ultimatum imposed by the Clinton White House upon what remained of Yugoslavia (Serbia and Montenegro)—declared: "The economy of Kosovo shall function in accordance with free market principles." There was to be no restriction on the movement of "goods, services, and capital to Kosovo," and all matters of trade, investment and corporate ownership were to be left to the private market.[34]

Another goal of U.S. policy was media monopoly and ideological control. In 1997, in what remained of Serbian Bosnia, the last radio station critical of NATO policy was forcibly shut down by NATO "peacekeepers" in order to advance democracy by "bringing about responsible news coverage."[35] Likewise, NATO bombings destroyed the two government TV channels and dozens of local radio and television stations, and killed sixteen newspeople in one instance. By the summer of 1999 the only TV one could see in Belgrade, when I visited that city, was German television, CNN and various U.S. programs. Yugoslavia's sin was not that it had a dictatorial media but that the publicly owned portion of its broadcasting system deviated from the Western media ideological monopoly that blanketed most of the world.

One of the great deceptions, notes Joan Phillips, is that "those who are mainly responsible for the bloodshed in Yugoslavia—not the Serbs, Croats or Muslims, but the Western powers—are depicted as saviors."[36]

In Croatia, Washington's choice separatist leader was Franjo Tudjman, who claimed in a book he authored in 1989, that "the establishment of Hitler's new European order can be justified by the need to be rid of the Jews," and that "only" 900,000 Jews, not six million, were killed in the Holocaust. Tudjman's government adopted the fascist Ustasha checkered flag and anthem.[37] Tudjman presided over the forced evacuation of over a half-million Serbs from Croatia between 1991 and 1995, replete with rapes and summary executions.[38] This included the 200,000 from Krajina in 1995, whose expulsion was propelled in part by attacks from NATO war planes and missiles. Tight controls were imposed on Croatian media, and anyone who criticized President Tudjman's reign risked incarceration. Yet the White House hailed Croatia as a new democracy.

In Bosnia, U.S. leaders supported the Muslim fundamentalist Alija Izetbegovic, an active Nazi in his youth, who called for strict religious control over the media and wanted to establish an Islamic Bosnian republic. Bosnia was put under IMF and NATO regency. It was not permitted to develop its own internal resources, nor allowed to extend credit or self-finance through an independent monetary system. Its state-owned assets, including energy, water, telecommunications, media and transportation, were sold off to private firms at giveaway prices.

In early 1999, the democratically elected president of Republika Srpska, the Serb mini-state in Bosnia, who had defeated the West's chosen candidate, was removed by NATO troops because he proved less than fully cooperative with NATO's "high representative" in Bosnia. The latter retained authority to impose his own solutions and remove elected officials who proved in any way uncooperative.[39]

None other than Charles Boyd, former deputy commander of the U.S. European command, commented in 1994: "Much of what the Croatians call 'the occupied territories' is land that has been held by Serbs for more that three centuries. The same is true of most Serb land in Bosnia. . . . In short the Serbs were not trying to conquer new territory, but merely to hold onto what was already theirs." While U.S. leaders claimed they wanted peace, Boyd concluded, they encouraged a deepening of the war.[40]

Kosovo presented a similar pattern. U.S. rulers aided separatist forces such as the self-styled Kosovo Liberation Army (KLA), previously considered a terrorist organization by Washington. The KLA was a longtime player in the heroin trade that reaches from Afghanistan to Switzerland, Austria, Belgium, Germany, Hungary, the Czech Republic, Norway, and Sweden.[41] KLA leaders had no social program other than the stated goal of cleansing Kosovo of all non-Albanians, a campaign that was pursued for decades. Between 1945 and 1998, the non-Albanian Kosovar population of Serbs, Roma, Turks, Gorani (Muslim Slavs), Montenegrins, and several other ethnic groups—subjected to systematic intimidation and expulsion—shrank from some 60 percent to about 20 percent. Meanwhile, the Albanian population grew from 40 to 80 percent (not the 90 percent repeatedly reported in the press), benefiting from a higher birth rate and a heavy influx of immigrants from Albania.

In 1987, the *New York Times* reported:

Ethnic Albanians in the [Kosovo provincial] government have manipulated public funds and regulations to take over land belonging to Serbs. . . . Slavic Orthodox churches have been attacked, and flags have been torn down. Wells have been poisoned and crops burned. Slavic boys have been knifed, and some young ethnic Albanians have been told by their elders to rape Serbian girls. . . . As the Slavs flee the protracted violence, Kosovo is becoming what ethnic Albanian nationalists have been demanding for years . . . an "ethnically pure" Albanian region. . . .[42]

While the Serbs were repeatedly charged with ethnic cleansing, they themselves have been the victims of such cleansing in Kosovo. Serbia itself is now the only multi-ethnic society left in the former Yugoslavia, with some twenty-six nationality groups, including thousands of Albanians who have lived in and around Belgrade for many years.

The Serbs were the designated enemy probably because they presented the biggest obstacle to the breakup of Yugoslavia. They were the largest ethnic group in the federation, the one most committed to keeping the country together, and with a working class that was most firmly socialist. The U.S. public was bombarded with stories demonizing the Serbian people and their elected leaders. The Serbs were accused of massacres, mass rapes, and even genocide. Yugoslavia's democratically elected president, Slobodan Milosevíç, was portrayed as a bloodthirsty tyrant and "Serbian nationalist." In fact, Milosevíç and his wife, Mira Markovíç, herself an active player in Yugoslav national politics, had long polemicized *against* nationalistic supremacy of any stripe (including Serbian nationalism), and *for* multi-ethnic unity.[43]

All sides in the secessionist wars committed atrocities, but the reporting seemed consistently one-sided. Incidents of Croat and Muslim war crimes against the Serbs rarely made it into the U.S. press, and when they did they were accorded only passing mention.[44] Meanwhile Serb atrocities were played up and sometimes even fabricated. John Ranz, chair of Survivors of the Buchenwald Concentration Camp, USA, asked where the TV cameras were when hundreds of Serbs were slaughtered by Muslims near Srebrenica.[45] The official line, faithfully parroted by many U.S. liberals and elements of the sectarian left, was that Bosnian Serb forces committed all the atrocities at Srebrenica.

Are we to trust U.S. leaders and the corporate-owned news media when they dish out atrocity stories? Recall the story about the five-hundred premature babies whom Iraqi soldiers laughingly ripped from incubators in Kuwait, a tale repeated and believed throughout the Gulf war of 1990-91, only to be exposed as a total fabrication years later. During the Bosnian war in 1993, the Serbs were accused of pursuing an official policy of rape. "Go forth and rape," a Bosnian Serb commander supposedly publicly announced to his troops. The source of that story never could be traced. The commander's name and the troop units to whom he spoke were never produced. The time and place of this supposed happening was never determined. Even the *New York Times* belatedly ran a tiny retraction, coyly allowing that "the existence of 'a systematic rape policy' by the Serbs remains to be proved."[46]

The "mass rape" theme was resuscitated in 1999 to justify the continued NATO attacks on Yugoslavia. A headline in the *San Francisco Examiner* boomed: "SERB TACTIC IS ORGANIZED RAPE, KOSOVO REFUGEES SAY."[47] No evidence or testimony was given in the story itself to support the charge of organized rape. Buried in the nineteenth paragraph, we read that reports gathered by an official mission of the Organization for Security and Cooperation (OSCE) found no such organized rape policy. The actual number of rapes were in the dozens, "and not many dozens," according to the OSCE spokesperson. A few dozen rapes is a few dozen too many, but can it serve as a justification for aerial assaults upon civilian populations and the destruction of a nation?

The Serbs were blamed for the Sarajevo market massacre. According to the report leaked out on French TV, however, Western intelligence knew that it was Muslim operatives who had bombed Bosnian civilians in the marketplace in order to induce NATO involvement. Even international negotiator David Owen, who worked with Cyrus Vance, admitted in his memoir that the NATO powers knew all along that it was a Muslim bomb.[48] On one occasion the *New York Times* ran a photo purporting to be of Croats grieving over Serbian atrocities when in fact the murders had been committed by Bosnian Muslims. The *Times* printed an obscure retraction the following week.[49]

Up until the NATO bombings began in March 1999, the conflict in Kosovo had taken some 2000 lives from both sides, according to Kosovo Albanian sources. Yugoslavian sources put the figure at about 800. Such casualties reveal a civil war, not mass genocide. Belgrade was condemned for the forced-expulsion policy of Albanians from Kosovo. But such expulsions began in discernible numbers only *after* the NATO aerial attacks commenced. Tens of thousands fled Kosovo because it was being mercilessly bombed by NATO, or because it was the scene of sustained ground fighting between Yugoslav forces and the KLA, or because they wanted to avoid conscription into the war or were just afraid and hungry. Asked by a news crew if she had been forced out by Serb police, an Albanian woman responded, "There

were no Serbs. We were frightened of the [NATO] bombs."[50]
Thus the refugee tide caused by the bombing was used by U.S.
officials as a justification for the bombing.

British journalist Audrey Gillan interviewed Kosovo refugees
about atrocities and found an impressive lack of evidence or cred-
ible specifics. One woman caught him glancing at the watch on
her wrist, while her husband told him how all the women had
been robbed of their jewelry and other possessions. A spokesperson for the U.N. High Commissioner for Refugees talked of mass
rapes and what sounded like hundreds of killings in three villages,
but when Gillan pressed him for more precise information, he
reduced it drastically to five or six teenage rape victims. Even in
regard to those six, he admitted that he had not spoken to any
witnesses, and that "we have no way of verifying these reports."[51]
Officials said there were refugees arriving who talked of sixty or
more being killed in one village and fifty in another, but Gillan
"could not find one eye-witness who actually saw these things
happening." Yet every day western journalists reported "hundreds" of rapes and murders. Sometimes they noted in passing
that the reports had yet to be substantiated. If so, why were such
unsubstantiated stories given such prominent play?

After NATO forces occupied Kosovo, the stories about mass
atrocities continued fortissimo. The *Washington Post* reported
that 350 ethnic Albanians "might be buried in mass graves."[52]
But mass graves of Albanian victims failed to materialize. The
few sites actually unearthed offered up as many as a dozen bodies
or sometimes twice that number, but with no clear evidence
regarding causes of death or even the nationality of victims. In
some cases there was reason to believe the victims might be
Serbs.[53]

On 19 April 1999, while the NATO bombings of Yugoslavia were in full swing, the State Department announced that up to 500,000 Kosovo Albanians were missing and feared dead. A few weeks later the Defense Department announced that 100,000 military-aged ethnic Albanian men had vanished and might have been killed by the Serbs.[54] Such widely varying but staggering figures from official sources went unchallenged by the media and by the many liberals and leftists who supported the "humanitarian rescue operation."

On June 17, just before the end of the war, British Foreign Office Minister Geoff Hoon said that "in more than 100 massacres" some 10,000 ethnic Albanians had been killed (down from the 500,000 and 100,000 bandied about by U.S. officials). A day or two after the bombings stopped, the Associated Press and other news agencies, echoing Hoon, reported that 10,000 Albanians had been killed by the Serbs. No one explained how this figure was arrived at. No war sites had yet been investigated and NATO forces had barely begun to roll into Kosovo.

On August 2, Bernard Kouchner, the United Nations' chief administrator in Kosovo and premier disinformationist, asserted that about 11,000 bodies had been found in common graves throughout Kosovo. He cited as his source the International Criminal Tribunal for the Former Republic of Yugoslavia (ICTY), the court that was set up by the Western powers to try Miloseviç et al. But the ICTY denied providing any such information. To this day, Kouchner has not explained how he came up with his numbers.[55]

As with the Croatian and Bosnian conflicts, so with Kosovo: unsubstantiated references to "mass graves," each purportedly filled with hundreds or even thousands of victims, were published in daily media reports for weeks on end. When it came down to hard evidence, the mass graves seemed to disappear. In mid-June 1999, the FBI sent a team to investigate two of the sites listed in the war-crimes indictment against Slobodan Miloseviç, one purportedly containing six victims and the other twenty. The team lugged 107,000 pounds of equipment into Kosovo to handle what was hailed as the "largest crime scene in the FBI's forensic history," but it came up with not a single report about mass graves. After two weeks the FBI team returned home empty-handed.[56]

Likewise a Spanish forensic team was told to prepare for at least 2,000 autopsies, but found only 187 bodies, usually buried in individual graves, and showing no signs of massacre or torture. Most seemed to have been killed by mortar shells and firearms. One Spanish forensic expert, Emilio Pérez Pujol, acknowledged that his team found not one mass grave. He dismissed the widely publicized references about mass graves as being part of the "machinery of war propaganda." All across Kosovo the search for killing fields continued, but bodies failed to materialize in substantial numbers—or any numbers at all.[57]

The worst incident of mass atrocities ascribed to Yugoslavian leader Slobodan Miloseviç allegedly occurred at the Trepca mine. As reported by U.S. and NATO officials, the Serbs threw a thousand or more bodies down the shafts or disposed of them in the mine's vats of hydrochloric acid. In October 1999, the ICTY released the findings of Western forensic teams investigating Trepca. Not one body was found in the mine shafts, not a shoe or belt buckle, or any evidence that the vats had ever been used to dissolve human remains.[58]

By late autumn of 1999, the media hype about mass graves had fizzled noticeably. The many sites unearthed, considered to be the most notorious, offered up a few hundred bodies altogether, not the tens of thousands or hundreds of thousands previously trumpeted, and with no evidence of torture or mass execution. In many cases, there was no reliable evidence regarding the nationality of victims. No mass killings means that the ICTY war crimes indictment of Miloseviç "becomes highly questionable," notes Richard Gwyn. "Even more questionable is the West's continued punishment of the Serbs."[59]

No doubt people in Kosovo were killed by NATO bombs and by the extensive land war between Yugoslav and KLA forces. Some of the dead may have expired from natural causes, as would happen in any large population over time, especially one under such stress. No doubt there also were grudge killings and summary executions as in any war, but not on a scale that would warrant the label of "genocide." The German Foreign Office privately denied there was any evidence that genocide or ethnic cleansing was ever a component of Yugoslav policy: "Even in Kosovo, an explicit political persecution linked to Albanian ethnicity is not verifiable. . . . The actions of the [Yugoslav] security forces [were] not directed against the Kosovo-Albanians as an ethnically defined group, but against the military opponent and its actual or alleged supporters."[60] Still, Miloseviç was indicted as a war criminal, charged with the forced expulsion of Kosovar Albanians, and with summary mass executions.

We repeatedly have seen how "rogue nations" are targeted. The process is predictably transparent and not very original. First and foremost, the leaders are demonized. Qaddafi of Libya was a "Hitlerite megalomaniac" and a "madman." Noriega of Panama was a "a swamp rat," "one of the world's worst drug thieves and scums," and "a Hitler admirer." Saddam Hussein of Iraq was "the Butcher of Baghdad," a "madman," and "worse than Hitler." Demonization of the leader then justifies U.S.-led sanctions and military attacks upon the leader's country and people. What such leaders really had in common was that each was charting a somewhat independent course of self-development not in compliance with the dictates of the global free market.[61]

In keeping with this practice, Yugoslav president Slobodan Miloseviç was described by Bill Clinton as "a new Hitler." Earlier he had not be considered so. Initially, Western officials, viewing the ex-banker as a bourgeois Serbian nationalist who might hasten the break-up of the federation, hailed him as a "charismatic personality." Only later, when they saw him as an obstacle rather than a tool, did they begin to depict him as the demon who "started all four wars." This was too much, even for the managing editor of the U.S. establishment journal *Foreign Affairs*, Fareed Zakaria. He noted in the *New York Times* that Miloseviç who rules "an impoverished country that has not attacked its neighbors—is no Adolf Hitler. He is not even Saddam Hussein."[62]

Miloseviç was elected as president of Yugoslavia in a contest that foreign observers said had relatively few violations. As of the end of 1999, he presided over a coalition government that included four parties, while opposition parties and publications openly denounced him and demonstrated against his government. These facts went almost unnoticed in the U.S. news media. To reject the demonized image of Miloseviç and of the Serbian people is not to idealize them or claim that Serb forces were faultless. It is merely to challenge the notions fabricated to justify NATO's aggression against Yugoslavia.

While professing to having been discomforted by the aerial destruction of Yugoslavia, many liberals and leftists were convinced that "this time" the U.S. national security state was really fighting the good fight. "Yes, the bombings don't work. The bombings are stupid!" they said at the time, "but we have to do *some*thing." In fact, the bombings were other than stupid: they were profoundly immoral. And in fact they did work; they destroyed much of what was left of Yugoslavia, turning it into a privatized, deindustrialized, recolonized, impoverished cluster of mini-republics, submissive wards of the free-market global empire. For U.S. foreign policy it was another smashing success.

32 TO KILL IRAQ

In October 2002, after a full-dress debate in the House and Senate, the U.S. Congress fell into line behind almost-elected president Bush Jr., giving him a mandate to launch a massive assault against Iraq, a nation already battered by twelve years of bombings and sanctions. The debate in Congress was marked by its usual evasions. Even many of the members who voted against the president's resolution did so on the narrowest procedural grounds, taking pains to tell how they too detested Iraqi dictator Saddam Hussein, how they agreed with the president on many points, how something needed to be done about Iraq and about fighting terrorism, but not quite in this way. Few members dared to question the imperial right of U.S. rulers to decide which nations shall live and which shall die.

PRETEXTS FOR WAR

Bush Jr. and other members of his administration gave varied reasons to justify the invasion of Iraq. They claimed it was to insure the well-being of the Middle East and the security of the United States itself, for Iraq was developing weapons of mass destruction, including nuclear missiles. In fact, right up to the U.S. invasion in March 2003, U.N. inspection teams maintained that Iraq had no such nuclear capability and actually had been in compliance with yearly disarmament inspections.

If the Iraqis had weapons of mass destruction, why didn't they use them against the invader? Why weren't they ever found by the occupying forces? Such questions were never answered. Iraq once did have factories that produced chemical and bacteriological weapons, but it was the United States that had supplied these materials to Baghdad. The quip circulating at the time was: "We know Saddam has weapons of mass destruction—we have the receipts." But according to United Nations inspection reports, Iraq's chemical warfare capability had been dismantled.

Still the White House kept talking about that country's dangerous "potential." Through September and October of 2002, the White House made it clear that Iraq would be attacked if it had weapons of mass destruction. In November 2002, Bush Jr. announced he would attack if Saddam *denied* that he had weapons of mass destruction. In sum, if the Iraqis admitted to having such weapons, they were to be invaded. If they denied having them, they still would be invaded—whether they had them or not.

Bush Jr. also charged Iraq with having close links with al-Qaeda and allowing terrorists to operate within its territory. But U.S. intelligence sources themselves let it be known that the Baghdad government was not connected to Islamic terrorist organizations. When a House committee in closed sessions asked administration officials whether they had information of an imminent terrorist threat from Saddam against the United States, they stated unequivocally that they had no such evidence.[63]

Bush and company seized upon another pretext for war: Saddam had committed war crimes and acts of aggression, including the war against Iran and the gassing of Kurds at Halabja. The Pentagon's own study, however, found that the massacre of Kurds was committed by the Iranians, not the Iraqis.[64] Another seldom-mentioned fact: U.S. leaders gave Iraq encouragement and military support in its war against Iran. If war crimes and wars of aggression are the issue, it might be recalled that U.S. leaders themselves had launched invasions of Grenada and Panama and sponsored wars of attrition against civilian targets in Mozambique, Angola, Nicaragua, El Salvador, Guatemala, Yugoslavia, and scores of other places, leaving hundreds of thousands dead. No communist state or "rogue nation" had a comparable record of military aggression.

With the various pretexts for war ringing hollow, the Bush administration resorted to the final indictment: Saddam was a dictator; the Iraqis needed democracy. The United States stood for democracy and human rights. Ergo, U.S. leaders were obliged to use force and violence to effect regime change and bring the blessings of democracy to Iraq. Again, questions leaped to the fore: There was no denying that Saddam was a dictator, but how did he and his cohorts come to power? Wasn't Saddam's conservative wing of the Baath party backed by the CIA? Weren't they enlisted to destroy the popular revolution, torturing and murdering every democrat, progressive, reformer, communist, and constitutionalist they could get hold of, including the left wing of their own Ba'ath party? During the years he was committing his worst atrocities, Saddam Hussein was Washington's poster boy. All this the U.S. press let slip down the memory hole.

A former U.S. Army special forces commando, Kevin Tillman, who served in Iraq and whose brother, famed NFL football star Pat Tillman, was killed in Afghanistan, summed up his frustration:

> Somehow we were sent to invade a nation because it was a direct threat to the American people, or to the world, or it harbored terrorists, or it was involved in the 9/11 attacks, or it received weapons-grade uranium from Niger, or it had mobile bio-weapons labs, or it had WMD, or it had a need to be liberated, or we needed to establish a democracy, or to stop an insurgency, or to stop a civil war we created that can't be called a civil war even though it is. Something like that.[65]

When policymakers keep providing new and different explanations to justify a particular action, they most likely are lying. When people keep changing their story, you can be fairly sure it's a story. Having seen that the reasons given by the White House to justify war were highly questionable, some observers incorrectly concluded that the administration had no sensible reasons for its policy, and was simply unwilling to admit its befuddlement. But just because the Bush people were trying to mislead and confuse the public does not perforce mean they themselves were confused. In fact there were some tempting and compelling reasons for war, kept from the American public because they reveal too much about what U.S. rulers are doing in the world. Consider the following.

GLOBAL POLITICO-ECONOMIC SUPREMACY

As enunciated by leading members of the Bush administration, a central goal is to advance U.S. global supremacy.[66] The objective is not just power for its own sake but power to insure plutocratic control of the planet, to privatize and deregulate the economies of every nation in the world, to foist upon people everywhere—including North America—the blessings of an untrammeled free-market globalism.

To achieve that goal, the emergence of any potentially competing superpower or, for that matter, any competing *regional* power must be prevented. Iraq is a case in point. In 1958 a popular revolution in Iraq kicked out the oil companies. Ten years later, the rightwing of the Baath party took power, with Saddam Hussein serving as point man for the CIA. His assignment was to undo the democratic revolution, which he did with vicious repression. But then, instead of acting as a comprador collaborator to Western investors in the style of Nicaragua's Somoza, Chile's Pinochet, Peru's Fujimora, and numerous others, Saddam committed economic nationalism, pursuing policies of public ownership and development, even retaining some of the social programs of the earlier progressive government. By 1990, Iraq had the highest standard of living in the Middle East.

A major goal of the U.S. invasion was to bring Iraq firmly within the free-market sphere, as a client state with a puppet government open to Western investors on terms entirely favorable to the investors. Things did not go quite that way. The invasion and occupation destroyed Saddam's secular military regime. The nationalist Baathist elements were systematically eradicated in assassination attacks, some of which were directed by the Ministry of Interior under CIA auspices.[67] Meanwhile the most retrograde sectarian elements in the region were incited. Sectarian terrorism, which had not been a problem before the invaders arrived, became a growth industry afterward.

PRIVATIZATION AND MONETARY CONTROL

Soon after the overthrow of the Soviet Union, U.S. rulers decided that Third World development no longer needed to be tolerated. The last thing the plutocrats in Washington wanted in the Middle East or any other region was independent, self-developing nations that controlled their own labor, capital, natural resources, and markets. The Iraq economy under Saddam was entirely state-owned, including the media. Secretary of Defense Donald Rumsfeld vented his alarm about Iraq's "Stalinist economy." Months before the March 2003 invasion, the White House had put together a committee whose purpose was to supervise the privatization and deregulation of the Iraqi economy.

In the subsequent years of U.S. occupation, the Iraqis may not have received much electricity, clean water, or human services but one "reform" was delivered to them in abundance: privatization. Just about every major component of the Iraqi economy was either destroyed, shut down, or privatized at easy prices. Poverty and underemployment climbed precipitously, so too the Iraqi national debt as international loans were floated in order to help the Iraqis pay for their own victimization.

The intervention also undid another act of troublesome independence. In October 2000, less than half a year before the invasion, Saddam Hussein dumped the U.S. dollar ("the currency of the enemy") and made the euro the reserve currency for his oil trade. Shortly after that, Iraq converted its $10 billion reserve fund at the United Nations to euros. Instead of buying up U.S. currency to keep it from collapsing, Saddam was now cashing in his dollars. For an oil-rich country to do that, perhaps inducing other OPEC countries to follow suit, could have had a shattering effect on U.S. currency markets. Saddam's ruling clique had to be replaced with a pliant puppet government that would revert to a dollar standard—as indeed happened. According to some critics, this was a central consideration behind the U.S. invasion and occupation.[68]

NATURAL RESOURCE GRAB

Another reason for targeting Iraq can be summed up in one word: oil. As of late 2002 Saddam had offered exploratory concessions to France, China, Russia, Brazil, Italy, and Malaysia. But with the U.S. takeover and a new puppet regime in place, all such agreements were pretty much forgotten. The Bush Jr. administration is composed in part of oilmen who are both sorely tempted and threatened by Iraq's oil reserve, one of the largest in the world. With 113 billion barrels of quality crude at $55 a barrel, Iraq's supply comes to over $6 trillion dollars, the biggest resource grab in the history of the world.

During the late 1990s, because of the slumping price of crude, U.S. leaders were interested in keeping Iraqi oil off the market. As reported in the *London Financial Times*, oil prices fell sharply because Iraq's agreement with the United Nations would allow Baghdad to sell oil on the world market in larger volumes "competing for market shares."[69] The *San Francisco Chronicle* headlined its story in no uncertain terms: "IRAQ'S OIL POSES THREAT TO THE WEST." In fact, Iraqi crude posed no threat to "the West," only to Western oil investors. If Iraq were able to reenter the international oil market, the *Chronicle* reported, "it would devalue British North Sea oil, undermine American oil production and—much more important—it would destroy the huge profits which the United States [read U.S. oil companies] stands to gain from its massive investment in Caucasian oil production, especially in Azerbajian."[70] Direct control of Iraqi oil was the surest way to keep it off the world market when the price was not right, and the surest way to profit from its eventual sale.[71]

WAR PROFITEERING

The aggression against Iraq was extremely good for the powerful military-industrial contractors and their many subcontractors. Billions of dollars in no-bid contracts resulted in astronomical profits for Halliburton, Bechtel, and some one hundred other companies, while producing paltry results for the Iraqi people. Most of the sewers remained unconnected, the utilities dysfunctional, and water supplies chancy or nonexistent. For the big companies, however, the combination of brazen corruption and lack of oversight made Iraq the place to be. As much as one-third to one-half of the immense funds allocated by Congress remained unaccounted for. It could not get any better than that for those feeding at the trough.

ISRAEL FIRST

The neoconservative officials in the Bush Jr. administration—Paul Wolfowitz, Douglas Feith, Elliot Abrams, Robert Kagan, Lewis Libby, Abram Shulsky, and others—were strong proponents of a militaristic and expansionist strain of Zionism linked closely to the right-wing Likud Party of Israel. With impressive cohesion these "neocons" played a determinant role in shaping U.S. Middle East policy.[72] In the early 1980s Wolfowitz and Feith were charged with passing classified documents to Israel. Instead of being charged with espionage, Feith temporarily lost his security clearance and Wolfowitz was untouched. The two continued to enjoy ascendant careers, becoming second and third in command at the Pentagon under Donald Rumsfeld.

For these right-wing Zionists, the war against Iraq was part of a larger campaign to serve the greater good of Israel. Saddam Hussein was Israel's most consistent adversary in the Middle East, providing much political support to the Palestinian resistance. The neocons had been pushing for war with Iraq well before 9/11, assisted by the well-financed and powerful Israeli lobby, as well as by prominent members of Congress from both parties who obligingly treated U.S. and Israeli interests in the Middle East as inseparable. The Zionist neocons provided alarming reports about the threat to the United States posed by Saddam because of his weapons of mass destruction. At that same time, reports by both the CIA and the Mossad (Israeli intelligence) registered strong skepticism about the existence of such weapons in Iraq.[73]

The neocon goal has been Israeli expansion into all Palestinian territories and the emergence of Israel as the unchallengeable, perfectly secure, supreme power in the region. This could best be accomplished by undoing the economies of pro-Palestinian states including Syria, Iran, Libya, Lebanon, and even Saudi Arabia. A most important step in that direction was the destruction of Iraq as a nation, including its military, civil service, police, universities, hospitals, utilities, professional class, and entire infrastructure, an Iraq torn with sectarian strife and left in shambles.[74]

DOMESTIC POLITICAL GAINS

As of 10 September 2001, Bush Jr.'s approval ratings were sagging woefully. The stock market was down, unemployment was up, wages remained flat, and a recession showed no sign of easing. But the next day's attacks on the World Trade Center and the Pentagon, swiftly followed by the newly trumpeted war against terrorism and the massive bombing and invasion of Afghanistan, sent Bush's approval ratings soaring.

Then came the corporate scandals of 2002. By July, both President Bush Jr. and Vice-President Cheney were implicated in fraudulent accounting practices with Harken and Halliburton respectively. The companies claimed false profits to pump up stock values, followed by heavy insider trading, selling at great profit (by Bush, Cheney and others) just before the stock was revealed to be nearly worthless and collapsed in price. By October 2002, the impending war against Iraq blew this whole issue out of the news. Daddy Bush had done the same thing in 1990–1991, sending the savings and loan scandal into media limbo by waging war against that very same country, thus keeping at least two of his sons from criminal prosecution.

Pegged as the party of corporate favoritism and corruption, the GOP again emerged as the party of strong patriotic leadership, fearlessly guiding America through perilous straits. Some of our compatriots, who are usually cynical about politicians in day-to-day affairs, display an almost childlike trust and knee-jerk faith when these same politicians trumpet a need to defend our "national security" against some alien threat, real or imagined. Many rallied around the flag, draped as it was around the president.

All through 2005–2006 Bush Jr. repeatedly intoned, "We are at war," inviting us thereby to suspend critical judgment and fall in line. In a speech before the U.S. Naval Academy's graduating class in 2005, he pointed enthusiastically to the brighter side of bloodletting: "Revolutionary advances in technology are transforming war in our favor. . . . put[ting] unprecedented agility, speed, precision, and power in your hands. . . . We can now strike our enemies with greater effectiveness, at greater range, with fewer civilian casualties. In this new era of warfare we can target a regime, not a nation."[75] Something to look forward to.

SUPPRESSING DEMOCRACY AT HOME

The statist psychology fostered by perpetual war makes democratic dissent difficult if not "unpatriotic" and provides an excuse to circumscribe our civil liberties, such as they are. Under newly enacted repressive legislation almost any critical effort against existing policy can be defined as "giving aid and comfort to terrorism." The Military Commissions Act of 2006 grants the president the power to incarcerate anyone at anytime without any accountability, a power that is dictatorial. Even the normally staid *New York Times* described the act as "a tyrannical law that will be ranked with the low points in American democracy, our generation's version of the Alien and Sedition Acts."[76]

Political democracy has historically been a weapon used by the people to defend themselves against the abuses of wealth. So it was in the ancient Greek and Roman republics and so it remains to this day. Consequently, the plutocrats wage war not only against the public sector and against the people's standard of living, but also against the very democratic rights that the populace utilizes to defend its well-being.

Some of the liberal cognoscenti are never happier than when, with patronizing smiles, they can dilate on the stupidity of Bush Jr. What I have tried to show is that Bush has been neither retarded nor misdirected. To be sure, his invasion of Iraq sank into an unanticipated insurrectionary quagmire not long after he announced "victory" was at hand. At the operational level his administration made gross miscalculations, yet his policy was anchored in some real material interests of much concern to him and his fellow plutocrats. On the eve of war, the White House was populated not by fools and bunglers but by liars and manipulators.

33 GOOD THINGS HAPPENING IN VENEZUELA

Even before I arrived in Venezuela for a recent visit, I encountered the great class divide that besets that country. On my connecting flight from Miami to Caracas, I found myself seated next to an attractive, exquisitely dressed Venezuelan woman. Judging from her prosperous aspect, I anticipated that she would take the first opportunity to hold forth against President Hugo Chávez. Unfortunately, I was right.

Our conversation moved along famously until we got to the political struggle going on in Venezuela. "Chávez," she hissed, "is terrible, terrible." He is "a liar"; he "fools the people" and is "ruining the country." She herself owned an upscale women's fashion company with links to prominent firms in the United States. When I asked how Chávez had hurt her business, she said, "Not at all." But many other businesses, she quickly added, have been irreparably damaged as has the whole economy. She went on denouncing Chávez in sweeping terms, warning me of the national disaster to come if this demon continued to have his way.

Other critics I encountered in Venezuela shared this same mode of attack: weak on specifics but strong in venom, voiced with all the ferocity of those who fear that their birthright (that is, their class advantage) was under siege because others below them on the social ladder were now getting a slightly larger slice of the pie.

In Venezuela over 80 percent of the population lives below the poverty level. Before Chávez, most of the poor had never seen a doctor or dentist. The neoliberal market "adjustments" of the 1980s and 1990s only made things worse, cutting social spending and eliminating subsidies in consumer goods. Successive administrations did nothing about the rampant corruption and nothing about the growing gap between rich and poor, and the worsening malnutrition and desperation.

Far from ruining the country, here are some of the good things the Chávez government has accomplished:

■ A land-reform program was designed to assist small farmers and the landless poor. In March 2005 a large estate owned by a British beef company was occupied by agrarian workers for farming purposes.

■ Even before Chávez there was public education in Venezuela, from grade level to university, yet many children from poor families never attended school, for they could not afford the annual fees. Education is now completely free (right through to university level), causing a dramatic increase in school enrollment.

■ The government set up a marine conservation program, and is taking steps to protect the land and fishing rights of indigenous peoples.

■ Special banks now assist small enterprises, worker cooperatives, and farmers.

■ Attempts to further privatize the state-run oil industry—80 percent of which is still publicly owned—were halted, and limits have been placed on foreign capital penetration.

■ Chávez kicked out the U.S. military advisors and prohibited overflights by U.S. military aircraft engaged in counterinsurgency in Colombia.

■ "Bolivarian Circles" were organized throughout the nation; they consist of neighborhood committees designed to activate citizens to assist in literacy, education, and vaccination campaigns, and other public services.

■ The government has been hiring unemployed men, on a temporary basis, to repair streets and neglected drainage and water systems in poor neighborhoods.

Then there is the health program. I visited a dental clinic in Chávez's home state of Barinas. The staff consisted of four dentists, two of whom were young Venezuelan women. The other two were Cuban men who were there on a one-year program. The Venezuelan dentists noted that in earlier times dentists did not have enough work. There were millions of people who needed treatment, but care was severely rationed by the private market, that is, by one's ability to pay. Dental care was distributed like any other market commodity, not to anyone who needed it but only to those who could afford it.

When the free clinic in Barinas first opened it was flooded with people seeking dental care. No one was turned away. Even opponents of the Chávez government availed themselves of the free service, suddenly being quite able to put aside their political aversions. Many of the doctors and dentists who work in the barrio clinics (along with some of the clinical supplies and pharmaceuticals) came from Cuba. Chávez also put Venezuelan military doctors and dentists to work in the free clinics.

That low-income people were receiving medical and dental care for the first time in their lives did not seem to be a consideration that carried much weight among the more "professionally minded" medical practitioners. Much of the Venezuelan medical establishment was vehemently and unforgivably opposed to the free-clinic program, seeing it as a Cuban communist campaign to undermine medical standards and physicians' earnings.

I visited one of the government-supported community food stores that are located around the country, mostly in low-income areas. These modest establishments sell canned goods, pasta, beans, rice, and some produce and fruits at well below the market price, a blessing in a society with widespread malnutrition. Popular food markets have eliminated the layers of intermediaries and made staples more affordable for residents. Most of these markets and stores are run by women. The government also created a state-financed bank whose function is to provide low-income women with funds to start cooperatives in their communities.

There are a growing number of worker cooperatives in Venezuela. One in Caracas was started by turning a waste dump into a shoe factory and a T-shirt factory. Financed with money from the petroleum ministry, the co-op put about a thousand people to work. The workers seem enthusiastic and hopeful. Surprisingly, many Venezuelans know relatively little about the worker cooperatives. Or perhaps it is not surprising, given the near monopoly that private capital has over the print and broadcast media. The wealthy media moguls, all vehemently anti-Chávez, own four of the five television stations and all the major newspapers.

The man most responsible for Venezuela's revolutionary developments, Hugo Chávez, has been accorded the usual ad hominem treatment in the U.S. news media. An article in the *San Francisco Chronicle* quotes a political opponent who called Chávez "a psychopath, a terribly aggressive guy."[77] The London *Financial Times* sees him as "increasingly autocratic" and presiding over what the *Times* called a "rogue democracy."[78] In 2005 ABC's *Nightline* labeled him "the leftist strongman" who "delivered a tirade in the United Nations against President Bush."[79] A *New York Times* news story reported that his government "is hostile to American interests."[80]

The following year Chávez reappeared at the United Nations General Assembly and lambasted George W. Bush again for his single-minded dedication to the rich and powerful, and for his aggressive war policies that were in violation of international law. House Democratic leader Nancy Pelosi rushed to Bush's defense, calling Chávez "an everyday thug." The next day the Venezuelan thug announced that Citgo, the U.S.-based subsidiary of Venezuelan state-run oil company, planned to more than double the amount of low-priced heating oil it was making available to needy Americans mostly in the Northeast United States, from forty million gallons a year to one hundred million gallons.[81]

In the *Nation*, Marc Cooper—one of those Cold War liberals who regularly defends the U.S. empire—wrote that the democratically elected Chávez spoke "often as a thug," who "flirts with megalomania." Chávez's behavior, Cooper rattled on, "borders on the paranoiac," was "ham-fisted demagogy" acted out with an "increasingly autocratic style." Like so many critics, Cooper downplayed or ignored Chávez's accomplishments and popular support, and used name-calling in place of informed analysis.[82]

Other media mouthpieces have labeled Chávez as "mercurial," "besieged," "heavy-handed," "incompetent," "dictatorial," a "barracks populist," a "firebrand," and, above all, a "leftist" and "anti-American." It is never explained what "leftist" means. A leftist is someone who advocates a more equitable use and development of social resources and human services, and who supports the kinds of programs that the Chávez government has been putting in place. Likewise a rightist is someone who opposes such programs and seeks to advance the insatiable privileges of private capital and the wealthy few.

Occasionally readers are allowed to challenge the demonizing barrage. When a report in the *San Francisco Chronicle* described Chávez as "a populist strongman with leftist leanings," an annoyed reader pointed out that these were loaded terms: "To be consistent, newspaper writers should refer to President Bush as 'an elitist oilman with far-right leanings who became president by political manipulation.'"[83] A *New York Times* article described Venezuela's efforts to aid poor people, including Mexicans needing eye surgery and Americans needing heating oil, as Chávez's "pet projects." A reader pointed out that the same article described similar efforts by the U.S. government as "development programs." He asked why were these not also described as "pet projects?" Why such asymmetry in reporting? He also asked, "Don't all countries seek foreign allies? Why is it particularly nefarious for Venezuela to do so?"[84]

Chávez's opponents, who staged an illegal and unconstitutional coup in April 2002 against Venezuela's democratically elected government, have been depicted in the U.S. media as champions of "pro-democratic" and "pro-West" governance. They were referring to the corporate-military leaders of Venezuela's privileged social order who killed more people in the forty-eight hours they held power in 2002 than were ever harmed by Chávez in his years of rule.[85]

When one of these perpetrators, General Carlos Alfonzo, was indicted by the Venezuelan government for the role he played in the undemocratic coup, the *New York Times* chose to call him a "dissident" whose rights were being suppressed by the Chávez government.[86] Four other top military officers charged with leading the 2002 coup were also likely to face legal action. No doubt, they too will be described not as plotters or traitors who tried to overthrow a democratic government, but as "dissidents" who supposedly were being denied their right to "disagree" with the government.

President Hugo Chávez, whose public talks I attended on three occasions in Caracas, proved to be an educated, articulate, remarkably well-informed and well-read individual. Of big heart, deep human feeling, and keen intellect, he manifested a sincere dedication to effecting some salutary changes for the great mass of his people, a man who in every aspect seemed most worthy of the decent and peaceful democratic revolution he was leading.

Millions of his compatriots correctly perceive him as being the only president who has ever paid attention to the nation's poorest areas. No wonder he is the target of calumny and coup from the upper echelons in his own country and from ruling circles up north. Chávez also charges that the United States government is plotting to assassinate him. I can believe it. And if U.S. rulers should succeed in that ever so foul deed, Nancy Pelosi, Marc Cooper, and the others will rush forth with assertions about how Chávez brought it on himself.

34 A WORD ABOUT TERRORISTS

Terrorism is a form of violent political action directed against innocent and defenseless people. Along with denouncing such murderous assaults, we must try to comprehend why they happen. A number of the U.S. corporate media's pundits maintain that "Islamic terrorists" have attacked us because we are prosperous, free, democratic, and secular. As CBS-TV anchorman Dan Rather remarked, "We are winners and they are losers, and that's why they hate us."

In fact, if we bother to listen to what the Islamic militants actually say, they oppose us not because of who we *are* but because of what we *do*—to them and their region of the world. The individuals who were convicted of bombing the World Trade Center the first time, in 1993, sent a letter to the *New York Times* declaring that the attack was "in response for the American political, economic, and military support to Israel . . . and the rest of the dictator countries in the [Middle East] region."[87]

In November 2001, in his first interview after 9/11, Osama bin Laden had this to say: "This is a defensive Jihad. We want to defend our people and the territory we control. This is why I said that if we do not get security, the Americans will not be secure either." A year later, a taped message from bin Laden began: "The road to safety [for America] begins by ending [U.S.] aggression. Reciprocal treatment is part of justice. The [terrorist] incidents that have taken place . . . are only reactions and reciprocal actions."[88] In November 2004, in another taped commentary, bin Laden argued that the war his people were waging against the United States was a retaliatory one. He explicitly addressed the assertion made by Western officials and media pundits that the United States is targeted because it is so free and prosperous. If so, he argued, then why haven't the jihadists attacked Sweden? Sweden is more prosperous and more democratic than the United States. Predictably the questions posed by bin Laden received no serious attention in the U.S. news media.

As early as 1989, former president Jimmy Carter offered a

fairly accurate explanation of why people in the Middle East see the United States as the enemy. He told the *New York Times*: "You only have to go to Lebanon, to Syria or to Jordan to witness first-hand the intense hatred among many people for the United States because we bombed and shelled and unmercifully killed totally innocent villagers—women and children and farmers and housewives—in those villages around Beirut [an attack ordered by President Ronald Reagan]. As a result of that . . . we became kind of a Satan in the minds of those who are deeply resentful. That is what . . . has precipitated some of the terrorists attacks."[89]

We critics of U.S. foreign policy have argued that the best road to national safety and security lies neither in police-state repression at home nor military invasions abroad but in a foreign policy that stops making the United States an object of hatred among people throughout the world.

The Iraqi resistance to the U.S. occupation, for instance, does not seem impelled by a hate-ridden envy of the United States as such but by a desire to get the Americans out of Iraq. The Iraqis resent the United States not because it is so free, prosperous, and secular but because U.S. forces have delivered death and destitution upon their nation. As exclaimed one Iraqi woman whose relatives were killed by U.S. troops, "God curse the Americans. God curse those who brought them to us."[90] Under the U.S. occupation, unemployment climbed to 50 percent or higher, and villages and towns continued to go without electricity, water, and sewage disposal. Meanwhile the country's public institutions were in shambles, and its economy was privatized and stripped bare.

An in-depth, five-year study of religiously motivated terrorism was conducted by Jessica Stern, who interviewed religious militants of all stripes. She found men and women who were propelled neither by hatred of America's prosperity and democracy nor by nihilistic violence. Rather they held a deep faith in the justice of their cause and in the possibility of transforming the world through violent sacrificial action.[91] The United States was not envied but *resented* for the repression and poverty its policies were seen to have imposed upon their countries.

To be sure, there have arisen cadres of extremist Islamic zealots, of whom the Taliban in Afghanistan are a prime example. The Taliban are dedicated to waging holy war in the hope of imposing their theocratic rule upon their country. In their maniacal intolerance, they pursue indiscriminate bloodletting, ghastly mistreatment of women, and a readiness to sacrifice themselves to their own acutely warped version of Islam. It might do well to remember that the Taliban were a product of the CIA-created, post-Soviet era in Afghanistan.

In various other parts of the world there are extremist Islamic sects and grouplets that teach their members to loathe all non-Muslims and detest even those Muslims who belong to the wrong sect and who indulge in such evil pursuits as shaving, listening to music, or allowing their women to leave their faces uncovered.[92] (This fanatical intolerance has its parallel among certain fundamentalist Christian sects that delightedly dwell on how all nonbelievers—as well as incorrect believers in competing sects—will writhe in eternal hellfire and are deserving of every ill-fated mishap here on Earth.) These kind of aberrant religious groups have long existed in various countries. The question is: what are the socio-political conditions that feed their accretion, thrusting them onto center stage in force and numbers?

In Iraq, as of 2007, fanatical sectarian elements have come to the fore but only *after* the U.S. invasion and occupation. This would suggest that the desperate conditions created by Western imperialism and globalization serve as fertile breeding grounds for such groups. The invasion of Iraq has created far more terrorists than ever previously existed in that country.

Meanwhile our rulers indulge in their own form of terrorism. They would have us believe that the terror bombings and invasions inflicted upon the peoples of other nations are for their own good. Why the targeted populations cannot see this remains a mystery to the chief sponsors of Washington's "humanitarian wars." When asked why he thought some populations have a "vitriolic hatred for America," George W. Bush offered his super-patriotic mystification: "I'm amazed that there's such misunderstanding of what our country is about that people would hate us. Like most Americans, I just can't believe it because I know how good we are."[93]

Even the Pentagon allowed that what U.S. leaders do abroad might have something to do with inciting terrorism. A 1997 Defense Department study concludes: "Historical data show a strong correlation between U.S. involvement in international situations and an increase in terrorist attacks against the United States."[94] Such "U.S. involvement," it should be noted, often consists of a state-sponsored terrorism that attacks popular movements throughout the world, exterminating whole villages and killing large numbers of labor leaders and workers, peasants, students, journalists, clergy, teachers, and anyone else who supports a more egalitarian social order for their own country.

People throughout the world are also discomforted by a U.S. superpower that possesses an unanswerable destructive capacity never before seen in human history, that can with impunity visit aerial death and destruction upon any nation that lacks a nuclear retaliatory strike force. With only five percent of the Earth's population, the United States expends more military funds than all the other major powers combined.[95] U.S.-sponsored terrorism—in the form of death squads, paramilitaries, invasions, and occupations—has taken millions of lives in scores of countries.

Whole societies have been undermined and shattered, not only by U.S. military assaults, but by U.S. sanctions and monetary policies that have imposed a debt peonage and poverty upon struggling nations. Maybe all this has something to do with why the terrorists oppose this nation. But to consider such things in any detail is to get too close to exposing the hypocrisies that sustain the U.S. global empire. Washington policymakers find it more convenient to pose as misunderstood paladins in shining armor puzzled by the ingratitude of those whom they purportedly rush to rescue.

NOTES

1. Karl Marx and Friedrich Engels, *The Communist Manifesto* (various editions).
2. The reference to China is prior to the 1979 modernization and rapid growth and prior to the one-child family program: see *Food First Development Report* no. 4, 1988.
3. Karl Marx and Friedrich Engels, *On Colonialism* (selected writings) (International Publishers, 1972), 319.
4. Italics added. When the text of Clinton's speech was printed the next day in the *New York Times,* the sentence quoted above was omitted.
5. *Washington Post,* 11 June 1990.
6. *New York Times,* 1 and 3 November 2006.
7. *New York Times,* 15 October 1995.
8. *New York Times,* 16 June 1996.
9. *New York Times,* 27 February 1990.
10. Vladimir Bilenkin, "Russian Workers Under the Yeltsin Regime: Notes on a Class in Defeat," *Monthly Review,* November 1996, 1–12; and Michael Parenti, *Blackshirts and Reds: Rational Fascism and the Overthrow of Communism* (City Lights, 1997), chapters 6 and 7.

11. See Eleanor Randolph, *Waking the Tempests: Ordinary Life in the New Russia* (Simon & Schuster, 1996).

12. CNN news report, 2 February 1992.

13. *Toronto Star*, 5 November 1995.

14. *New York Times*, 6 April 1994.

15. NPR news, 21 July 1996.

16. K.L. Abeywickrama, "The Marketization of Mongolia," *Monthly Review*, March 1996, 25–33, and reports cited therein.

17. *Nation*, 7 December 1992.

18. *Los Angeles Times*, 17 January 1996.

19. *San Francisco Chronicle*, 14 August 1990.

20. *Wall Street Journal*, 19 May 1994.

21. *New York Times*, 8 April 1996.

22. AP report, 28 October 1996.

23. Bilenkin, "Russian Workers Under the Yeltsin Regime"; italics added.

24. *Los Angeles Times*, 3 August 1996.

25. *Los Angeles Times*, 10 March 1990.

26. *Washington Post*, 1 January 1996.

27. *Modern Maturity*, September/October 1994.

28. Richard Pipes, "Flight from Freedom: What Russians Think and Want," *Foreign Affairs* (May/June, 2004).

29. Information and quotations in the above paragraph are from Laura Petricola, "Czech Gov't Bans Youth Group, Torpedoes Democracy," *People's Weekly World*, 28 October 2006.

30. Michael Parenti, *Inventing Reality* (St. Martin's Press, 1986), 145.

31. *New York Times*, 8 July 1998.

32. Sean Gervasi, "Germany, US and the Yugoslav Crisis," *CovertAction Quarterly*, winter 1992–93.

33. Michel Chossudovsky, "Dismantling Former Yugoslavia, Recolonizing Bosnia," *CovertAction Quarterly*, Spring 1996; and Chossudovsky's "Banking on the Balkans," *THIS*, July-August 1999; see also see the collection of reports by Ramsey Clark, Sean Gervasi, Sara Flounders, Nadja Tesich, Michel Choussudovsky, and others in *NATO in the Balkans: Voices of Opposition* (International Action Center, 1998).

34. *Interim Agreement for Peace and Self-government in Kosovo* (the "Rambouillet Agreement"), February 23, 1999, reproduced in full in *The Kosovo Dossier*, 2ND ed.(Lord Byron Foundation for Balkan Studies, 1999).

35. *New York Times*, 10 October 1997; for more details of this incident, see selection 3, "Methods of Media Manipulation."

36. Joan Phillips, "Breaking the Selective Silence," *Living Marxism* April 1993, 10.

37. *Financial Times* (London), 15 April 1993.

38. See for instance, Yigal Chazan's report in the *Guardian* (London/Manchester), 17 August 1992.

39. Michael Kelly, "The Clinton Doctrine is a Fraud, and Kosovo Proves It," *Boston Globe* 1 July 1999.

40. *Foreign Affairs*, September/October 1994.

41. *San Francisco Chronicle*, 5 May 1999 and *Washington Times*, 3 May 1999.

42. *New York Times*, 1 November 1987.

43. For example, Mira Marković, *Night and Day, A Diary* (Dragiša Nikolič, 1995).

44. For instance, Raymond Bonner, "War Crimes Panel Finds Croat Troops 'Cleansed' the Serbs," *New York Times*, 21 March 1999, a revealing report by a reputable correspondent that was largely ignored.

45. John Ranz, paid advertisement, *New York Times*, 29 April 1993.

46. "Correction: Report on Rape in Bosnia, " *New York Times*, October 23, 1993.

47. *San Francisco Examiner*, 26 April 1999.

48. David Owen, *Balkan Odyssey* (Harcourt, 1997), 262.

49. *New York Times*, 7 August 1993.

50. Brooke Shelby Biggs, "Failure to Inform," *San Francisco Bay Guardian*, May 5, 1999.

51. Audrey Gillan, "What's the Story?" *London Review of Books*, 27 May 1999.

52. *Washington Post*, 10 July 1999.

53. Carlotta Gall, "Belgrade Sees Grave Site as Proof NATO Fails to Protect Serbs," *New York Times*, 27 August 1999.

54. Both the 500,000 and 100,000 were reported in the *New York Times*, 11 November 1999.

55. Stratfor.com, Global Intelligence Update, "Where Are Kosovo's Killing Fields?" weekly analysis, 18 October 1999.

56. Reed Irvine and Cliff Kincaid, "Playing the Numbers Game" (www.aim. org/mm/1999/08/03. htm).

57. Perez Puhola quoted in *London Sunday Times*, 31 October 1999; see also Stratfor.com, Global Intelligence Update, "Where Are Kosovo's Killing Fields?" weekly analysis, 18 October 1999.

58. For a fuller discussion of the atrocity lies and related issues, see Michael Parenti, *To Kill a Nation: The Attack on Yugoslavia* (Verso, 2000).

59. Richard Gwyn's report in the *Toronto Star*, 3 November 1999.

60. Intelligence reports from the German Foreign Office, 12 January 1999 and 29 October 1998 to the German Administrative Courts, translated by Eric Canepa, Brecht Forum, New York, 20 April 1999.

61. For further discussion of this point, see Michael Parenti, *Against Empire* (City Lights Books, 1995).

62. *New York Times*, March 28, 1999.

63. *San Francisco Chronicle*, 20 September 2002.

64. *New York Times*, 24 January 2003.

65. Kevin Tillman, "The Day After Pat's Birthday: A Plea to Speak Up for Democracy," CommonDreams.org, 19 October 2006, www.commondreams.org/views06/1020-23.htm.

66. See the report *Rebuilding America's Defenses* promulgated by Project for a New American Century, the right-wing think tank that provided the top policymakers of the Bush Jr. administration.

67. Max Fuller, "Ghosts of Jadiriyah," 14 November 2006, www.brusselstribunal.org/FullerJadiriyah.htm.

68. W. Clark, "The Real Reasons for the Upcoming War with Iraq," Independent Media Center www.indymedia.org, 6 March 2003; and Coilin Nunan, "Currency and the War on Iraq," www.feasta.org/documents/papers/oil, 27 March 2003.

69. *London Financial Times*, 24 February 1998.

70. *San Francisco Chronicle*, 22 February 1998.

71. On paper, Iraq's oil industry was still state owned as of 2006.

72. James Petras, *The Power of Israel in the United States* (Clarity Press and Fernwood Books, 2006), 61–62 and passim.

73. Petras, *The Power of Israel in the United States*, 21 and passim.

74. See Yahya Sadowski, "No War for Whose Oil?" *Le Monde Diplomatique*, April 2003; Patrick Seale, "A Costly Friendship," *Nation*, 21 July 2003, and Petras, *The Power of Israel in the United States*.

75. *New York Times*, 12 June 2005.

76. *New York Times* editorial, 28 September 2006.

77. *San Francisco Chronicle*, 30 November 2001.

78. *Financial Times*, 12 January 2002.

79. ABC's "Nightline" 16 September 2005.

80. *New York Times*, 19 October 2006.

81. Associated Press report, 22 September 2006.

82. *Nation*, 6 May 2002.

83. *San Francisco Chronicle* report, 16 April 2002; and response by Donald Scott, 18 April 2002.

84. *New York Times* article, 4 April 2006; and response by Robert Daiman, 5 April 2006.

85. See Gregory Wilpert, ed., *Coup Against Chávez in Venezuela: The Best International Reports of What Really Happened* (Fundación por Un Mondo Multipolar, 2003).

86. "Venezuelan Court Rules Against Dissident," *New York Times*, 16 April 2005.

87. *New York Times*, 9 January 1998.

88. *Los Angeles Times*, 13 November 2002.
89. *New York Times*, 26 March 1989.
90. *San Francisco Chronicle*, 11 January 2004.
91. Jessica Stern, *Terror in the Name of God* (Ecco, 2003).
92. For example, Daveed Gartenstein-Ross, *My Year Inside Radical Islam* (Tarcher, 2007).
93. *Boston Globe*, 12 October 2001.
94. U.S. Department of Defense, Defense Science Board 1997 Summer Study Task Force on DOD Responses to Transnational Threats, October 1997, Final Report, Vol.1. www.acq.osd.mil/dsb/trans.pdf, cited.
95. On the U.S. military empire, see the collection of articles in Carl Boggs (ed.) *Masters of War: Militarism and Blowback in the Era of American Empire* (Routledge, 2003).

VIII.
THE REST IS HISTORY

35 DOMINANT HISTORY

History has many enemies, including some who profess to serve its cause. The struggle to define the past is part of the struggle to control society itself. Too often history is used not to enlighten but to indoctrinate. The study of history is too important to be left exclusively in the hands of historians. In fact, all sorts of people, including political leaders, publicists, press pundits, clergy, textbook publishers, moneyed investors, semiliterate editors, professors, and school teachers are involved in the manufacturing and marketing of mainstream history.

Many historians who claim to be disciples of impartial scholarship have little sense of how they are wedded to ideological respectability and how inhospitable they are to counter-hegemonic views. This synchronicity between their individual beliefs and the dominant belief system is treated as "objectivity." It follows that a departure from this ideological orthodoxy is itself dismissed as ideological.

The term "history" refers both to the actual course of past events and the study of those events, that is, making history and writing it. But the distinction between these two meanings is not absolute, for those who *write* history have an impact upon events in that they help control history's course by defining its dominant themes, thereby influencing our understanding of what has happened. Conversely, those who *make* history, especially those who occupy elite policy positions, often manipulate the materials needed for recording it. They sometimes destroy or repress information, introducing distortions at the point of origin well before the history is written or even played out. In an unguarded moment Winston Churchill told William Deakin, who had helped him write *The Second World War*, "This is not history, this is my case."[1] With that same intent to make their case, numerous political leaders have produced self-justifying memoirs and official histories whose contribution to the truth has been parsimonious.

The process of controlling history at the point of origin is not left to chance but is pursued systematically by policymakers and official agencies. This point was brought home to Carroll Quigley, who for twenty years studied the Cecil Rhodes–Alfred Milner Round Table. The Milner Group, as they were known, was a coterie of elite decision makers who had a definitive influence on British policy from 1891 through World War II. Quigley himself was close to establishment figures in the United States and Great Britain. After teaching at Princeton and Harvard he spent the rest of his career at Georgetown's School of Foreign Service, was a consultant for the Brookings Institution, the Pentagon, and the State Department, and taught western civilization and history. Not surprisingly, he was in agreement with most of the policies of the Round Table elites but he was bothered by some of their methods and thought their inherited wealth and power held "terrifying" implications for democratic governance. If anything, Quigley was bothered not so much by their influence over events but by their control over the recording of these events. To quote him:

> No country that values its safety should allow what the Milner Group accomplished in Britain—that is, that a small number of men should be able to wield such power in administration and politics, should be given almost complete control over the publication of the documents relating to their actions, should be able to exercise such influence over the avenues of information that create public opinion, and should be able to monopolize so completely the writing and teaching of the history of their own period.[2]

The examples of how history is changed, distorted, suppressed and fabricated at the point of origin are too numerous to record.[3] Any researcher who has spent much time in government archives soon discovers that many documents are missing; others are not available or have never been catalogued; many remain classified for fifty years or more. The War Department Records on President Abraham Lincoln's assassination were kept secret for sixty years, finally placed in the public domain in the mid-1930s. When researching the conspiracy behind Lincoln's murder, Theodore Roscoe discovered that some Civil War records of the "U.S. Army secret intelligence" were still classified almost one hundred years after the assassination.[4] What question of national security could be involved here? How many Confederate spies were prowling behind Union lines in 1960?

There are the dramatic vignettes such as during the Iran-Contra affair when Lieutenant Colonel Oliver North shredded documents while FBI agents lackadaisically thumbed through files at the other end of the office. There are the thousands of documents related to the assassination of President John Kennedy still under lock and key, the physical evidence that disappeared or showed signs of being tampered with, and the limousine in which he was shot, whose insides—the scene of the crime—were immediately stripped and destroyed. There are the classified documents and disappeared materials and many unanswered questions relating to the mind boggling events of 9/11. One could go on.

This leads us to another point: No society of any complexity speaks with one voice. There are a variety of perspectives in the intellectual community and elsewhere. The opinions most likely to prevail are not necessarily most representative of the great mass of people. Rather it is the select few who are usually best endowed with the material means to produce the literature of history. In short, history is written by those who can afford to write it.

If it is true that people tend to perceive reality, past and present, in accordance with the position they occupy in the social structure, then it is likely that most of the history that has been handed down to us is from elitist sources. The writing of history has been principally a privilege of the victor, written from within the court, church, government, and academy, at the very least written by persons of property and leisure. Who else had the time or means?

So in every age we have what might be called "dominant history," the product of the prevailing institutions of whatever epoch we are looking at, which still exercises an influence over our perceptions. Consider what our history books still tell us about peasants in the Middle Ages, specifically their deep involvement with religion. To this notion the historian E. H. Carr poses an interesting question:

I wonder how we know this, and whether it is true. What we know as the facts of medieval history have almost all been selected for us by generations of chroniclers who were professionally occupied in the theory and practice of religion, and who therefore thought it supremely important, and recorded everything relating to it, and not much else. The picture of the Russian peasant as devoutly religious was destroyed by the revolution of 1917. The picture of medieval man as devoutly religious, whether true or not, is indestructible, because nearly all the known facts about him were preselected for us by people who believed it, and wanted others to believe it, and a mass of other facts, in which we might possibly have found evidence to the contrary, has been lost beyond recall.[5]

Indeed, during those feudal times, the keepers of the faith were also the keepers of the records, a historic fact still embodied in the French word *clerc,* which can mean clergyman, scholar, or clerk; and in the English "clerical," an adjective pertaining both to clerks and clergy. As Henry Charles Lea writes, the ecclesiastics "monopolized . . . the educated intelligence of the age."[6] For more than a millennium, Europe was ruled by a totalitarian system known as Christendom.

With the recording of history so thoroughly controlled by one favored estate, the peasants had virtually no opportunity to speak for themselves. While there do exist numerous studies of feudal communities, they rarely offer any *direct* testimony from the common folk. But, in 1965, not long after Carr voiced his regret that all contrary evidence "has been lost beyond recall," the three surviving volumes of the Inquisition Register of Jacques Fournier,

Bishop of Pamiers, transcribed in 1318–1325, happened to have been retrieved from the Vatican Library and published. These tomes contain exhaustive verbatim depositions elicited by the inquisitional courts from the peasantry of Montaillou, a village in southern France suspected of being a hotbed of Albigensian heresy. Sociologist Emmanuel Le Roy Ladurie extracted from the volumes a detailed description of village life in Montaillou originally recorded directly from the mouths of the peasants themselves.

The picture that emerges is of a people who were concerned with much else besides religion, including property, farming, cooperative communal services, crafts, festivals, family relations, and love affairs.[7] The peasants of 1318 were inclined to be affectionate toward their children, and wept more easily than we, both in happiness and sorrow. Of special interest for our inquiry: less than half of the Montaillou parishioners attended church, according to one of the religious dissidents, and many did so without any special enthusiasm.[8] One villager remarks to a group of men in the community, "Instead of burning heretics they ought to burn Bishop Fournier himself, because he demands that we pay tithes in lambs."

This statement was treated as a blasphemy against God. In fact, it was a secular criticism of class exploitation, a denunciation of a parasitic, high-living cleric. Bishop Fournier also imposed onerous tithes on previously exempt agricultural products. Not without cause did some of the village heretics claim that the "Pope devours the blood and sweat of the poor. And the bishops and priests, who are rich and honored and self-indulgent, behave in the same manner."[9] Heresy in Montaillou seems to have stemmed less from theological disputes and more from a resistance to the economic thievery of the church hierarchy.[10] The impression one gets is that these peasants were not involved in church affairs so much as the church was involved in their affairs.

They were preoccupied not with eternal salvation but earthly survival. Carr's suspicions seem to be confirmed.

The point to remember here is that the evidence put together by Le Roy Ladurie regarding Montaillou is not likely to overturn the dominant history, the one that treats the feudal peasantry as composed of devout, simple bumpkins and stolid serfs who accepted their station in life in symbiotic vassalage with their superiors. The prevailing image of the common people was created by the churchmen themselves. And it remains the image embraced to this day by elitist scribes.

Who then speaks for the people of history? Through the centuries there have been scarcely anyone to record their glory and misery, no one to take note of the Roman commoners who wept for loved ones lost in Caesar's war, the peaceful villages obliterated by the conqueror's holocaust, the women torn from their hearths by the military rapists and plunderers, the men enslaved in Charlemaigne's mines.

Few chroniclers over the centuries have recorded how the course of history was changed in a positive way by the peaceful women and men who created the crafts and generated the skills of society, those who developed horticulture and designed the first wagons, seafaring vessels, and fishing nets, the first looms, lathes, and kilns, who cultivated the first orchards, vineyards, and terraces and invented the written word, more than once in more than one place—those who did what Thorstein Veblen called "the work of civilization." Not then, not now are they celebrated for their contributions to history, for the inventiveness and positive contributions that have made life bearable and even possible.

To the princes and presidents, plutocrats and prime ministers, we owe the horrors of war and conquest, the technologies of destruction and control, and the rapacious expropriation that has enriched the few and impoverished the many through so many epochs. Real history should give us not only accounts of popular struggles against oppression but also exposés of the crimes and abuses of ruling interests, so many of which have been glossed over by mainstream historians.

The dramatic struggles of working people in North America, extending over the better part of three centuries, are absent from most of our history texts, as are the armed revolts of farmers, slaves, and Native Americans ("Indians"). Dominant history has little to say about the pitched battles between workers and militia, the factory takeovers, and the gunning down of strikers by company gun thugs, police, and army. In his 1,122-page tome on U.S. history, Samuel Eliot Morison—one of America's "official" historians, so to speak—has little or nothing to say about these struggles, not a word about the champions of labor such as John Swinton, Charles Steinmetz, Albert Parsons, Henry George, W. E. B. Du Bois, Bill Haywood, Clarence Darrow, Mother Jones, Carlo Tresca, Elizabeth Gurley Flynn, and Emma Goldman. Morison's history is a celebration of establishment leadership, generously larded with Eurocentric, ruling-elite apologetics.[11]

A study of seventeen widely used high-school U.S. history textbooks, covering the period from the Civil War to World War I, finds that, despite the claim to objectivity, the books offer an ideologically slanted pro-business, anti-labor view of events. The author of the study, Jean Anyon, notes that all the textbooks are marketed by "a publishing industry that is big business—with annual sales of several billion dollars—and that is increasingly owned by corporate conglomerates."[12]

Historians will go on at length about the historical method, about how history relates to other social sciences; how historians must grapple with research problems, sift carefully through the evidence, accepting little on faith while letting the chips fall where they may; how they must immerse themselves in the historical context of their subject yet keep their perspective and detachment, showing imagination and caution, skill and sagacity, and other such sterling qualities of creative scholarship.

Hardly a word can be found in all this literature about the *marketing of history*, specifically the ideological forces within the corporate economy that help determine the distribution of historical studies—-and which thereby influence what is produced. Little is said about why certain books win foundation funding, are elaborately promoted and widely reviewed, earn awards and book-club adoptions, and are kept in print for long periods, while other volumes never emerge from an obscurity that seems no more deserved than the former's celebrity. Big publishers, big distributors, and chain retailers largely determine which books are carried in bookstores and how they are displayed, which ones are highlighted at a front table or hidden away on a dusty shelf. Surely, one of the major factors determining this parsing is ideology.

Consider some classic cases. Osborne Ward wrote an amazing book, *The Ancient Lowly* (1888), about trade unions, guilds and strikes in the ancient world, which attempted to demonstrate that class struggle was the name of the game even then. For almost twenty years Ward was unable to find a publisher because, as Charles H. Kerr explained, "no capitalist publishing house would take the responsibility for so revolutionary a book, and no socialist publishing house existed."[13] In 1907, Ward's work was published by Kerr's socialist collective and received an enthusiastic reception among those limited numbers who heard of its existence.

In 1920, American socialist Upton Sinclair wrote a scathing critique of the business-owned press, *The Brass Check*. An acquaintance told him it was inconceivable that publication of this book would be permitted in America. After exasperating experiences with Doubleday and Macmillan, Sinclair decided to publish it himself. The book enjoyed six printings and sold 100,000 copies within a half-year.[14]

Recall also the critical works produced by the aforementioned Carroll Quigley who blew the whistle on the transatlantic policy plutocrats. Quigley's first book, *The Anglo-American Establishment*, was rejected by fifteen publishers, and finally appeared posthumously more than thirty-two years after its completion. His major work, *Tragedy and Hope*, supposedly went out of print immediately after publication in 1966. Quigley was entitled to recover the plates from Macmillan, but after much stalling, the publisher claimed that the plates had been "inadvertently" destroyed.[15]

Ideological bias comes through clearly in which books get reviewed in the major media. Critical progressive titles are far less likely to receive attention, except perhaps to be savaged. A regular reviewer for the *Boston Globe*, a reputedly liberal newspaper, told a South End Press editor that she "would be fired" if she reviewed writers with a radical perspective.[16] Publications like *Choice*, *Kirkus*, *Library Journal*, and *Publishers Weekly*, used by libraries and bookstores to determine purchases, are also biased in what they review, tending to ignore—or denounce—titles that stray beyond the ideological norm.

Librarian Charles Willett points out that titles acquired by both university libraries and public libraries are slanted toward a conventional view of past and present, selected by librarians and faculty "who tend to accept large corporate and university press publishers as objective and trustworthy, while rejecting small nonprofit publishers as 'political' and unreliable." If any change has occurred, it is in a more regressive direction, as libraries, faced with declining budgets, acquire even fewer alternative titles.[17]

To conclude, history is not just what the historians say it is, but what government agencies, corporate conglomerates, chain-store distributors, mass-media pundits, editors, reviewers, and other ideological gatekeepers want to put into circulation. In this sense we can speak of a dominant history. The deck is stacked to favor those who deal the cards.

36 FASCISM, THE REAL STORY

We should study history with the intention of trying to get at the real story, not the sanitized myths that too often are passed along. Most people are never exposed to real history. In school we rarely read history. We read history textbooks, mostly ones that avoid the underlying realities and propagate all sorts of improbable scenarios. Fascism is a good example of how a fearsome political movement of momentous scope can be diluted and misrepresented. Here is a turn at the real story.

Fascism is the name given to the political movement that arose in Italy under the leadership of Benito Mussolini, who ruled that country from 1922 to 1943. Nazism was a movement led by Adolph Hitler, who was Germany's dictator from 1933 to 1945. Nazism is considered by most observers to be a variant of fascism, as to a lesser degree was the militaristic government that controlled Japan from 1940 to 1945; so too the Falangist movement led by Francisco Franco, who in 1939 took over Spain after a protracted civil war, with the military aid of the Italian and Nazi fascists.

Self-avowed fascist movements also arose in Great Britain, the United States, France, and much of Eastern Europe. During the early 1990s, the press carried numerous reports about how countries such as Bulgaria, Romania, Hungary, Lithuania, Poland, and Croatia were overthrowing "the yoke of communism" and "returning to their democratic roots." In fact these countries had been under right-ist autocratic rule in their pre-communism days. With the exception of Poland, all had been openly allied with Nazi Germany.

Fascism offers a deceptive mix of revolutionary-sounding mass appeals and reactionary class politics. Hitler's party, for instance, was called the National Socialist German Workers Party (NSDAP) or Nazis, a leftist-sounding name designed to win broad support among working people even while the Nazis were destroying work-ing-class organizations. The original Italian and German variations of fascism made a revolutionary appeal without making a revolu-tion, promising to solve the ills of the many while in fact protecting the special interests of the few with violence and terror. Fascism propagated a false revolution with a new political consciousness, a new order to serve the same old moneyed interests. Let us briefly consider the major characteristics of the fascist ideology.

First, the leadership cult, the glorification of an all-knowing, supreme and absolutist leader.

Second, the idolatrous worship of the nation-state as an entity unto itself, an absolute component to which the individual is sub-sumed. Everything for the state, nothing against the state, nothing outside the state. That was Mussolini's and Hitler's dictum. Hitler's henchman Rudolf Hess once said, "Adolf Hitler is Ger-many, and Germany is Adolf Hitler," thereby wrapping both the leadership cult and the state cult in one. The leader is the embod-iment of the state, and the state is supreme.

Third, glorification of military conquest and jingoism: the state is vitalized and empowered by subduing, conquering, and enslaving other peoples and territories.

Fourth, propagation of a folk mysticism, with its concomitant xenophobia and racism. The Nazi slogan was *ein Volk, ein Reich, ein Führer* (one people, one empire, one leader), an atavistic celebration of the special blood lineage and wondrous legacy of the people. Along with this comes a disdain for other peoples and nationalities. For the Nazis and most other Eastern European fascists, the core enemy was the Jew, who was seen as the perpetrator of all societal ills. Behind the trade unionists, communists, homosexuals and others were the Jews, wickedly alien creatures who would pollute the pure-blooded and undermine the state.

Fifth, on behalf of the interests of the giant business cartels, there was a concerted suppression, both by the Italian fascists and German Nazis, of all egalitarian working-class loyalties and organizations, including labor unions.

Of these various characteristics of fascism, the last one is rarely talked about by mainstream historians, political scientists and journalists who usually ignore the link between fascism and capitalism, just as they tend to ignore the entire subject of capitalism itself when something unfavorable needs to be said about it. Instead, they dwell on the more bizarre components of fascist ideology: the "nihilist revolt against Western individuality," the mystic *volk* attachment, and so forth. Fascism was those things, but along with its irrational appeals it had rational functions. It was a key instrument for the preservation of plutocratic domination.

After World War I, Italy had a parliamentary government that seemed incapable of solving the country's economic crises. Profits were declining, banks were failing, unemployment was rising. To ensure profits, the big industrial giants and landowners needed higher prices for their commodities, massive government subsidies, tax exemptions, and tariff protections. To finance this, the population had to be taxed more heavily; their wages had to be rolled back and their social welfare expenditures drastically cut.

But the government was not totally free to apply these measures. Italian workers and peasants were fairly well organized with their own political organizations, cooperatives, unions, and publications. Through the use of demonstrations and strikes, boycotts, factory takeovers, and forcible occupation of farmlands they often won some real concessions. Even in the face of the worsening economic crisis they were able to mount a troublesome defense of their modest living standard. The only solution was to smash the worker and peasant organizations, in effect destroying all political and civil liberties, including the right to organize, agitate and propagandize. The state would have to be more authoritarian in order to keep the populace more firmly subservient to the interests of big capital.

Enter Benito Mussolini. Born in 1883, the son of a blacksmith, Mussolini had an early manhood marked by street brawls, arrests, jailings, and violent, radical political activities. Before World War I, he was a socialist. A brilliant organizer, agitator, and gifted journalist, he became editor of the Socialist Party's official newspaper. Yet many of his comrades suspected him of being less interested in advancing socialism than in advancing Mussolini. Indeed, when the Italian industrialists and financiers tempted him with recognition, financial support, and the promise of power, he was not long in doing a volte-face.

By the end of World War I, Mussolini the socialist who had organized strikes for workers and peasants had become Mussolini the fascist who broke strikes on behalf of financiers and landowners. Using the huge sums he received from them, he projected himself onto the national scene as the acknowledged leader of *i fasci di combattimento*, a movement composed of black-shirted ex-army officers and sundry toughs who were guided by no clear political doctrine other than a militaristic patriotism and dislike for anything associated with socialism and organized labor.

Between January and May 1921, the fascist blackshirts destroyed 120 labor headquarters, attacked 243 socialist centers and other buildings, killed 202 workers (in addition to 44 killed by the police and gendarmerie), and wounded 1,144 others. During this time 2,240 workers were arrested and only 162 fascists. In the 1921–22 period up to Mussolini's seizure of state power, "500 labor halls and cooperative stores were burned, and 900 socialist municipalities were dissolved."[18]

In 1922, the leaders of industry, along with representatives from the banking and agribusiness associations, met with Mussolini to plan the "March on Rome," contributing 20 million lire to the undertaking. With the additional backing of Italy's top military officers and police chiefs, the fascist "revolution"—really a coup d'état—took place. In the words of Senator Ettore Conti, himself a very loyal representative of the moneyed interests, "Mussolini was the candidate of the plutocracy and the business associations."[19]

Within two years after seizing state power, *il Duce* had shut down all opposition newspapers and crushed the Socialist, Liberal, Catholic, Democratic, and Republican parties, which together had commanded some 80 percent of the vote. Labor leaders, cooperative farm leaders, parliamentary delegates, and others critical of the new regime were beaten, exiled, or murdered by fascist terror *squadristi*. The Italian Communist Party endured the severest repression of all, yet managed to maintain a courageous underground resistance that eventually evolved into armed struggle against the *fascisti* and the German occupation force.

In Germany, a similar pattern of complicity between fascists and capitalists emerged. In the period following World War I, under the Weimar Republic, workers and farm laborers won the eight-hour day, unemployment insurance, and the right to unionize. But the nearly total collapse of the German economy in 1929–30 presented the owning class with a momentous investment crisis. Only massive state aid could revive their profits. Wages, social welfare, and human services had to be cut. Union contracts had to be abrogated. The crisis in agriculture was equally severe, and the large land proprietors, the Junker class, demanded higher subsidies, heavier duties on foreign agriculture imports, and an end to farm unions that were protecting wage levels and thereby cutting into profits.

During the 1920s, the Nazi *Sturmabteilung* or SA, the brown-shirted "stormtroopers," subsidized by business, were used mostly as an anti-labor paramilitary force whose function was to terrorize workers, farm laborers, socialists, and communists. In the words of Nazi leader Herman Goering, they were the "bodyguard of capitalism."

By 1930 most of the influential landowners and big industrialists and bankers had concluded that the Weimar Republic no longer served their interests, being too accommodating to the working class and to certain sectors of light industry. They greatly increased their subsidies to Hitler and propelled the Nazi party onto the national stage.

In the July 1932 electoral campaign, fortified with vast sums of money from the German cartels, the Nazis gleaned about 37 percent of the vote, the highest they ever won in an election. Their reliable base was among the more affluent strata along with substantial numbers of petty bourgeoisie and lumpenproletarians who served as strong-arm party thugs. As with the fascists in Italy, the Nazis in Germany never had a majority of the people on their side. The great majority of the German working class supported the Communists or Social Democrats to the very end.

True to form, the Social Democrat leaders refused the Communist Party's proposal to form an eleventh-hour coalition against Nazism. As in many other countries past and present, so in Germany, the Social Democrats would sooner ally themselves with the reactionary Right than make common cause with the Reds. Earlier in 1924, Social Democratic government officials in the Weimar Ministry of Interior used fascist paramilitary troops to attack left-wing demonstrators. They imprisoned seven thousand workers and suppressed Communist Party newspapers.[20] Then in January 1933, a number of right-wing parties coalesced behind the Nazis and, just weeks after the election, Hindenburg invited Hitler to become chancellor.

Upon assuming state power, Hitler and his Nazis pursued an agenda not unlike Mussolini's. They crushed organized labor and eradicated all elections, opposition parties, and independent publications. Hundreds of thousands of opponents were imprisoned, tortured, or murdered. In Germany, as in Italy, the communists endured the severest political repression of all groups.

Neither in Italy nor Germany was the left ever strong enough to effect a revolution. But popular forces had developed enough strength to resist the austerity and the rollback that the capitalists tried to impose in order to maintain their own profit levels. The bourgeoisie resorted to fascism less out of a response to the proletarian disturbances in the street and more as a response to the contradictions within their own economic system.

The Italian and German cartels looked to huge armament contracts and related public works as an expanded source of profitable investment. This also fit with their desire for a more aggressive foreign policy that might open new markets and put them on a better footing with their French and English competitors. So the fascists became a very useful ally against the capitalists' two worst enemies: the workers in their own country, and the capitalists in other countries.

Not all the big industrialists and financiers supported fascism with equal fervor. Some, like Thyssen, were early and enthusiastic backers of Hitler. The aged Emil Kurdoff thanked God that he lived long enough to see the Führer emerge as the savior of Germany. Others contributed money to the Nazis but also to other anti-socialist parties on the right. They backed Hitler only when he appeared to be the most effective force against the left. Many of them remained privately critical of the more extreme expressions of Nazi propaganda and were uneasy about the anti-bourgeois rhetoric enunciated by some of the plebeian brownshirts.

Some business elements were not that enamoured with Hitler. Light industry had lower fixed costs and more stable profits than heavy industry, and was more dependent on consumer buying power. Consequently, light industrialists were not that keen about a more aggressive foreign policy and subsidies to heavy industry. But when push came to shove, they may not have been close to the fascists, but they were not about to ally themselves with the proletariat against the business class, of which they were a part. They either sided with the cartels or kept their mouths shut.

There was another element in these two societies that not only tolerated the rise of fascism but supported it: the capitalist state itself. Not the parliament as such, but the instruments of the state that had a monopoly on the legal use of force and violence, the police, the army, and the courts. In Italy years before Mussolini emerged victorious, the police collaborated with the fascists in attacking labor and peasant organizations. They recruited criminals for the fascist *squadristi*, promising them immunity from prosecution for past crimes. While applications for gun permits were regularly denied to workers and peasants, police guns and cars were made available to Mussolini's goons.

Likewise in Germany immediately after World War I, the military police and the judiciary tended to favor the rightists while suppressing the leftists, a pattern of collaboration that continued into Hitler's day. In other words, these liberal capitalist democracies—that supposedly were "equally opposed to totalitarianism of the left and right"—were not really equally opposed. They often collaborated with the extreme right, those who were protecting the interests of big capital and the existing class structure. If defeating socialism and communism also entailed destroying democracy, so much the worse for democracy.

The literature on who supported fascism and Nazism is long and much debated. But a much neglected question is: *whom did fascism support when it came to power?* How did fascist Italy and Nazi Germany deal with social services, taxes, business, and the conditions of labor? For whose benefit and at whose expense? Most of the mainstream western literature on fascism and Nazism has little to say about such things.[21]

Fascist-sponsored "unions" were set up. Their function was to speed up production and prevent wildcat strikes and apply punitive regulations, including fines, dismissals and imprisonment for those workers who complained of shop conditions. Even a Nazi labor-front newspaper had to admit, "Some shop regulations are reminiscent of penal codes." Workers could be shifted from one employment to another regardless of their wishes. They could be conscripted for any work assumed useful for the nation's economy, with no guarantee of wages equal to previous earnings. In both Italy and Germany the government exercised compulsory arbitration in regulation of work and wages. Any worker who contested such an arrangement was declared an enemy of the state.

These measures had the intended effect. According to figures supplied by the Italian press itself, the already meager wages for Italian workers in 1927 were cut in half by 1932. By 1939 the cost of living had risen an additional 30 percent. Taxes on wages were introduced. Regulations were instated against minimum wages. There was no more increased pay for overtime. In some regions, sanitary and safety regulations were dropped. Occupational-safety regulations were eliminated in factories. In many areas child labor was reintroduced. Many of the evils that the Italians thought belonged to a past generation now returned under fascism.

In Germany, it was the same story. Between 1933 and 1935 wages were lowered anywhere from 25 to 40 percent, a harsh cut for ordinary workers trying to make ends meet. Wage taxes were instituted. Municipal poll taxes were doubled and other payroll deductions were imposed. The nonprofit mutual-assistance and insurance associations that had existed before the Nazis were abolished. Their funds were taken over by private insurance companies that charged more while paying out smaller benefits. And in Germany, just as in Italy, inflation substantially added to the workers' hardships.

In both Italy and Germany, perfectly solvent publicly owned enterprises, such as power plants, steel mills, banks, railways, insurance firms, steamship companies, and shipyards, were handed over to private ownership. Corporate taxes were reduced by half in both Italy and Germany. Taxes on luxury items for the rich were cut. Inheritance taxes were either drastically lowered or abolished. In Germany between 1934 and 1940 the average net income of corporate businessmen rose by 46 percent. Enterprises that were floundering were refloated with state bonds, recapitalized out of the state treasury. Once made solvent, they were returned to private owners. With numerous enterprises, the state guaranteed a return on the capital invested and assumed all the risks. The rich investor did not have to worry about any losses; if a business did poorly, the investor would be recompensed from the state treasury.

What the fascist state attempts is a final solution to the problem of class conflict. It obliterates the democratic forms that allow workers some room for an organized defense of their interests. But this final solution proved very far from final. In fascist Italy and Germany, industrial sabotage and sporadic wildcat strikes continued, inflation increased, whole sectors of the economy remained stagnant. There was widespread corruption, mismanagement, underemployment, and vital social services deteriorated—but profits climbed.

The Italian economy remained in a troubled, stagnant condition right up to the Second World War. In Germany, thanks to the booming armaments industry, the standard of living, most notably the terrible unemployment problem, showed modest improvement, but it never came close to 1928 levels. Under the Weimar Republic, for all its troubles, the levels of food, textiles, and other areas of consumption and production were much better than ever achieved under Nazi Germany.

Here then were two peoples, the Italians and Germans, with different histories, cultures, and languages, and supposedly different temperaments, who ended up with the same repressive solutions because of the compelling similarities of economic power and class conflict that prevailed in their respective countries. Likewise in countries with such diverse histories and cultures as Lithuania, Croatia, Rumania, Hungary, Japan, and Spain a similar fascist pattern emerged to do its utmost to save corporate business from the troublesome impositions of democracy.[22] Fascism's savage service to big capital remains almost entirely a hidden history.

37 THE COLD WAR IS AN OLD WAR

It is commonly believed that the rivalry between the United States and the Soviet Union, known as the "Cold War," began after World War II. Both nations had been allies in the struggle against the Axis powers, but in short time an otherwise friendly Washington had to adopt a "containment policy" in order to counter Moscow's expansionist thrusts and military buildups, or so the story goes.

The truth is something else. The capitalist nations, including the United States, treated Soviet Russia as a threat virtually from the first days of its existence. What is called the "Cold War" is really an old war, a continuation of an antagonism prevailing from the first days of the Bolshevik Revolution in Russia in 1917. Long before the Soviets could ever have been a military threat to the West, they posed a *political* threat, the danger of an alternative system. Most Americans remain completely unfamiliar with this history.

In the century before World War II, U.S. rulers had already piled up a record of violent intervention in various countries, starting with the war of aggression against Mexico ending in 1848 that led to the annexation of almost half of Mexico's territory. U.S. expansionists then wiped out the last resistant Native American nations and closed the frontier. Some years later, in 1899–1903, they launched a bloody and protracted war of conquest in the Philippines. U.S. expeditionary forces intervened in China along with other Western armies to suppress the Boxer Rebellion and keep the Chinese under the heel of European and North American colonialists. U.S. marines invaded and occupied Nicaragua in 1912 and again in 1926–1933, Cuba in 1898–1902, Mexico in 1914 and 1916, Panama in 1903–1914, Haiti in 1915–1934, and Honduras six time between 1911 and 1925. So it was not an altogether unprecedented step when the United States joined other capitalist nations in an invasion of revolutionary Russia in 1918.

Years before the Russian Revolution, U.S. officials were taking repressive measures at home against syndicalists, anarchists, socialists, and communists who sought, in the words of one official, to "reduce all economic classes to one dismal level."[23] When revolutionary workers, under the leadership of Lenin's Bolshevik party, seized state power in Russia in 1917, some American labor organizations offered expressions of solidarity.[24] But among the moneyed classes of this and other capitalist nations the fear was palpable. The plutocracy's worst nightmare was coming true: here was a successful socialist revolution by the unlettered and unwashed masses against the natural leaders of society, the persons of talent and property. Unless drastic measures were taken, might not other countries follow suit?

Beginning in August 1918, fourteen capitalist nations, including the United States, Great Britain, France, and Japan, invaded Soviet Russia in an attempt to overthrow the Bolshevik government. In addition to using their own troops, they provided aid to the reactionary pro-czarist White Guard armies. To justify their action, Western leaders initially announced that the intervention was an attempt to keep Russia in the war against Germany. But the World War ended shortly after the invasion, yet the allies continued in their military campaign against the Bolshevik government for almost another two years. Western rulers also announced that the invasion was an attempt to rescue Czech prisoners-of-war marooned inside Russia. But the plight of the Czech prisoners developed well after the decision to intervene had been contemplated and was seized upon more as an after-the-fact excuse, a rather lame one at that.[25]

In truth, the allied leaders intervened in revolutionary Russia for the same reason conservative rulers have intervened in revolutionary conflicts before and since: to protect the existing social order. Recall how various European monarchs colluded against the French Revolution at the end of the eighteenth century. All the bitter rivalries that plagued the courts of Europe weighed less than the aristocracy's shared interest in class survival. Recall also, almost a century later in 1871, how Bismarck mobilized the same French army he had just defeated so that it could be used by the French ruling class against the revolutionary workers of the Paris Commune.

Likewise, after the 1918 armistice, the victorious Western allies allowed the German militarists to retain 5,000 machine guns to be used against German workers "infected with Bolshevism." The allies made clear that they would not tolerate a socialist workers' government in Germany nor permit diplomatic relations between Berlin and the newly installed Soviet government in the Kremlin."[26]

While President Woodrow Wilson contemplated sending American troops to Russia, his secretary of state, Robert Lansing, recorded in a confidential memorandum the administration's concerns. Lansing perceived Lenin and the Bolsheviks to be revolutionary socialists who sought "to make the ignorant and incapable mass of humanity dominate the earth." The Bolsheviks wanted "to overthrow all existing governments and establish on the ruins a despotism of the proletariat in every country." Their appeal was to "a class which does not have property but hopes to obtain a share by process of government rather than by individual enterprise. This is of course a direct threat at existing social order [i.e., capitalism] in all countries." The danger was that it "may well appeal to the average man, who will not perceive the fundamental errors." The Bolsheviks appealed "to the proletariat of all countries . . . to the ignorant and mentally deficient, who by their numbers are urged to become masters." Furthermore, the Bolsheviks had actually "confiscated private property" in Russia. For the patrician Lansing, Bolshevism was the "most hideous and monstrous thing that the human mind has ever conceived."[27]

General Alfred Knox, chief British military advisor in Russia, warned: "Distribute the land in Russia today, and in two years we'll be doing it in England." The U.S. ambassador to Russia, David Francis, urged armed intervention because the socialist elements organized into councils or *soviets* "composed of workingmen and soldiers . . . are advocating abolition of classes and the right of soldiers to disobey their officers."[28]

Concerned that the allied invasion would be ineffective, President Wilson was more hesitant to intervene than some other leaders. But he never made secret his distaste for the Bolsheviks. He told British leaders that he supported intervention even "against the wishes of the Russian people knowing it was eventually for their good. . . ."[29] Wilson dreaded the doctrine of social equality posed by the Russian Revolution and the effect it might have in other countries. Some of his worries about class (and racial) leveling were recorded by his physician:

> [President Wilson was concerned] that if the present government of Germany is recognizing the soldiers and workers councils, it is delivering itself into the hands of bolshevists. He said the American negro returning from abroad would be our greatest medium in conveying bolshevism to America. For example, a friend recently related the experience of a lady friend wanting to employ a negro laundress offering to pay the usual wage in that community. The negress demanded that she be given more money than was offered for the reason that "money is as much mine as it is yours."[30]

Wilson also feared that Bolshevism would affect the way business in America was conducted; business leaders might have to accede to having workers on their boards of directors, and other such scandalous arrangements.[31]

The class nature of the allied invasion of Soviet Russia became apparent to some of the invaders themselves. Members of the expedition to Archangel, in Northwestern Russia, observed that the cheering crowds greeting the British and American troops "consisted entirely of the bourgeoisie and that there was not a workman to be seen."[32] A British colonel stationed in a Siberian urban center angrily complained that "the [Russian] bourgeoisie makes one almost a Bolshevik oneself." In a town "full of quite rich people" not one of the affluent residents dreams of sparing just an hour to meet the trainloads of wounded and offer them a cup of tea. Instead they go "nightly to the opera and then on to

dance or what not until four or five even."[33] An American ser-
geant in Murmansk registered his loathing for the "lying, thieving,
murdering, tsarist army officials who keep their people in this
ignorance and poverty." Most of the Russian people, he maintained, were in sympathy with the Bolsheviks "and I don't blame
them."[34]

The allied intervention involved hundreds of thousands of military personnel. U.S. participation was more than "token" (as it
was falsely described in subsequent years). U.S. troops in Siberia
and in Archangel and Murmansk conservatively estimated at
40,000, not counting naval forces, engaged in extensive hostilities
and suffered several thousand casualties, including 436 fatalities.
American and other allied troops participated regularly in atrocities. Widespread pillaging and killing of civilians, including the
massacre of thousands of Jews, were carried out by the reactionary White Guard armies. The White armies were assisted by
a German expeditionary force under General Von der Goltz, who,
with U.S. and British funding, joined his former adversaries
against the common class enemy. Von der Goltz reportedly executed 3,000 persons in Riga alone.[35]

By 1919, the White Guard armies were wholly dependent on
American and British financial aid. In a report to Congress in January 1921, Herbert Hoover admitted that humanitarian relief
funds voted by Congress to feed starving civilians had been used
by him to supply these armies. Hoover withheld aid intended for
Hungary until the short-lived revolutionary Bella Kun government was overthrown and Admiral Worthy was installed, backed
by the bayonets of a Romanian army that executed hundreds of
revolutionaries and Hungarian Jews. Hoover also placed large
sums at the disposal of Polish militarists to support their invasion
of Soviet Russia in April 1920.[36]

Russia's immense natural wealth was very much on the minds of Western investors. Corporate investments in the country were slated to be nationalized by the Bolsheviks. Hoover alone had secured a major interest in no less than eleven Russian oil companies. Wherever the allied armies invaded, they were followed by Western business people. Coal, grain, timber, ores, furs, gold, oil, and machinery were extracted from the occupied areas and shipped to capitalist countries.[37]

During the 1980s, millions of Americans were treated to movies like *Red Dawn* and *Invasion USA* and television series like ABC's *Amerika*, which portrayed imaginary Soviet invasions of the United States. Most Americans would probably have been surprised to hear that in real life the reverse had happened. Even some of our presidents seemed unaware of the real history. Appearing on Soviet television while on a visit to the USSR in 1972, President Nixon announced: "Most important of all, we have never fought one another in war." In his 1984 State of the Union message, President Reagan said the same thing: "Our sons and daughters have never fought each other in war."[38] The Soviets, of course, remembered it differently.

In the United States one must search hard for historians and political scientists who have given attention to the West's invasion of revolutionary Russia. The scholarly literature is meager. Little mention, if any at all, of this extraordinary episode is made in textbooks and mainstream media. But imagine the treatment had it happened the other way around. Suppose that in 1920 or so, the young Soviet government had sent an expeditionary force across the Bering Strait down to Seattle, Portland, and California, in support of American strikers and labor agitators. Imagine that for two years this expeditionary force engaged in pitched battles, massacred many thousands of our citizens and destroyed properties, farms, and homes before being forced to retreat back to Russia. We would still be hearing about it in books, movies, and documentaries, and it would have remained a subject of lively study in U.S. schools from the first grade up through the doctoral level. Politicians and pundits would still be treating it as everlasting proof that Moscow was out to get us. But since the invasion happened the other way around, hardly any Americans have been informed of it.

The antagonism that plutocrats, presidents, prime ministers, and popes displayed toward Soviet Russia persisted through the two decades after World War I, in marked contrast to the forbearance and even admiration shown toward the fascists in Italy and the Nazis in Germany. While Hitler and Mussolini sent troops and armaments to help Generalissimo Franco crush the Spanish Republic in 1936–39, the United States, Great Britain, and France maintained an embargo against that beleaguered democracy, effectively contributing to its defeat. The Soviet Union and Mexico were the only nations to aid the Republic. Soviet shipments had to run a gauntlet of German and Italian submarines, with a loss of tons of munitions and arms, while the French government blocked Soviet overland deliveries into Spain. But fuel supplies from U.S. companies continued to flow to Franco's invading army.[39] Western leaders preferred to see Franco's fascist dictatorship installed in 1939 rather than risk the survival of a democratic republic that seemed to be moving too far to the left.

When Hitler annexed Austria in 1938, the Western leaders acted as if nothing too terrible had happened. With the active cooperation of U.S. officialdom, American corporations continued to expand their investments in German heavy industry and arms production.[40] That same year, British and French leaders hurried to

Munich to grant Hitler his claim to the Sudetenland, the heavily industrialized western portion of Czechoslovakia that contained a large German population. Less than half a year after Munich, Hitler marched his troops into all of Czechoslovakia. The day after this takeover, British leaders handed the Nazi dictator millions in Czech gold that had been deposited in the Bank of England.[41]

Some Western leaders had hoped to direct German expansionism eastward against the Soviet state. With few exceptions, they were more concerned with the Bolshevik specter than the fascist reality. They grew increasingly uncomfortable about Hitler's emergent power but they did not look upon fascism with the same fear and loathing as they did communism. Unlike the communists, the fascists were not a threat to business enterprise; if anything, the fascists had crushed worker organizations in Germany and Italy and had made those countries safer and more profitable than ever for private capital.[42]

Furthermore, the ruling circles in the West saw Hitler as a bulwark against communism in Germany, and Nazi Germany as a bulwark against communism in Europe. Their collaboration with Hitler has since been condemned as "appeasement." More accurately it was an active complicity born of a mutual class hatred for revolutionary socialism.[43] For western leaders the goal was to get the Nazis to attack the Soviets. At the same time, the United States and Great Britain did little to deter Japan's aggressions in Manchuria and China. Here too the anticipation was that Tokyo might eventually move against the USSR, as indeed occurred. In 1938, Japan entered an "Axis alliance" with Germany and Italy (the Anti-Comintern Pact), explicitly avowing a joint struggle against "World Communism." Japanese imperial forces then attacked the Soviet Union near the Outer Mongolian area, only to be beaten back with heavy casualties.

Repeated overtures by Moscow to conclude collective-security pacts with the Western democracies in order to contain Axis aggression were rebuffed, including Soviet attempts to render armed assistance to Czechoslovakia. Frustrated in its attempts to form an anti-Nazi alliance, and believing (correctly) that it was being set up as a target for Nazi aggression, the USSR signed an eleventh-hour nonaggression treaty with Hitler in 1939 to divert any immediate attack by German forces.

To this day, the Hitler-Stalin pact is paraded as proof of the USSR's diabolic affinity for Nazism and its willingness to cooperate with Hitler in the dismemberment of Poland. Conservative news columnist George Will was only one of many when he mistakenly described the Soviet Union as a regime that was "once allied with Hitler."[44] The Soviets were never allied with Hitler. The pact was a treaty, not an alliance. It no more denoted an alliance with Nazism than would a nonaggression treaty between the United States and the Soviets have denoted an alliance between the two. On this point, British historian A. J. P. Taylor is worth quoting:

> It was no doubt disgraceful that Soviet Russia should make any agreement with the leading Fascist state; but this reproach came ill from the statesmen who went to Munich . . . . [The Hitler-Stalin] pact contained none of the fulsome expressions of friendship which Chamberlain had put into the Anglo-German declaration on the day after the Munich conference. Indeed Stalin rejected any such expressions: "the Soviet Government could not suddenly present to the public German-Soviet assurances of friendship after [we] had been covered with buckets of filth by the Nazi Government for six years."

The pact was neither an alliance nor an agreement for the partition of Poland. Munich had been a true alliance for partition: the British and French dictated partition to the Czechs. The Soviet government undertook no such action against the Poles. They merely promised to remain neutral, which is what the Poles had always asked them to do and which Western policy implied also. More than this, the agreement was in the last resort anti-German: it limited the German advance eastwards in case of war. . . . [With the pact, the Soviets hoped to ward] off what they had most dreaded—a united capitalist attack on Soviet Russia. . . . It is difficult to see what other course Soviet Russia could have followed.[45]

When Hitler attacked Poland in September 1939, thus setting off World War II, the Soviets moved into Latvia, Lithuania, and Estonia, the Baltic territories that had been taken from them by Germany, Britain, and Poland in 1919. They overthrew the pro-fascist dictatorships that the Western powers had installed, and incorporated the Baltic states as three republics of the USSR. The Soviets also invaded and annexed eastern Poland. This has been portrayed as proof that they colluded with the Nazis to gobble up that beleaguered nation, but the Soviets reoccupied only the land that had been taken from them by the Polish dictatorship in 1921: Western Byelorussia, the Western Ukraine, and some other areas. History offers few if any examples of a nation refusing the opportunity to regain territory that had been seized from it. In any case, as Taylor notes, by reclaiming their old boundaries, the Soviets drew a line on the Nazi advance which was more than what Great Britain and France seemed willing to do.

When Hitler subsequently invaded France and then the Soviet

Union, he forged in war the East-West alliance that London and Washington had repeatedly rejected and Moscow had long sought. But even then British leaders seriously considered coming to peace terms with Berlin so that they might make common cause with the Nazis against their real bête noir, Russian Bolshevism.[46] For instance, while ostensibly at war with Germany, British Tory leaders sought passage of Allied forces through Scandinavia and Finland in order to launch an attack against the Soviet Union— an action Churchill supported even after the Finns had signed a peace treaty with Moscow in March 1940 and at a time when the Nazis were overrunning Europe.[47] As in earlier years, the British elites were more concerned with undoing the Soviets than with stopping the Nazis. Most British and American accounts of the war ignore the major role played by the USSR in Nazism's defeat, and the horrendous losses in life and property sustained by the Soviets fighting a war that was many times greater than anything on the Western front. More than 80 percent of all German casualties were sustained on the Russian front.[48]

Well before hostilities ceased, the West was preparing to resume the crusade to make Eurasia safe for capitalism. Kim Philby, the British agent who defected to the USSR, reports that between the wars, the greater part of British intelligence's resources were "devoted to the penetration of the Soviet Union." When the defeat of the Axis was in sight, British espionage focused once again on "Bolshevism."[49]

The August 1943 minutes of the combined chiefs of staff, made public in London and Washington in 1970, reveal that ten months before the end of hostilities in Europe, "military strategists discussed the possibility of repelling the Russians if they suddenly began overrunning Nazi Germany." Both U.S. chief of staff General George Marshall and British chief of staff Sir Alan Brooke were interested in ascertaining whether Germany would help allied troops enter Europe "to repel the Russians."

On the eve of the first atomic test, President Truman's first thoughts were of the Russians: "If [the atomic bomb] explodes, as I think it will, I'll certainly have a hammer on those boys." According to one visitor, Truman asserted that "the Russians would soon be put in their places" and that the United States would then "take the lead in running the world in the way that the world ought to be run."[50] General Groves, head of the Manhattan Project that developed the bomb, testified: "There was never—from about two weeks from the time I took charge of the project—any illusion on my part but that Russia was the enemy and that the project was conducted on that basis."[51]

The conventional explanation of how the Cold War began, the one given to the U.S. public is something else. As pronounced by Mose Harvey, a member of the State Department's Policy Planning Council: "The Soviets had chosen to, as it were, declare war on us—much to our surprise. We had little choice but to concentrate on the various threats thrusted before us."[52] Of the various threats, the most menacing was said to be the Red Army itself, massively arrayed across Central Europe at the end of World War II, supposedly deterred from invading the West only by U.S. possession of the atomic bomb. As Winston Churchill asserted, "Nothing preserves Europe from an overwhelming military attack except the devastating resources of the United States in this awful weapon."[53]

Worse still, while the United States engaged in large-scale demobilization after the war, the Soviets purportedly retained their forces at full strength. Political scientists Arora and Lasswell claim: "There was, in fact, a period of such rapid withdrawal of American forces abroad that communist forces were given a new lease on life in many countries."[54] It is not clear where the rapid U.S. withdrawal took place; certainly not from West Germany, France, Italy, Austria, Korea, or Japan, nor from the hundreds of U.S. military bases that were being set up around the world, nor from the seas and oceans patrolled by U.S. fleets, nor from the many newly constructed U.S. air bases with their long-range bombers armed with nuclear bombs.

It is true that Western armies were not kept anywhere at wartime strength. The same holds for the Red Army. By 1948, the USSR had demobilized its forces from 11.3 million to 2.8 million and had withdrawn its troops from Manchuria, Korea, Norway, Denmark, Austria, and elsewhere. Most Western observers now agree that the Red Army's strength was "considerably exaggerated in the West during the early postwar years."[55] Soviet divisions were much smaller and lacked the extensive logistical supports of Western divisions. Also, a large portion of the Red Army was composed of noncombat units engaged in mending the extensive war damage, rebuilding industries and housing complexes.[56]

The Soviets lost more than 22 million citizens in World War II, and suffered massive destruction of its cities, utilities, industries, railways, bridges, and collective farms.[57] Following a trip to the USSR in 1947, British Field Marshal Montgomery wrote to General Eisenhower: "The Soviet Union is very, very tired. Devastation in Russia is appalling and the country is in no fit state to go to war."[58] While U.S. cold warriors took steps to remilitarize Germany and form a military pact of Western nations (NATO), a CIA report stated: "There is no conclusive evidence of Soviet preparation for direct military aggression during 1949."[59] Yet the threat was conjured for decades to justify U.S. military build-ups in Europe and elsewhere. Recent research indicates that top U.S.

defense officials in the postwar era did not expect a Soviet military attack. Their real fear was that they would lose control of Europe and Asia to socialist revolutions caused by widespread poverty and economic instability.[60]

If our rulers were capable of misleading us for so long about Soviet intentions and capabilities in order to justify their own expansionist policies during the postwar era, is it not unreasonable to entertain the possibility that they are capable of misrepresentations today about other "mortal threats" and "adversaries?"

38 THE PEOPLE AS "RABBLE" AND "MOB"

Mainstream historians have seldom thought well of the common people of history, when they bothered to think about them at all. Take, for example, the impoverished commoners of ancient Rome. In the first century B.C., Cicero was part of an already established tradition when he described the *plebs urbana* as the "city dirt and filth," "a starving, contemptible rabble." And whenever the people mobilized against class injustice, they became in his mind that most odious of all creatures, the "mob."[61] Cicero regarded the people as worthless groundlings, akin to criminals and degenerates, "many of them simply out for revolution." He denounced those of pedestrian occupation, "the artisans and shopkeepers and all that kind of scum" who align themselves with dangerous demagogues, "the wretched half-starved commoners who attend mass meetings and suck the blood of the treasury."[62] To him, their restiveness was an outgrowth of their own personal malevolence rather than a response to unforgiving material circumstances. Privately Cicero referred to "my army of the rich" and noted that "the safety of the state is to the advantage of all good men, but most clearly benefits men of fortune"—which was as he thought it should be.[63]

Long before Cicero, Polybius was asserting that "the masses are always fickle, filled with lawless desires, unreasoning anger and violent passions."[64] Later on Asconius referred to the supporters of the popular reformer Clodius Pulcher (Caesar's ally) as "a great crowd of slaves and rabble," an "ignorant mob."[65] In a similar mode Appian wrote of "the poor and hotheaded," and criticized Julius Caesar for "introducing laws to win the favor of the mob," or as Plutarch commented, Caesar aligned himself with "the numerous diseased and corrupted elements in the polity."[66]

Down to the present day, classical historians continue to describe the Roman proletariat as "the mob," "the idle city rabble," the "emotional masses" who were "no more than the tool of power," "the stupid . . . selfish, good-for-nothing mob," "the parasitic mob of the metropolis," "the worthless elements."[67]

H.H. Scullard sniffs at the "increasingly irresponsible . . . idle urban mob," as if their idleness were purely of their own choosing. Meanwhile the aristocratic idlers—so well supported by the labor of slaves and plebs—earn not a harsh word from him or most other writers.[68] Theodore Mommsen refers to "the lazy and hungry rabble"; for him the people's assemblies were agitated by "special passions, in which intelligence was totally lost." "That terrible urban proletariat" was "utterly demoralized . . . sometimes stupid and sometimes knavish."[69] Christian Meier, agreeing with the Roman nobles who referred to the urban mass as "the bilge of the city," denounces "Rome's laborers, traders and artisans" for trying to assume a level of political participation "that was far beyond their capacity."[70] Even radical journalist-cum-classical historian I.F. Stone characterized the Roman plebs as "a rabble," comparing them unfavorably to Athens' "citizenry."[71] And the liberal Lewis Mumford referred to Rome's "parasitic mob."[72]

Historians have been ever alert to the corrupting influence that state assistance might have upon the Roman poor. Sallust, who wrote during Caesar's day, spoke of "the populace who are now demoralized by largesse and the public distribution of grain." Forced into idleness, they become "infected with vicious principles" and need to "be prevented from disturbing the government."[73] Appian was convinced that the grain ration attracted "the idly destitute and hotheaded elements of the Italian population to the capital," who contrast unfavorably with "those who possessed property and good sense."[74] Juvenal wrote scornfully of the mob's preoccupation with *"panem et circenses"* (bread and circuses), a phrase that has echoed down through the ages, adding to the image of Rome's proletariat as a shiftless, volatile mass addicted to endless rounds of free victuals and free entertainment.[75]

Centuries later, Scullard denounced "the city mob" as "far too irresponsible to exercise political power: rather it wanted '*panem et circenses*.'" Mumford saw only parasitism in "the dual handout of bread and circuses."[76] And John Dickinson denounced Julius Caesar for appealing to "the cupidity and self-interest of those who desired to be supported at the expense of the state."[77] Dickinson saw the plebs as acting from their "baser motives" when they demanded subsidized bread prices, land reform, public jobs, and rent easement. He voices no reproach of the nobility for their expropriation of the public lands, their usury, rent gouging, and plundering of the provinces. In a similar spirit Scullard was certain that a free grain dole "hastened the demoralization of the people." In contrast, he describes the dictator Sulla's abolition of grain distribution as a "reform," and invites no critical comment for the severe hardship it must have inflicted upon the poor.[78]

Contrary to the image propagated by past and present historians, dole recipients did not live like parasites off the "bread" they received—actually a meager grain ration used for making bread and gruel. Man (and woman) cannot live by bread alone, not even at the simple physiological level. The plebs needed money for rent, clothing, cooking oil, and other necessities. Most of them had to find work, low-paying and irregular as it might be. As a necessary supplement, the bread dole often was the difference between survival and starvation, but it never served as a total support allowing people to idle away their days.

In any case, we might wonder why so many scholars have judged the Roman commoners as venal and degraded because they demanded affordable bread to feed themselves and their children. Alan Cameron is one of the few writers, along with the great G. E. M. de Ste. Croix, who takes issue with the historical image of the freeloading plebs: "That notorious idle mob of layabouts sponging off the state is little more than a figment of middle-class prejudice, ancient and modern alike." As with bread, so with circuses. "It was not the people's fault that public entertainments, being in origin religious festivals, were provided free," Cameron adds.[79]

At any one time, Lewis Mumford reckoned, almost half the free adult population of Rome could be accommodated in its circuses, arenas, and theaters. Mumford seems to think that attendance at the amphitheater became the proletariat's principle occupation. With a touch of psychobabble, he tells us that the commoners sought to escape their "own self-loathing" and "desire for death" by pursuing "a violent desire to impose a humiliating death on others" in the Roman arena.[80]

It may well be that the games and races helped the poor to forget their grievances for awhile, acting as a popular distraction, not unlike mass sporting events today. The emperors seemed well aware of the diversionary social control function that the spectacles served, which probably explains why they continued to produce them regardless of cost.[81]

The poor were not the only ones to attend the awful bloodletting of the amphitheater. Probably a higher proportion of wealthy nobles and equestrians frequented the games, ensconced in reserved front-row stalls that afforded them the best view. A contemporary report from Juvenal tell us that "all the best seats are reserved for the classes who have the most money."[82] Likewise in the Colosseum the front rows were reserved for magistrates, foreign dignitaries, and senators. The rows directly behind them were set aside for the upper social classes, with additional seats for priests, military officers, and other special groups. Women were consigned to the worst seats in the house at the very top. And behind them was standing room for the common "rabble."[83]

Emperor Augustus himself admitted to enjoying the games.[84] And Tacitus tells us that Emperor Tiberius's son eagerly presided over the gladiatorial contests, displaying an "inordinate delight . . . in the slaughter, though it be of men who mattered little."[85] The rich and well-born occasionally participated in the arena games. Patrician children displayed their horsemanship. Young peers vied with one another in chariot races. Some knights and the son of an erstwhile praetor voluntarily engaged in displays of combat in a grand spectacle produced by Julius Caesar.[86]

Portrayed as nothing more than a blood-lusting rabble, the plebs actually were sometimes critical of what they witnessed at arena spectacles. For example, the ceremonies to dedicate Pompey's theater included a battle between a score of elephants and men armed with javelins. The event did not go as intended. The slaughter of the elephants proved more than the crowd could countenance. One giant creature, brought to its knees by the missiles, crawled about, ripping shields from its attackers and tossing them into the air. Another, pierced deeply through the eye with a javelin, fell dead with a horrifying crash. The elephants shrieked bitterly as their tormentors closed in. Some of them refused to fight, treading about frantically with trunks raised toward heaven, as if lamenting to the gods. In desperation, the beleaguered beasts tried to break through the iron palisade that corralled them. When they lost all hope of escape, they turned to the arena crowd as if to beg for their assistance with heartbreaking gestures of entreaty and a pitiful wailing. The spectators were moved to tears and brought to their feet cursing Pompey, overcome with feeling for these great mammals.[87]

In an another instance, in 46 B.C., to celebrate his Gallic triumph and his third consulship, Caesar produced a series of violent spectacles. In the grand finale, two armies respectively composed of war captives and condemned criminals—each side consisting of hundreds of foot soldiers, cavalry, and a score of elephants—waged a battle to the death. But the Roman commoners were more distressed than enthralled by the bloody performance. As Dio Cassius records, they criticized Caesar for the great number who were slain, charging that "he had not himself become satiated with slaughter and was exhibiting to the populace symbols of their own miseries." In addition, an outcry was raised because Caesar had collected most of the funds unjustly and had squandered them on such a wanton display.[88]

Who actually composed the Roman proletariat, this "heartless mob" who wept for tormented elephants and deplored the arena's dissipation of blood and treasure? Who might be this "idle rabble" who organized into political clubs and workers' guilds, and engaged in Forum meetings, demonstrations, and street insurgencies?

The "mobs" of eighteenth- and nineteenth-century England and France are described by the upper-class critics of those times as composed of beggars, convicts, and other low-life detritus. But records reveal that rebel crowds in both countries consisted of farm laborers, and various kinds of craftsmen, along with shopkeepers, wine merchants, cooks, porters, domestic servants, miners, and laborers; almost all of fixed abode, some temporarily unemployed, only a handful of whom were vagrants or had criminal records.[89]

The rebels of the Paris Commune of 1871, sentenced to death or imprisonment, consisted of carpenters, tinworkers, watchmakers, bookbinders, teachers, house painters, locksmiths, tailors, tanners, stonecutters, bricklayers, cobblers, dressmakers, and numerous other occupations. Still others listed themselves as medical student, accountant, cashier, man of letters, and head of primary school. About half the craftsmen and skilled workers of Paris fell in the summary mass executions of 1871.[90]

The longstanding stereotype of popular mobs as fickle, brutish, rootless, and senselessly destructive was elaborately promoted by Gustave Le Bon in his *La Foule*, translated into English in 1869 as *The Crowd*, a book that has been kept in print and assigned to generations of students for over 135 years, long declared a classic. "Although Le Bon wrote in the relatively tranquil late nineteenth century," remarks Leonard Richards, "he managed to sound like an aristocrat dashing off a passionate indictment of the French Revolution several hours before it became his turn to meet the guillotine."[91] Also challenging Le Bon is George Rudé who maintains that the "mobish actions" of the eighteenth century were not wanton mindless affairs but forms of social protest against unaffordable rents, food prices, and crushing taxes. The riots often were coordinated actions, targeting particular officials, merchants, granaries, landlords, and other culpable persons and places, depending on the issue. They agitated not only for bread but for decent wages, the security of their homes, and the right to dissent and organize unions. Rudé concludes that rioters did not consist of the lawless riffraff "imagined by those historians who have taken their cue from the prejudiced accounts of contemporary observers."[92]

(Parenthetically it might be added that, of course, not all crowd actions have been directed toward democratic goals. One need only draw examples from our own history of lynchings, race riots, anti-immigrant riots, jingoist attacks on peace protesters, and the like. Keep in mind that in the early nineteenth century, anti-abolition mobs often were mobilized and prodded by community leaders, prominent slaveholders, and other affluent individuals.[93])

Returning to ancient Rome, we find Cicero gazing down from his senatorial heights, characterizing the activist elements among the plebs as "exiles, slaves, madmen," runaways, criminals, and "assassins from the jail." In fact, they were mostly masons, carpenters, shopkeepers, scribes, glaziers, butchers, blacksmiths, coppersmiths, bakers, dyers, rope makers, weavers, fullers, tanners, metal workers, scrap dealers, teamsters, dockers, porters, and various day jobbers—the toiling proletariat of Rome.[94]

In the slim record that comes down to us, there is evidence indicating that these commoners were quite capable of exercising critical judgment at crucial times. For instance, in July 45 B.C., as Cicero himself relates, the people showed their displeasure at Caesar's monarchical pretensions, refraining from applauding his statue when it was being carried with those of the gods in a procession.[95]

Many of Rome's commoners were ex-slaves or the sons of slaves. Most were almost as poor as slaves. They sometimes worked alongside slaves, and were inclined to feel a common interest with the servile population on many basic issues. In parts of Sicily, free farmhands joined in common cause with slaves to rebel against big planters.[96] An incident from Tacitus speaks volumes. In A.D. 61, the city prefect was murdered in his bed chamber by one or more of his slaves. By ancient custom, when a master was murdered by a slave all *servi* in the household had to be put to death. In this instance it meant the extermination of some four hundred souls, including women and children. The possibility of such a mass execution caused a public outcry, compelling the Senate to hold a formal debate on the issue. One of the senior members of the Senate spoke at length in support of the executions, maintaining that the slaveholder's interest demanded that there be no departure from ancient practice no matter how harsh the outcome. "If all four hundred slaves are not executed, who among us will be safe?" he argued. There were a few uneasy outcries, but no senator took the floor to denounce the measure, which passed without further debate.[97]

This mass execution however did evoke furious protests from the plebs, who assembled outside the Senate House armed with rocks and torches. Emperor Nero had to bring out the troops to line the route over which the condemned passed. The sense of moral outrage expressed by the protesters signaled a sympathetic bond between impoverished slaves and impoverished plebs. Tacitus refers to the protesters as "the mob" but offers no critical description of the mob mentality that prevailed *within* the Senate House among those who sanctioned this mass murder.

Rather than being a mindless rabble, the poor joined battle on a number of issues that affected them, showing a keen sense of their own interests. Not without reason did Cato the younger, a fierce conservative, fear restiveness among the very poorest, for they "were always the first to kindle the flame among the people."[98] Yavetz cites over fifty mass political actions known to have occurred during the Republican era.[99] The Roman commoners provided support to the various reform-minded leaders (*populares*), including Julius Caesar who was able to win their backing less because they were mesmerized by his demagogic style and more because they strongly favored his luxury taxes on the rich, and his programs for land reform and resettlement of deracinated families. Caesar canceled rents for a year, abolished about 25 percent of all debts, and initiated public works projects that eased the underemployment. He also required that free labor replace one-third of the slave workforce on the plantations. These and other initiatives won him much popular regard.

What evidence we have of proletarian activism is virtually ignored by almost all modern-day classical historians. Almost a century before Caesar there was Tiberius Gracchus who as a people's tribune championed agrarian reform. Plutarch writes, "It was above all the people themselves who did most to stoke Tiberius's energy and ambitions by inscribing slogans and appeals on porticoes, monuments, and the walls of houses, calling upon him to recover the public land for the poor." Tiberius and some three hundred of his supporters were massacred in 133 B.C. by a gang of assassins led by conservative senators, most notably Nasica. The common people felt bitterly about the killings and spoke openly of revenge. When they encountered Nasica, reports Plutarch, "they did not try to hide their hatred of him, but grew savage and cried out upon him wherever he chanced to be, calling him an accursed man and a tyrant." Fearing for Nasica's safety, the Senate voted to send him to Asia though it had no need of him there. Nasica wandered about ignominiously in foreign lands for a brief period, then took his own life.[100]

About ten years after Tiberius's death, his younger brother, Gaius Gracchus, a people's tribune, left his home on the fashionable Palatine Hill to live among the poor near the Forum. After he put forth his reform legislation, "a great multitude began to gather in Rome from all parts of Italy to support him." Gaius won "the wholehearted devotion of the people, and they were prepared to do almost anything in the world to show their goodwill."[101] But he too, along with some 250 of his supporters were killed by the senatorial oligarchs' death squads in 121 B.C.

After the Gracchi were assassinated, public acknowledgment of their existence was officially proscribed. The oligarchs were intent upon expurgating the collective historical memory. Yet the populace continued to commemorate the brothers. Plutarch offers a moving vignette: "The people were cowed and humiliated by the collapse of the democratic cause, but they soon showed how deeply they missed and longed for the Gracchi. Statues of the brothers were set up in a prominent part of the city, the places where they had fallen were declared to be holy ground, and the first-fruits of the season were offered up there throughout the year. Many people even sacrificed to the Gracchi every day, and worshipped their statues as though they were visiting the shrines of gods."[102]

In 62 B.C. another popular leader, Catiline, was hunted down and killed along with others in a northern province by an army under orders from Rome's leading consul of that day, none other than Cicero. A few years later, the plebs adorned Catiline's tomb "as formerly that of the Gracchi, with flowers and garlands," writes Mommsen.[103] As far as can be said, the people never offered memorial tributes to Cicero, Cato, Sulla, Catulus, Brutus, Cassius, or any other prominent senatorial oligarch.

In 70 B.C. and again in 67, 66, and 64, radical tribunes packed the assemblies and launched demonstrations and electoral campaigns by mobilizing the *collegia*, those guilds of freedmen, slaves, and free poor. Such mass actions were enough to cause the Senate to pass a decree dissolving all but a few of the more innocuous *collegia*, depriving the popular movement of its key organizations.

In all, the proletariat played a crucial but much ignored role in the struggle for democratic policies. They showed themselves to be neither a mindless mob nor a shiftless rabble but a politically aware force capable of registering preferences in accordance with their interests, able to distinguish friend from foe. That their efforts have been deemed worthy of little more than passing condemnation is but a further reflection of the elite biases shared by ancient and modern historians alike.

We hear that we must avoid imposing present values upon past experience, and we must immerse ourselves in the historic context under study. But few present-day historians immerse themselves in the grim and embattled social experience of the Roman commoners. If anything, they see the poor—especially the rebellious poor—through the prism of their own elitist bias, the same bias shared by ancient historians. In the one-sided record that is called history, it has been standard practice to damn popular agitation as the work of riffraff and demagogues.

The common people of ancient Rome had scant opportunity to

leave a written record of their views and struggles. Still, what we know of them suggests that they displayed a social consciousness and sense of justice that was usually superior to anything possessed by their would-be superiors. The anonymous masses, upon whose shoulders stood such great reform leaders as the Gracchi, come down to us most usually as a disreputable mob.

They who struggled against formidable odds with the fear and courage of ordinary humans, whose names we shall never know, whose blood and tears we shall never see, whose cries of pain and hope we shall never hear, to them we are linked by a past that is never dead nor ever really past. And so, when the best pages of history are finally written, it will be not by princes, presidents, prime ministers, or pundits, nor even by professors, but by the people themselves. For all their faults and shortcomings, the people are all we have. Indeed, we ourselves are the people.

NOTES

1. As quoted by Kenneth Harris in *New York Times Book Review*, 27 April 1997.
2. Carroll Quigley, *The Anglo-American Establishment* (Books in Focus, 1981), xi, 197.
3. For a more extensive discussion, see Michael Parenti, *History as Mystery* (City Lights, 1999), especially chapter four.
4. Theodore Roscoe, *The Web of Conspiracy: The Complete Story of the Men Who Murdered Abraham Lincoln* (Prentice-Hall, 1959, 1960), ix.
5. Edward Hallett Carr, *What is History?* (Random House, 1961), 12–13.
6. Henry Charles Lea, *The Inquisition of the Middle Ages: Its Organization and Operation* (Citadel Press, 1961), 5.
7. Emmanuel Le Roy Ladurie, *Montaillou, The Promised Land of Error* (Vintage, 1979). The original Inquisition record from the Vatican Library is cited by Le Roy Ladurie as: Jean Duvernoy (ed.), *Le Registre d'Inquisition de Jacques Fournier, evêque de Pamiers (1318-1325)*, 3 vols. (Toulouse, 1965).
8. Le Roy Ladurie, *Montaillou*, 246.
9. Le Roy Ladurie, *Montaillou*, xi, 317, 321, 333. In 1334 Bishop Fournier was elected Pope of Avignon under the name of Benedict XII.

10. Le Roy Ladurie, *Montaillou*, 231, 243.
11. Samuel Eliot Morison, *The Oxford History of the American People* (Oxford University Press, 1965).
12. Jean Anyon, "Ideology and United States History Textbooks," *Harvard Educational Review*, 49 (August 1979): 361–364.
13. Publisher's Note to C. Osborne Ward, *The Ancient Lowly* (Charles H. Kerr Cooperative, 1907), v.
14. Upton Sinclair, *The Brass Check: A Study of American Journalism* (published by the author, n.d. [c. 1920]); John Ahouse, *Upton Sinclair Bibliography* (Mercer & Aitchison, 1994), ix; Upton Sinclair, *The Autobiography of Upton Sinclair* (Harcourt, Brace & World, 1962), 223.
15. Carroll Quigley, *Tragedy and Hope: A History of the World in Our Time* (MacMillan, 1966); also Daniel Brandt, "Philanthropists at War," *NameBase NewsLine*, no. 15 (October–December 1996).
16. Ellis Goldberg, "Bookstores Have Their Own Censorship," *Guardian* (New York), 15 March 1989.
17. Charles Willet, "Librarians as Censors," *Librarians at Liberty*, (CRISES Press), June 1995.
18. R. Palme Dutt, *Fascism and Social Revolution* (International Publishers, 1935), 124.
19. Quoted in Daniel Guerin, *Fascism and Big Business* (Monad Press/Pathfinder Press, 1973), 33.
20. Richard Plant, *The Pink Triangle* (Henry Holt, 1986), 47.
21. Among the thousands of books that deal with fascism, there are a few that do not evade questions of political economy and class power. Most of the information that follows is from: Gaetano Salvemini, *Under the Ax of Fascism* (Howard Fertig, 1969); Guerin, *Fascism and Big Business*; James Pool and Suzanne Pool, *Who Financed Hitler* (Dial Press, 1978); Palmiro Togliatti, *Lectures on Fascism* (International Publishers, 1976); Franz Neumann, *Behemoth* (Oxford University Press, 1944); and Dutt, *Fascism and Social Revolution*.
22. This is not to gainsay that cultural differences can lead to important variations. Consider, for instance, the horrific role played by anti-Semitism in Nazi Germany as compared to fascist Italy.
23. William Preston, Jr., *Aliens and Dissenters* (Harvard University Press, 1963); Sidney Fine, *Laissez-Faire and the General Welfare State* (University of Michigan Press, 1956).
24. Richard Boyer and Herbert Morais, *Labor's Untold Story* (United Electrical, 1972), 202, 215.
25. Lloyd Gardner, *Safe For Democracy, The Anglo-American Response to Revolution*, 1913–1923 (Oxford University Press, 1984), 170, 180; William Appleman Williams, "American Intervention in Russia: 1917–1920," in

David Horowitz, ed., Containment and Revolution (Beacon Press, 1967), 62.

26. Gardner, *Safe For Democracy*, 198–200.

27. Quoted in William Appleman Williams, "American Intervention in Russia: 1917–1920," in David Horowitz (ed.), *Containment and Revolution* (Boston: Beacon Press, 1967), 36, 38, 42–43, 61; Gardner, *Safe for Democracy*, 161.

28. Quotations from Gardner, *Safe For Democracy*, 133–134, 148, 151.

29. Both Wilson quotations from Williams, "American Intervention," 61 and 57 respectively.

30. Gary Grayson's diary, quoted in Gardner, *Safe For Democracy*, 242.

31. Gardner, *Safe For Democracy*, 242.

32. Christopher Dobson and John Miller, *The Day They Almost Bombed Moscow* (Atheneum, 1986), 64.

33. Dobson and Miller, *The Day They Almost Bombed Moscow*, 239–240.

34. Dobson and Miller, *The Day They Almost Bombed Moscow*, 189–190.

35. Michael Sayers and Albert Kahn, *The Great Conspiracy, The Secret War Against the Soviet Union* (Proletarian Publishers, 1946) chapters 6, 7, 8 and passim; Dobson and Miller, *The Day They Almost Bombed Moscow*, 23, 248, 270. For a more complete account of White Army atrocities, see George Stewart, *The White Armies of Russia* (Macmillan 1933).

36. W. W. Liggett, *The Rise of Herbert Hoover* (H. K. Fly 1932), 255, 260–267; also B. M. Weissman, *Herbert Hoover and Famine Relief to Soviet Russia* (Hoover Institution Press, 1974), 34, 37, 215.

37. John Hamill, *The Strange Career of Herbert Hoover under Two Flags* (William Faro, 1931), 298–300.

38. For the Nixon and Reagan statements, see Dobson and Miller, *The Day they Almost Bombed Moscow*, 200.

39. Arthur Landis, *Spain, The Unfinished Revolution* (International Publishers, 1975).

40. Charles Higham, *Trading with the Enemy* (Dell, 1983).

41. See Jacob Oser's essay in Judith Joel and Gerald Erickson, eds., *Anti-Communism: The Politics of Manipulation* (Marxist Educational Press, 1987)

42. See herein selection 36, "Fascism, the Real Story."

43. For a superb history of the politics behind Munich, see Clement Leibovitz, *The Chamberlain-Hitler Deal* (Les Editions Duval, 1993).

44. See Will's columns in the *Washington Post*, 16 November 1986, also 21 May 1987.

45. A. J. P. Taylor, *The Origins of the Second World War* (Hamilton, 1961), 262.

46. Well demonstrated by Leibovitz, *The Chamberlain-Hitler Deal* passim.

47. Clive Ponting, *1940: Myth and Reality* (Ivan R. Dee, 1991), 50.

48. John Newsinger, "Churchill: Myth and Imperialist History," 56–57; and Clive Ponting, Churchill (Sinclair Stevenson, 1994).

49. Kim Philby, *My Silent War* (Ballantine Books, 1968), 101.

50. William Appleman Williams, *The Tragedy of American Diplomacy* (World Publishing, 1959), 168–69. On how Truman reneged on the Yalta agreements, see Diana Shaver Clemens, *Yalta* (Oxford, 1971).

51. Quoted in Bert Cochran, *The War System* (Macmillan, 1965), 42–43.

52. Mose Harvey, "Focus on the Soviet Challenge," lecture recording, Westinghouse Broadcasting, 1964.

53. Churchill quoted in Matthew Evangelista, "Stalin's Postwar Army Reappraised," *International Security*, 7, Winter 1982–83, 110.

54. Satish Arora and Harold Lasswell, *Political Communication: The Public Language of Political Elites in India and the United States* (Holt, Rinehart & Winston, 1969).

55. Evangelista, "Stalin's Postwar Army . . . ," 115 and the official US reports cited therein; see also Tom Gervasi, *The Myth of Soviet Military Supremacy* (Harpercollins, 1987).

56. Evangelista, "Stalin's Postwar Army . . . ," 117–19, 125.

57. D. F. Fleming, *The Cold War and Its Origins* (Doubleday, 1961).

58. Evangelista, "Stalin's Postwar Army . . . ," 134.

59. Evangelista, "Stalin's Postwar Army . . . ," 134.

60. Melvin Leffler, "The American Conception of National Security and the Beginnings of t he Cold War, 1945–48," *American Historical Review*, 90, Feburary 1985, 363–64.

61. Cicero, *To Atticus* 1.16,11 and 1.19,4; *To His Friends*, XI.7.1; *Philippics*, II.116 and VIII.9.

62. *To Atticus* 1.16 and VIII.3; and Cicero's *For Flaccus* 15–18, and *To His Friends* VII.1.

63. *To Atticus* 1.19,4; II.6.

64. Polybius, *Histories* VI.56

65. Asconius Pedianus, commentary on Pro Milo, in his *Orationum Ciceronis*.

66. Appian, *The Civil Wars*, 1.59 and II.13; Plutarch, *Cato the Younger* XXVI.1–2.

67. For these and other such negative labeling, see the writings of John Dickinson, P.A. Brunt, Matthias Gelzer, Cyril Robinson, Dero Saunders, Zwi Yavetz, John H. Collins, J. F. C. Fuller, and others too numerous to list.

68. H. H. Scullard, *From the Gracchi to Nero* (Methuen, 1963), 30, 32, and passim.

69. Theodore Mommsen, *The History of Rome*, (Meridian Books, 1958) 23, 48, 73–74.

70. Christian Meier, *Caesar* (Basic Books, 1982), 41, 151.

71. In a talk before the Washington Press Club carried on National Public Radio in 1988. Stone had just authored *The Trial of Socrates* (Little, Brown, 1988).
72. Lewis Mumford, *The City in History* (Harcourt, Brace & World, 1961) 228–229.
73. Sallust, *Epistle to Caesar* II.5,7.
74. Appian, *The Civil Wars* II.120 and 1.59 respectively.
75. Juvenal, *Satires* X.77–81.
76. Scullard, *From the Gracchi to Nero*, 235; Mumford, *The City in History*, 229.
77. Dickinson, *Death of a Republic*, 331.
78. Scullard, *From the Gracchi to Nero*, 85 and 120.
79. Alan Cameron, "Bread and Circuses, The Roman Emperor and his People," Inaugural Lecture, King's College, 1973, quoted in G.E.M. de Ste. Croix, *The Class Struggle in the Ancient Greek World* (Cornell University Press, 1981), 371.
80. Mumford, *The City in History*, 229, 231, 233–234.
81. On the importance of the organized spectacles, see Roland August, *Cruelty and Civilization: The Roman Games* (Routledge, 1994).
82. Juvenal, *Satires* III.159; Casson, *Everyday Life in Ancient Rome*, rev. ed., 100; and Stewart Perowne, *Caesars and Saints* (W. W. Norton, 1962), 86.
83. Casson, *Everyday Life in Ancient Rome*, 104.
84. Suetonius, *Augustus* 44.
85. Tacitus, *Annals* 1.76.5.
86. Dio Cassius, *Roman History* XLIII.23.
87. Pliny, *Natural History* VIII.7.20–21; Dio Cassius, *Roman History* XXXIX.38; Cicero, *To His Friends* VII.1.
88. Dio Cassius, *Roman History* XLIII.24.
89. George Rudé, *The Crowd in History*, 1730–1848 (John Wiley & Sons, 1964), 199–201, 210.
90. P.-O Lissagary, *History of the Commune of 1871* (International Publishing Co., 1898 [1876]), 382–465, 499–500; and Graham Robb, *Victor Hugo* (W.W. Norton, 1997), 466-469.
91. Leonard L. Richards, *"Gentlemen of Property and Standing": Anti-Abolition Mobs in Jacksonian America* (Oxford University Press, 1970), 82–85.
92. Rudé, *The Crowd in History*, 30, 45, 55–56, 60–61, 68, 178, 189.
93. See Richards, *"Gentlemen of Property and Standing": Anti-Abolition Mobs in Jacksonian America*, passim; also herein selection 12, "Racist Rule, Then and Now."
94. On the occupations of freedmen in ancient Rome, see Brunt, *Social Conflicts in the Roman Republic*, 137; Neal Wood, *Cicero's Social and Political Thought* (University of California Press, 1988), 19; and Jérôme Carcopino

Daily Life in Ancient Rome (Yale University Press, 1940), 179–180. Cicero allows that there were shopkeepers among Clodius's followers, but he labels them criminals.

95. Cicero, *To Atticus* XIII.44,1.
96. Appian, *The Civil Wars* I.116.
97. Tacitus, *Annuls* XIV.42–45.
98. Plutarch, *Caesar* VIII.3–4. Also note Ste. Croix's comment in *The Class Struggle in the Ancient Greek World*, 353.
99. Zwi Yavetz, *Plebs and Princeps* (Oxford University Press, 1969).
100. Plutarch, *Tiberius Gracchus* XXI.2–3.
101. Plutarch, *Tiberius Gracchus* VIII.1–2,5; and *Gaius Gracchus* VIII.1–2,5 and XII.1.
102. Plutarch, *Gaius Gracchus* XVIII.2. The people also erected a bronze statue to Cornelia, with the inscription: "Cornelia, mother of the Gracchi": *Gaius Gracchus* IV.2–4.
103. Mommsen, *The History of Rome*, 488.

INDEX

385

ABOUT THE AUTHOR

Michael Parenti is an internationally acclaimed, award-winning writer, scholar, and social commentator who has published some twenty books and hundreds of articles, covering a vast range of topics, including politics, class power, empire, history, culture, media, lifestyle, and ecology. His most recent works are: *Democracy for the Few,* 8th edition (Wadsworth/Thomson, 2007), *The Culture Struggle* (Seven Stories, 2006), *Superpatriotism* (City Lights, 2004), and *The Assassination of Julius Caesar* (New Press, 2003). Describing himself as a "recovering academic," Parenti now devotes all his time to writing and lecturing across North America and abroad. For further information, visit his Web site: www.michaelparenti.org.